2-

To Kay

With friendship and
in appreciation of loyal
outstanding work for
AMA

Franco Di Blasi

NYc   4-23-01

The
Leadership
Investment

The Leadership Investment

How the World's Best Organizations Gain Strategic Advantage through Leadership Development

Robert M. Fulmer
Marshall Goldsmith

AMACOM
American Management Association

New York • Atlanta • Boston • Chicago • Kansas City • San Francisco • Washington, D.C.
Brussels • Mexico City • Tokyo • Toronto

This publication is designed to provide accurate and authoritative information in regard to the subject matter covered. It is sold with the understanding that the publisher is not engaged in rendering legal, accounting, or other professional service. If legal advice or other expert assistance is required, the services of a competent professional person should be sought.

Library of Congress Cataloging-in-Publication Data

Fulmer, Robert M.
    The leadership investment : how the world's best organizations gain strategic advantage through leadership development / Robert M. Fulmer, Marshall Goldsmith.
        p.   cm.
    Includes bibliographical references and index.
    ISBN 0-8144-0558-4
    1. Executives—Training of—Case studies.   2. Leadership—Study and teaching—Case studies.   I. Goldsmith, Marshall.   II. Title.
HD30.4.F84   2000
658.4'07124—dc21   00-033157

Printing number

10   9   8   7   6   5   4   3   2   1

Contents

2 Arthur Andersen: The Search for Qualification   31

3 General Electric: Staging Ground for Corporate Revolution   52

5   Johnson & Johnson: FrameworkS of Leadership   111

List of Abbreviations

I. General terms

American Productivity & Quality Center (APQC)
American Society for Training & Development (ASTD)
computer-based training (CBT)
customer satisfaction index (CSI)
electronic distance learning (EDL)
IESE
INSEAD
Keilty, Goldsmith & Company (KGC)
KSA (knowledge, skills, and attitudes) Model
return on investment (ROI)

II. Company-specific terms

Andersen Worldwide
    Partner Development Program (PDP)

General Electric (GE)
CI & CII reviews
Corporate Research & Development (R&D)
    BOCA
    Business Management Courses (BMC)

Change Acceleration Program (CAP)
Corporate Executive Council (CEC)
Corporate Leadership Development (CLD)
Executive Development Courses (EDC)
Experienced Manager Course (EMC)
Leadership Course (LC)
Manager Development Course (MDC)
Management Development Institute
New Manager Development Course (NMDC)
S1 Strategy & S2 Budget Sessions
RAAMP Matrix: (Reports, Approvals, Meetings, Measures,
    Policies, Practices)
CTQs (Critical to Quality)
statistical process control (SPC)
Strategic Business Units (SBUs)

Hewlett-Packard (HP)
Business Leadership Development (BLD)
Leadership Development and Review (LD&R)
LeaRN (Learning Resource Network)
management by objectives (MBO)
management by wandering around (MBWA)
Product Process Organization (PPO)
request for proposal (RFP)
Sales and Services Group (SSG)

Johnson & Johnson (J&J)
Corporate Education and Development (CED)
FOLIOMAP
FrameworkS

Saturn
Education Tracking System (ET)
Individual Training Plan (ITP)
Management Leadership Team (MLT)
People Systems Training & Development (PSTD)
Subject Matter Experts (SMEs)
train-the-trainer (T3)
UAW

Shell International
Committee of Managing Directors (CMD)
Leadership and Performance program (LEAP)
   Business (one of three divisions of LEAP)
   Business Framework Implementation (BFI)
   Career Assignment Summary (CAS)
CAR (Capacity, Achievement, Relationships)

World Bank
European Bank for Reconstruction and Development (EBRD)
Executive Development Program (EDP)
Grass Roots Immersion Program (GRIP)
international financial institutions (IFIs)
International Monetary Fund (IMF)
United Nations Development Program (UNDP)
   International Bank for Reconstruction (IBRD)
   International Development Association (IDA)
   International Finance Corporation (IFC)
   Multilateral Investment Guarantee Agency (MIGA)

Acknowledgments

While we retain responsibility (and some credit) for this work, it would not have been completed without the collaboration and assistance of several individuals and organizations.

First, our appreciation and debt to the American Productivity & Quality Center must be expressed. C. Jackson Grayson and Carla O'Dell provided executive leadership for the research and helped create the research methodology employed for much of the data collection. In the final stages of putting the book together, Ron Webb was most helpful in providing permissions, contacts, and other information. Justin McMorrow, Belinda Schmidt, and Joe Camillus made the original research happen with their attention to detail, logistics, and content. George Hollenbeck (SME), Wesley Vestal (APQC), and Jay Conger (Special Project Advisor) were instrumental in making the 1999 project assessable and successful.

Our hosts for the various site visits were both hospitable and insightful. In the original research, Scott Cheney and Stacey Wagner represented the study's cosponsor, the American Society for Training & Development (ASTD), and provided leadership, analysis, contacts, and publicity for the work. At Arthur Andersen, Susan E. Bumpass, Marshall J. Gerber, and Michelle K. Miller; at GE, Jacquie Vierling, John Lawson, Steve Kerr, Hank Meincke, Betty Disch, Amy Howard, and Jim Edler; at Johnson & Johnson, Allen C. Anderson, Charley Corace, and Jim DeVito, Myron Goff and Ron Bossard; at HP, Kathy Hendrickson, Paulina Mustazza, and Sherry Cox; at Shell International, Mac

McDonald, John Hofmeister, Paul Crowley, and Paul van Schaik; at Saturn, Mike Schlacter, Gary Grider and Peggy Berger; and at the World Bank, Alberto Bazzan, Mark Baird, Maury Sterns, Dorothy Berry, and Surinder Deol were all outstanding representatives of their organizations and excellent conduits of information about how the best firms in the world develop their leaders.

Charlie Walton helped translate our notes and mumblings about the best practice partners into (mostly) intelligible prose. Sarah McArthur helped complete that transition and provided outstanding editorial suggestions and revisions. John Wheaton was tremendous at helping us confirm sources of information, update data, secure permissions, and check footnotes.

It was a pleasure to work with AMACOM throughout the effort. Our thanks to Adrienne Hickey who saw the potential for the project and made us feel that it was important to her and AMACOM and to Christina McLaughlin who coordinated the production process and was patient with our need to make improvements (changes) at the last minute. While our colleagues at the various business schools and consulting firms discussed in chapters 9 and 10 are referenced there, we do appreciate their candor and cooperation. Finally, we appreciate the interest and sense of inquiry demonstrated by our readers and hope you will find our journey educational and enjoyable.

The
Leadership
Investment

Introduction

Leadership Development Lessons from the Best

his book is based on the authors' work with senior corporate executives, business academics, and principals in consulting firms that specialize in leadership development. It incorporates a decade of research conducted by Robert M. Fulmer with organizations such as Columbia University, the MIT Center for Organizational Learning, The College of William and Mary, American Society for Training and Development (ASTD), and American Productivity and Quality Center (APQC). It builds on Bob's previous work with Albert Vicere, *Leadership by Design*,[1] and emphasizes the findings of two studies: a global best-practices study sponsored by APQC and ASTD (1998);[2] and a subsequent study concerning the organizational development of leaders at all levels (1999).[3] Marshall Goldsmith has been actively involved as a consultant to many of the best-practice partners through his work as founding director of Keilty, Goldsmith & Company (KGC), one of the world's leading leadership development firms. This work includes the conclusions of more than a decade of focus by Marshall concerning the characteristics that will be required for leadership in the future.

Anyone interested in gaining the ultimate source of competitive advantage—"an ability to learn faster than the competition"—will find this book of value. Those who will find this book practical, insightful, and timely include senior line executives interested in gaining leverage for strategic change or in addressing the projected critical shortfall of qualified leaders, individuals associated with one of the more than 1,000 corporate universities, and human resources executives who have responsibility for management or leadership development.

This book draws from data from the 1998–1999 research studies involving best-practice partners: Arthur Andersen (Andersen), General Electric (GE), Hewlett-Packard (HP), Johnson & Johnson (J&J), Royal Dutch Shell–Shell International Division (Shell), Saturn, and the World Bank. It contains comparisons of the practices utilized by these world-class exemplars, the thirty-five organizational sponsors of the research, and observations from bellwether organizations who seem to represent the best of the future.

Importance of Learning

Business historians are likely to judge the most lasting realization of the 1990s to be encapsulated in the statement, "Learning is the only source of sustainable competitive advantage." At the beginning of a new century, leader development is more than a set of aspirational words. It represents a major commitment of time, money, and energy in the world's leading global enterprises.

Smart CEOs are making strategic investments in leadership development to ensure that their key executives produce consistent and positive results. Companies spent an estimated $60.7 billion on training in 1998 and an estimated $65 + billion in 1999, according to *Training* magazine.[4] *Business Week* estimates that companies spend one-fourth of the total ($16.5 billion) annually on executive education and leadership development.[5]

Of course, it is easier to commit budget dollars than the time and energy of top management. That is why CEO time allotment to leadership development is much more revealing than the impressive sums that are dedicated. Roger Enrico of Pepsico, Jack Welch of GE, and Larry Bossidy of AlliedSignal are representative of the top guns who now devote significant amounts of their business days to personally guiding and mentoring future leaders within their organizations. It is becoming increasingly clear that developing leaders is not a luxury. Leadership development is a strategic necessity.

An oft-quoted truism of leadership is that "to effectively lead a country or a company, you must take control of three entities: its press, its police, and its schools." Astute captains of best-practice corporations see instinctively that the press equates to corporate communications; the corporate equivalent of the police includes succession planning, compensation, and performance management; and the corporate school system is the company's education program.

The need for good leaders is undisputed. The subject about which heated discussion does continue is how best to develop current and future leaders. How do the exemplary organizations select and groom their leaders? What are the processes that transform managers into leaders—leaders who can make the decisions and set the strategies that will be victorious in an arena in which there are no second chances? Which are the companies that are designing, managing, and delivering world-class leadership programs today?

Current Leadership Development Programs

Today's leadership development programs are designed to provide participants with a variety of experiences that broaden their perspectives, skills, flexibility, and overall effectiveness. Included are experiences that enhance understanding, respect, and value for cultural differences; that foster greater creativity and help leaders think "out of the box," create a broader, more systemic view of organizations and their issues, and explore nontraditional approaches to problem-solving. Some programs incorporate physical challenges that foster risk-taking, require decisions and actions in unpredictable and ambiguous situations, and force mutual interdependence and shifts in roles and responsibilities. Debriefing of all these experiences, discussions, and lessons is extensive. Executives must identify what they have learned and what insights those learnings have provided.

There may first be a need to unlearn some assumptions, beliefs, and conclusions that underpin the leader's current behavior. It is only when a leader realizes that these paradigms are barriers that he or she can begin to acquire the knowledge and experience that will lead to new beliefs and conclusions and ultimately to new, more productive behaviors.

There is a growing demand that executive education should result in immediate actions that leaders can take to improve company performance. To accomplish this, corporate representatives are far more active in the education of their leaders. Although in-house executive development staff members continue working with universities and other executive development providers, they are often directly involved with vendors in the determination of content and course or program design. Some in-house executive development staffers design the programs and then use different vendors to deliver key content and provide the insight, advice, and expert coaching that the executives will need to address real organizational issues during and following the course.

The Search for Excellence

In January 1998, the APQC and ASTD, together with this work's senior author joined forces to develop a consortium benchmarking study to investigate best practices in leadership development. Again, in 1999, APQC expanded the original study to explore how firms such as Saturn "develop leaders at all levels." Bob Fulmer and Jay Conger of the London Business School were advisors for this project.

Thirty-five businesses (see Table I.1) participated in the study by attending a planning session, completing data-gathering surveys, and attending or hosting on-site interviews. The six companies shown in Table I.2 were chosen by the consortium from a dozen firms identified as having strong or innovative leadership development processes in place. These six organizations were invited to participate in the study as best-practice

Table I.1 Study Sponsors

◆ AARP	◆ Lutheran Brotherhood
◆ Aerojet	◆ Medrad
◆ Allstate Insurance	◆ Nortel
◆ American General	◆ North American Coal
◆ Ameritech	◆ PDVSA-CIED
◆ Amoco	◆ Pharmacia & Upjohn
◆ Buckman Laboratories	◆ Royal Dutch Shell
◆ Canadian Imperial Bank of	(Shell International Division)
Commerce	◆ Smith & Nephew
◆ Celanese	◆ Sprint
◆ Chevron	◆ Thomas Cook Group
◆ Compaq Computer	◆ The Timken Company
◆ Deere & Company	◆ U.S. Dept. of Treasury
◆ Eastman Chemical	◆ U.S. Postal Service
◆ Honda of America Manufacturing	◆ USA Group
◆ Johns Hopkins University—	◆ USDA Graduate School
Applied Physics Lab	◆ Wachovia Corporation
◆ Johnson & Johnson	◆ Warner-Lambert
◆ Lucent Technologies	◆ Ziff-Davis

Table I.2 Best-Practice Partner Organizations

◆ Arthur Andersen	◆ Royal Dutch Shell
◆ General Electric	(Shell International Division)
◆ Hewlett-Packard	◆ The World Bank
◆ Johnson & Johnson	

partners. Best practices were established using a benchmarking process explained in Appendix A.

The six best-practice partners for this study are diverse exemplars of excellence in leadership development. While all of them exhibit commitment to developing leaders, there is tremendous diversity in their approaches, emphases, and cultures. The following pages highlight the major conclusions relevant for senior executives and strategists. It is important to recognize that the practices of these outstanding firms do not necessarily provide templates for the reorganization of other companies. One of the most important characteristics of all six companies is the extreme care taken to ensure that their leadership development processes are tailored to their own strategic initiatives and specific cultures.

Diversity in Excellence

As the study's site visits progressed, it became clear that each of the best-practice, leadership development processes was built on key leverage points. While these centers of excellence vary from firm to firm, each is closely tied to the culture of its organization. Furthermore, each serves as the foundation of excellence that permeates the entire process.

Among the firms, Arthur Andersen was the most precise in measuring the impact of its programs—a characteristic that reflects the nature of its business and the importance of quantifiable data in its culture. J&J is well known for its commitment to its corporate Credo. At J&J, selection, assessment, succession planning, and education build upon, review, and challenge the assumption of the Credo. GE's long commitment to management development enables it to operate with a strong emphasis on results that are less measured and controlled than other cost centers in the company.

The studies' summary of findings identified other core elements of leadership development among its best-practice partners. The summary's emphasis was that, while all excellent programs differ, together they provide a "patchwork of excellence" in the development of their leaders. Arthur Andersen may have better measurement methods than GE. GE may be more oriented toward action learning and results than the World Bank. HP may be more focused on creating on-the-job learning initiatives, while J&J's values are the glue that allows the world's most diversified health care organization to maintain strategic alignment of its 190 operating companies around the world. Each best-practice partner has key strengths that are highlighted in the chapters that follow.

Each of these leadership training efforts began with a commitment that was unique to its organization. Each built superb programs (and processes) upon that solid foundation. In each case, the excellence referenced two key pillars: a tone of overall quality was part of the original commitment; and each leadership development process was created to fit its own specific organization. It is unthinkable that GE would spend as much time on measurement as Arthur Andersen. Senior partners at Andersen naturally need more data to support the value of leadership development than GE, with its long-standing success at using education as a lever of strategic change.

Throughout the site visits, the study staff members were impressed with the professionalism of the leadership development people at each of the best-practice partners. They had excellent backgrounds in various aspects of human resource development. They had line business operations experience. They were enthusiastic and articulate in discussing their approaches. And, even more impressively, they were good listeners! Even though they were being designated as "world class," they were curious about what their visitors were doing. It was clear that they listened to their CEOs, line managers, students, and the outside experts they engaged to build program initiatives. They were masters of networking and keeping their fingers on the pulse of their constituencies.

The following chapters will introduce and discuss some of the most important concepts revealed or confirmed by the study.

Notes

1. *Leadership by Design*. Boston: Harvard Business School Press, 1998.
2. Robert M. Fulmer, Joe Camillus and Justin McMorrow, editors, *Leadership Development: Building Executive Talent*, (Houston: American Productivity & Quality Center and American Society for Training & Development, 1999).
3. George Hollenback & Wesley Vestal, editors, *Developing Leaders At All Levels*, (Houston: American Productivity & Quality Center, 1999).
4. Anonymous, "Industry Report 1998: Training Budgets," *Training*, October 1998, pp. 47–52.
5. Extrapolated from Jennifer Reingold, "Learning to Lead," *Business Week* (Oct. 18, 1999) p. 77; and Lori Bongiorno, "Corporate America's New Lesson Plan," *Business Week* (Oct. 25, 1993), p. 102.

1

The Competitive Advantage of Leadership Development

I f the leadership development process is to be an effective part of the change process, it must be aligned with all of the strategic objectives of the organization. Successful leadership development initiatives have gone to great lengths to understand and help implement overall corporate strategy. Only by aligning with corporate strategy will new leaders be prepared to meet new business challenges and global market constraints.

Seeking Adjustment

To meet Arthur Andersen's (Andersen) needs to continue diversifying and globalizing, its Partner Development Program (PDP) links closely to its business strategy. PDP constantly reviews strategy documents from the business, as well as Andersen's Four Cornerstones model, which is to be "simply the best" in people, market share/growth, exceeding client expectations, and quality/risk management.

At Hewlett-Packard (HP), Carly Fiorina's appointment as CEO was evidence of the firm's commitment to creating a new generation of leaders that had many of the talents and values of founders Dave Packard and Bill Hewlett but with more diversity than the first generation of leaders who make HP great. In this context, she is both the "effect" of a commitment to leadership and the cause of its continuing evolution.

Johnson and Johnson (J&J) believes it is critical to start any education and development discussion with the business objectives of the company. The current chairman has focused on three basic objectives:

1. *Top-line growth*—The company's history of double-digit, top-line growth requires innovation, whether it be through heavy research and development investments, new alliances, or mergers and acquisitions.

2. *Enhanced competitiveness*—This must come through aggressive cost-reduction, but without increased prices.

3. *Organizational excellence*—To find and develop great people, or the other objectives become moot points.

Leadership development is closely aligned with, and is used to support, corporate strategy. Issues such as globalization, decentralization, and the rapid pace of today's marketplace have forced companies to evaluate the ways in which they operate. Paradigms that have worked for years suddenly become ineffective when an organization's largest customer is thousands of miles away. Realizing the need for change is an important first step. However, determining exactly *how* to turn the new challenges into opportunities keeps many a CEO awake at night. In many cases, bold, new strategic initiatives are under way to revamp the way organizations do business, while re-creating the workforce undertaking these efforts.

The best-practice organizations discussed in this book are no different. Each organization addresses business issues that have created needed changes. Their leadership development efforts reflect their responses to these opportunities. A majority of study participants reported the presence of a "defining situation" in their organization that led to the (re-)creation of the leadership development process. In this chapter, we present an overview of themes associated with the best practices in leadership development. In subsequent chapters, we develop the practices of the exemplar firms in greater detail.

In a sense, the best-practice organizations view the leadership development process as a way to increase their competitive advantages. For example, General Electric (GE) Crotonville, GE's central education function, is described as a "staging ground for corporate revolutions." From 1981 to 1997, GE more than tripled its revenues, while decreasing its worldwide employment from 404,000 to 240,000. Naturally, this type of growth caused an enormous cultural shift within GE, including the Crotonville operation.

James Wolfensohn joined the World Bank as president in 1995. Acknowledging both the internal and external challenges, he felt that the World Bank offered a number of great opportunities. The fall of the Berlin Wall in 1989 meant that many new clients and potential funders could join the organization. The information revolution meant that knowledge could be transferred at a much more rapid pace to the member countries and to clients of the World Bank. Wolfensohn saw new leadership development efforts as one of the tools he could use to reshape the culture of the organization.

About ten years ago, senior executives at J&J decided that the organization had to change its culture. J&J had more than 100 years of success operating in a decentralized manner. However, the decentralization inherent in its move into the global marketplace was leading to high overhead costs. Internal competition was actually becoming a roadblock to growth. As a result, the organization encouraged its 190 operating companies to partner with each other to compete on a global basis. Ralph Larsen, chairman and CEO at J&J, champions the Executive Conference program. He uses decentralized decision-making to flush out the details of conference themes, and then exercises his leadership by articulating concerns and themes that he feels the entire corporation needs to address.

Royal Dutch Shell/Shell International (Shell) has long understood that developing leaders is a significant source of competitive advantage. The foundations of its developmental planning lie within its core business strategies and values of integrity, professionalism, respect for people, long-term focus, and pride without arrogance.

Shell's Leadership and Performance program (LEAP) used these business strategies as guidelines for its leadership development journey into undefined and uncertain territory. Shell admitted that it did not know exactly what its future leaders would look like. The company simply knew that a transformation had to happen for it to remain competitive in the constantly changing global economy. It dedicated itself to the pursuit of breakthrough performance in order to realize the full potential of its new opportunities.

Focusing on Core Issues

Corporate leadership development focuses on core issues, such as values and strategic change, that are vital to the entire organization. At the same time, the corporation's business units are focusing on challenges specific to their operations. All the best-practice organizations studied had created a separate corporate leadership development function that focused on leadership skills and usually left the management skills and business-specific skill development to the businesses themselves.

In the eyes of these organizations, management skills deal with the basics, with skills and behaviors that enable employees to make their numbers. Leadership development builds on these core attributes. For example, at GE the ability to influence peers is critical. At J&J, building leaders involves giving employees the tools to make tough ethical decisions. Corporate leadership development efforts more often focus on applying corporate values to specific strategic initiatives. Teaching management and supervisory skills is usually handled at the business level.

This split of responsibility seems to work well. Corporate leadership efforts in best-practice organizations complement, rather than compete with, those within the business. Generally, the business operations are much better equipped to handle their own management and training needs. However, best-practice organizations saw corporate leadership programs providing the decision-making framework to effectively use the tools provided by the businesses.

J&J feels that the expertise for management development in a particular operating company often resides within that business. As a result, it makes no sense for the corporate division to have full responsibility for this activity. Top-level leadership development, on the other hand, is consistent across the company, and, as a result, it makes sense to have a central group take the lead on this issue.

Connecting Resource Development with Business Experience

Best-practice organizations carefully build leadership development teams by emphasizing the importance of both human resources development and business experience. Each of the study's best-practice organizations had key leaders with extensive line experience. At Andersen, J&J, and Shell, the heads of the leadership development process had senior-level business experience before assuming responsibility for this function. The use of business leaders in key human resource development positions does not imply a lack of respect for unique aspects of the discipline. Rather, it is based on a feeling that the presence of business leaders in the functions helps ensure the practicality of programs and buy-in from the businesses.

Building on the concept of "hiring from the field," a number of best-practice organizations have found innovative ways of bringing additional business experience on board. GE and Shell bring in high-potential individuals on two-year rotating assignments. HP recruits key people from line positions to ensure that knowledge of the HP Way (the company's values and objectives) and the pragmatic needs of the business are addressed in an adequate manner. These assignments help leadership development ground its efforts in business realities and also assist those individuals who come in from the business units. Often, a person will start an assignment with knowledge of only one line of the business but leave with an understanding of the entire organization.

While representation from the business units may be critical, best-practice organizations do not ignore experience in corporate education, human resources, or academia. The director of Crotonville came from a university setting. The World Bank's Executive Development Program (EDP) is run by someone with a background in corporate education. Creating a business and education mix seems to enable best-practice organizations to build programs based on sound theory, but focused on results vital to the organization.

Internally Focused, Externally Aware

Best-practice leadership development processes are internally focused and externally aware. New business demands dictated the need for change within each of the best-practice organizations but certainly did not provide a framework for how to create the change. Whether started by the CEO or bubbling up throughout the organization, the focus on building the skills of current and future leaders surfaced as a potential enabler of change. Creating a process to build leadership skills, abilities, and techniques has pushed best-practice organizations to look both internally and externally for answers.

The best-practice organizations realized that to enable change, the leadership development process must fit the culture of its organization. A first step for those designing the leadership development process was to ensure this linkage by soliciting the direct input of their customers. Input from key customers is an ongoing process for best-practice organizations.

To conduct a proper needs analysis, best-practice organizations rely on a number of tools, including:

1. Use of line executives in key human resource development positions
2. Program "steering committees"
3. Formal links with strategic planning efforts

4. Extensive conversations with business leaders
5. Internal and external customer surveys.

These formal needs assessments may seem like an obvious step in creating a leadership development process. Unfortunately, they are not done universally. All best-practice partners reported conducting formal business-unit needs assessments—only about half of the sponsor group reported doing the same.

Identifying the Leadership Pool

A majority of the best-practice organizations have identified leadership competencies or, at least, tried to define characteristics and qualities of successful leaders. Any discussion of leadership competencies can easily become controversial. Many contend that the identification of competencies helps organizations to understand those qualities, characteristics, and skills that lead to outstanding performance and outcomes. Others question whether competencies can be defined at all.

Not all of the best-practice partners in this study define competencies, but each does try to define the characteristics and qualities of successful leaders within its particular organization. The same is true with the majority of study sponsors. However, partners were more likely to have developed their competencies internally or with a limited use of outside consultants than to have sponsored extensive, formal competency studies. Best-practice organizations also make sure that their competencies are kept up-to-date through both internal and external research.

The vast majority of organizations surveyed in the study believe that, once competencies are defined, the results should be consistent throughout the company, regardless of position, business unit, or geographic location. At best-practice organizations, all these variables were taken into consideration before the competencies were finalized. For example, J&J sent a team around the world to make sure that what made a successful leader in one country would translate to another country. Although J&J found that some of the wording for its competency model had to be changed from location to location, the behaviors were, in fact, globally consistent.

Andersen defines a competency as a statement of the behaviors necessary to perform a job task. Competencies are composed of knowledge, multiple skills, traits, and attributes.

GE's values play a key role in determining each person's performance. All employees at GE discuss their performance and career goals during a review meeting with their managers, and are then rated on a chart. One axis of the chart rates an employee's performance, and the other axis rates his or her adherence to company values.

Growing Leaders Instead of Buying Them

Best-practice organizations grow leaders as opposed to buying them. Best-practice organizations, such as those involved in this study, are often seen as large candidate pools for executive-level positions in Fortune 500 companies. Aspiring companies want to know the secret of making "leaders their most important product." Throughout the course of this benchmarking effort, best-practice organizations emphasized that their top leadership came from within the company. Senior executives tended to be products of the leadership development system, groomed from the beginning to take on increasing responsibilities.

In stark contrast to the situation in many companies today, buying top-level talent occurs occasionally. Best-practice organizations lean toward internal leaders because of the powerful and distinct cultures in which they work. These organizations see their strong cultures as critical to continued success. Still, they realize that not everyone can thrive in these unique situations. Executives brought in from other organizations may have all the right experience and skills, but they may not be a good fit with J&J's Corporate Credo or HP's decentralized structure. Leaders who have come up through the organization are a proven fit, because they have successfully accomplished assignments in the way that the organization has chosen for its leaders.

While a robust pipeline of talent helps to distinguish best-practice companies, these organizations also realize that some executive positions must be filled externally to avoid stagnation and "inbreeding." In some cases, buying talent is a competitive must. As organizations transform themselves to deal with new markets, technology, or customers, hiring externally is often the fastest way to expand the base of competencies and skill sets. When best-practice organizations do hire from the outside, they rely on the development function to fill the role of cultural assimilator by exposing learners to the organization's culture and values.

Ninety-five percent of Shell's current executives come from within the organization. Currently, the World Bank has only 23 managers who did not rise through the bank system, which makes its EDP a critical piece in the organizational puzzle for change. This means that the entire management team knows the traditions and culture of the organization, but it presents a major challenge when there is a perceived need to change the culture.

The Right People in the Right Programs

Best-practice organizations focus on getting the right people into the right programs. They are clear about the type of individual and the type of program they want for their leadership development processes. They look to the goals of their leadership development process to determine who will be selected as a participant. At Shell, the goal of the program is to create leaders at all levels. Therefore, its LEAP programs are open to anyone within the organization (even though certain programs are targeted for the highest potential individuals). The World Bank's EDP and Andersen's PDP focus only on those currently at the leadership level. Others, like GE and HP, are more selective about entrance into their key leadership programs. They focus on their "A players"—those who have the potential to move up through the ranks quickly.

Diversity Is Critical

Whatever the specific criteria may be, best-practice organizations spend a great deal of time deciding who needs to be involved in leadership development. An increasing point of interest for best-practice partners is to bring a diverse population into the leadership development process. Each of the best-practice partners operates in the global marketplace and consequently must look to the leadership development process to help its organization build a more diverse workforce. Moreover, the diversity of the classes adds different perspectives that improve the learning. Most best-in-class organizations report trying to get a mix of different countries, cultures, and business-unit reports into their corporate development efforts.

Crotonville's leadership development offerings are for high-potential individuals, "A players" who have been identified through the succession-planning process. Philosophically, the organization feels that it should spend the majority of its time developing its best and brightest. The company employs approximately 240,000 people worldwide. Crotonville only trains about 10,000 (or 4 percent) of them a year.

At Andersen, each program team is responsible for managing vendors and working with them to modify existing courses. The team provides each vendor with a study guide and stated objectives before a course is designed and then works closely with the vendor in the program design phase. Arthur Andersen never uses 100 percent of anyone's off-the-shelf products.

At the World Bank, all of the modules of EDP are delivered by the university consortium (Harvard Business School, John F. Kennedy School of Government, Stanford Business School, INSEAD, and IESF). These programs have been tailored to meet the specific needs of the bank's managers, but all are influenced by the universities that deliver them. This was precisely what the bank had in mind when it decided on these universities as vendors. Since the World Bank operates in a culture in which many employees hold advanced degrees, the organization needed to provide a program delivered by highly regarded faculty.

Engaging Leaders in the Process

Action, not knowledge, is the goal of best-practice leadership development processes. In preparing their leaders to make critical decisions, these organizations have realized the need to do more than simply provide their leaders with knowledge and information. The right knowledge can build a strong foundation, but the leadership development process must also equip participants with the skills, qualities, and techniques to apply that knowledge in ambiguous situations.

Therefore, best-practice partners emphasize *action learning*—the use of real-time business issues for learning and development. With such an approach, content cannot be sacrificed for simplistic solutions, and the answers cannot be found in the instructor's head or in the back of a book. Creative and realistic answers must be developed on the spot by the learners, and they must be answers that will work in corporate application. What's more, it is the leadership development participants themselves who are charged with the job of implementing their recommendations. They and their superiors are going to see clearly whether or not their proposals work.

It may sound complicated and costly for global corporations to turn their real-time challenges into "class projects," and it may be risky. More often, however, it is the one sure way to assay the ability of promising future leaders to solve actual business problems. Action learning is the best way to deliver a learning experience that is tailored to both the organization and the learner's own development. For organizations that are serious about producing meaningful results from their leadership development processes, it is often the most effective path.

Andersen uses a great many problem-solving activities with the small groups in its leadership development activities. Each course has a prescribed content, but the lecture is not emphasized. Other learning techniques include case methods, simulations, action learning, experiential learning, and executive coaching. Some of Arthur Andersen's courses involve a modified, action-learning approach that incorporates both pre- and post-work.

Some higher-level courses in the GE leadership development core curriculum are designed to help provide direction for the company—from a regional strategic standpoint and even from a worldwide company standpoint. Chairman and CEO Jack Welch personally chooses the action-learning topics for each Business Management Course (BMC), of which there are three per year, and each Executive Development Course (EDC), of which there is one per year. As a result, when GE employees hear that a certain initiative was a recommendation from the BMC or EDC, they make every effort to ensure that it becomes a reality. In most instances, recommendations made by GE's leadership development participants have been implemented.

For example, students in the BMC recently went to Russia and developed a set of recommendations for GE's operations in this area. The students then shared their recommendations with top leadership and then decided on a course of action. A mid-1990's BMC report on quality spearheaded the Six Sigma initiative that drives GE today, one of the biggest changes to occur at GE (see Chapter 3).

To create the new style of "walk the talk" leadership, Shell's LEAP programs feature compressed action learning that empowers teams and individuals to resolve issues for themselves. Each program consists of a mix of classroom days and team-based projects that take place over a 90- to 120-day period. While the approximately 11 classroom days are tremendous for the purposes of networking and best-practice sharing, a majority of the learning takes place in the team-based projects. No more than nine teams participate in a program at one time, and depending on the specific program, the team can come from within a business or consist of individuals across businesses and functions.

Nothing Teaches Like Experience

Technology can be useful for knowledge dissemination, but it cannot replace the teaching power of putting leaders together to solve a real problem. Companies across the globe acknowledge that technology has enormous potential in creating a learning organization. Today, top companies use technology to disseminate knowledge, keep people connected throughout the organization, expedite and facilitate team learning, and allow access to the knowledge capital of the organization.

On the other hand, the experience of getting leaders away from their jobs and providing face-to-face exposure to colleagues from across the world is an essential part of the best programs. According to American philosopher and psychologist William James (1842–1910) "genius is simply the ability to see the world from a different perspective." Corporate programs can provide learners with this opportunity.

Currently, best-practice organizations feel they cannot fully achieve the benefits of networking via technology. When asked about their favored methods of delivery, best-practice partners indicated that a majority of their programs were delivered face-to-face. At present, technology is often perceived as a plug to fill gaps in the learning process. For instance, part of J&J's strategy is to create an organization of 90,000 leaders. The company realizes that it cannot put 90,000 people through its top development programs. But it can provide the technology for employees around the world to interact and learn from each other. In this case, technology is seen as a potential bridge between leaders within the organization.

With the importance Andersen places on face-to-face interaction, technology-based education is not a big part of the PDP program but, rather, is primarily used for sophisticated leadership simulations (i.e., flight simulator work). PDP is also currently searching for software to facilitate pre-course work and post-event follow-up. It is in these two areas that the organization believes technology can be most effective.

HP's emphasis on creating learning that takes place on the job has led the company to create an online learning resource. LeaRN is a Web-based database for locating pre-qualified development resources. These resources are either recommended by HP employees or identified by the Business Leadership Development (BLD) staff. The reference is listed within the Web site database. Employees drive their own education, but BLD has made it possible to search for solutions by topics, with links to competencies. This has helped tremendously, as BLD also has been marketing the concept of career self-reliance. The LeaRN system enables HP employees to build learning solutions that will help them develop the competencies HP has identified as critical to success.

In Executive Conference II (one of J&J's first, formal, corporate development programs), the company challenged senior managers with several exercises requiring the use of laptop computers. The benefits were twofold. The computers tabulated participant responses, data analysis, and information retrieval. These exercises provided leaders inexperienced with computer applications with non-threatening coaching and hands-on experience. Coincidentally, the exercises provided the leaders with the skill base they needed to move on to more sophisticated challenges.

As J&J moves toward using technology more in leadership offerings, it has created a four-point strategy for implementation:

1. *100 percent access*—Every employee worldwide should have access to what he or she needs to know to be effective on the job.

2. *Experiment*—Since it is not clear what the best educational technologies are, J&J must experiment with various design and delivery modes.

3. *Benchmark and partner*—Internally, CED partners with the information technology function and the advanced communication group to leverage resources and determine the best strategies for using educational technology. Externally, the organization does a significant amount of benchmarking to keep up to date.

4. *Business Value*—Learning and experience has to focus on compelling and critical performance issues.

Realizing constraints such as cost and time, Shell has begun to use existing technologies. The various teams throughout the 120-day period use laptop computers, e-mail, and Internet forums, but no effort has been made to replace the face-to-face workshops with distance learning. The most effective use of technology to date has been in collecting the knowledge generated by participants as a result of the LEAP programs. A knowledge-management tool called *Silent Dialogue* has been created to capture knowledge and is being used throughout the organization. This forum is a virtual magazine that not only discusses what LEAP is doing, but also highlights best practices discovered by the project teams. *Silent Dialogue* helps market the LEAP program, as well as provide solutions for Shell employees.

Connecting Leadership Development and Leadership Succession

The leadership development process is linked to the organization's succession-planning efforts. As part of the alignment between leadership development and other corporate systems, best-practice organizations have a tie between educational efforts and the formal succession process. A few of the best-practice partners have the leadership development function reporting to the same executive; others have a more informal relationship. Regardless of the method, the natural linkage is clearly present.

Top developmental functions all discussed the usage of 360-degree evaluations as a part of their leadership development process, whether it be simply for development or for actual selection purposes. In some cases, partners are open in discussing the fact that program participants are assessed. "Aren't top executives always assessing people?" they ask. "Surely, everyone understands that if they make a good impression on the CEO when he or she visits a program, that is going to be helpful when the CEO reviews their potential for promotion."

At J&J, the 360-degree feedback instrument was designed to reflect the characteristics of future leaders needed by the organization. Coaching and developmental plans growing out of this feedback are encouraged as part of the Executive Conference process, but the results of the assessment are not fed directly into the succession-planning process.

The leadership development process at GE is tied directly to succession planning. Each employee participates in a mandatory annual performance review with his or her manager. Each review includes a discussion about performance and adherence to GE values. To ensure fairness and accuracy, this discussion is later interpreted by someone at a higher management level. To prevent managers from holding back talented employees, GE's performance appraisals include a negative values variable.

Although the study data were not conclusive, it seems that leadership development is integral to ensuring that top talent is tracked and allowed to flourish. The best firms are beginning to formalize this linkage and tie together assessment, development, feedback, coaching, and succession planning into one aligned and integrated system.

Impact of Leadership Development

The leadership development process is a symbiotic tool of effective leaders. For the best-practice partners, top-level support was a consistent key to developing leaders and sustaining the process. Without that support the processes would flounder. Yet, the success of leadership development engenders even more high-level support. As top leadership development functions help their organizations meet current and future competitive demands, they win further support from the organization's top leaders. Corporate executives are more likely to support leadership efforts that are clearly helping them get results. Through monitoring the effectiveness of leadership development processes, capitalizing on quick wins, and communicating their successes throughout the organization, best-practice organizations keep this "virtuous cycle" going.

Groups such as Andersen's PDP and GE Crotonville remain successful with a customer-focused strategy, in which careful listening, diligent program crafting, and constant monitoring and communication play a role in creating senior-management buy-in. This makes it easier for senior executives to understand how the leadership development process helps shape and disseminate their organization's culture. It also helps executives overcome resistance to change and achieve their strategic goals.

To maintain a high level of buy-in, Corporate Leadership Development (CLD) surveys GE leaders around the world to ascertain future business needs and the requirements of future leaders. Additionally, CLD identifies and uses "early adopters" of the leadership process. Throughout GE, certain developmental initiatives excite some business leaders sooner than others. By identifying these champions and leveraging their support, the company has been able to attain a critical mass of support for its efforts. This early identification and rallying was used with both the Work-Out™ program and the Change Acceleration Process (CAP).

HP has garnered support for its leadership development process by involving both the CEO and senior management as participants in its programs. These executives serve as mentors, faculty, and sponsors for the design and process of these programs. For example, HP's former CEO, Lew Platt, opened and closed every Accelerated Development Program (ADP) with a dialogue session about the HP Way and the expectations of those participating in the process. CFO Bob Wayman sponsors a worldwide broadcast and facilitates a panel discussion.

From the outset, LEAP staff members realized that to effect and accelerate Shell's transformation, staff champions would be needed to communicate the program's value. The group looked inside Shell's business units to identify leaders and set about negotiating "contracts" that would bring together teams to participate in LEAP. Shell believes that as the process moves throughout the organization, the program's success will engender leader support, and leader support will, in turn, strengthen the process.

The World Bank's EDP was initiated after Jim Wolfensohn created the strategic compact with the board of directors. In the compact, he outlined a number of integrated initiatives, including increased focus on executive and management talent. This compact, which began the movement toward the present-day EDP, evidenced Wolfensohn's support from the beginning. As initial positive results have been attained, this support continues even though the program is costly. Senior-level support for EDP is further engendered by executives' participation as champions and coaches of EDP's project teams.

Assessing Success of Leadership Development Programs

Although the assessment efforts vary from company to company, all best-practice organizations assess the impact of their leadership development processes. For instance, Arthur Andersen, who puts strong emphasis on quantification, found that PDP graduates had more satisfied clients and higher per-hour supervised net fees than partners who had not attended PDP; at Shell, if team projects do not generate revenues at least 25 times the project costs, LEAP staff do not feel that their program is adding value; the World Bank hired an external consultant to perform an objective assessment of its efforts; and follow-up research conducted by J&J determines whether or not subordinates and peers see improvements after an Executive Conference.

Assessment is also seen as a means of generating buy-in and keeping efforts focused on the right objectives. The type and intensity of assessment depends on the objectives of the leadership development process and the culture of the firm. Of all the best-practice organizations, Andersen probably had the most dedicated assessment efforts, and it has certainly reaped the benefits. The vast amounts of data the firm collects not only helps to demonstrate the PDP's correlation with improved business results, but also shows in which direction the organization needs to head in the future. Though expensive and sometimes tricky, the benefits of measurement cannot be discounted.

To collect this vital information, best-practice partners use a number of tools and techniques. While the Four-Level Model of Evaluation (participant reaction, knowledge acquired, behavioral change, business results) is but one of the means organizations use to determine the impact of leadership development efforts, it is nonetheless common and important.

In general, best-practice partners are more aggressive about measuring and evaluating the effectiveness of their programs. The most striking difference between partners and sponsors is the greater use of customer- and employee-satisfaction information by best-practice partners. Andersen's evaluation system is composed of two parts and is more data-oriented than most other benchmark firms. Attendees in the partners' programs fill out forms before they go to class, right after the class is finished, and then again three months later. These forms contain both course evaluation and needs-assessment questions. After the course is completed, partners are asked to assess themselves in terms of knowledge gained from the course. Arthur Andersen has found this type of self-assessment to be very accurate.

The company has compared partners who have attended PDP with those who have not (on a course-by-course basis). The results show a link between PDP and both increased client satisfaction and higher per-hour supervised net fees. This impact research is done in a two-year cycle; information is gathered on partners a year before they enter the program and extends to a year after the program is completed.

The use of both participant satisfaction and impact research helps provide a balanced set of results. For instance, Andersen found that one of its programs was not getting a high participant-satisfaction rating, but an impact analysis report showed that the program was having greater impact than any of the other courses.

GE's leadership development process is not driven by typical measures, such as cost and return on investment (ROI). Steve Kerr, chief learning officer, suggests that "Crotonville may be the only unmeasured and uncontrolled cost center in GE." Instead of traditional attempts to measure impact, the organization relies on feedback from a number of sources to make sure it is staying on the right track. For example, more than half of the senior executive development courses at the company are run by the leaders of the corporation. They are a great source of feedback about the effectiveness of course design. The organization also relies heavily on student feedback.

GE is currently working on a number of initiatives to measure its learning. To establish a model that may be used across all courses, the organization is piloting a Level-Three analysis on one of its programs. The organization is using 360-degree feedback before the training, immediately after the training, and then six months later to see what the long-term effect of the course is. The 360-degree feedback method is used to start the participants on a development plan, for which they choose no more than two objectives for the year. The development plan drives their mentor match and the external university program that they will take.

In terms of measurement, Shell has a unique situation in that all of the LEAP programs have goals and real deliverables. During the initial contracting process, a member of the LEAP staff and the leader within the business determine project outcomes. As part of this discussion, the business leader expresses his or her objectives in sending the candidate to the program. In many cases, this discussion defines the program and the problem the team or candidate will address. The LEAP staff tracks these specific goals, and the teams report results to the business leader throughout the 120-day period. In addition to this, LEAP looks at the financials at the start and end of the program to identify any changes. It also scans for factors that may have played a role in any changes.

In early 1998, the World Bank asked an outside firm to conduct an interim evaluation of EDP, based on the experiences of the first two cohorts to participate in EDP. They found that, overall, EDP was effective, and that six to eight months after attending EDP, 20 to 30 percent of participants usually changed behaviors, policies, and procedures.

Worth Every Penny

Best-practice organizations see leadership development as a costly undertaking but also as a worthwhile investment. The old adage "you get what you pay for" seems to apply to the leadership development processes within best-practice organizations. As each of these best-practice partners encountered change, they saw value in investing in their future leaders. Costs were considered in the process, but the larger focus was the value that the program could provide. When asked to rank the importance of certain criteria when selecting an outside partner or vendor for the leadership development process, "fees" tended to be ranked as one of the least important factors.

The key for best-practice organizations was viewing their leadership development process as a long-term investment. While each tried to ramp up quickly so the effects would be felt throughout the organization, they realized that major payoffs would take time.

This feeling was reflected when comparing the responses of the best-practice partners to questions in the detailed questionnaire. When asked if they attributed cost savings to the leadership development process, 60 percent said yes, as opposed to only 17 percent of the sponsoring organizations. Additionally, when asked if they attributed increased profitability or productivity to the leadership development process, 80 percent said yes, as opposed to only 17 percent of the sponsoring organizations.

Since 1997 Arthur Andersen has invested more than $300 million per year in education, approximately 6 percent of total revenue. The company spends this amount because it believes that to deliver a best-practice program, it must focus on value and not on cost.

Andersen operates a zero-based funding model—all the program wants to do is recover its costs. Program development costs are allocated to each office based on that office's percentage of total partners. The delivery costs, which are usually $3,000 to $5,000 per partner, are charged back to the local offices, while transportation costs are adjusted to equalize costs across the globe. To ensure that offices send partners to PDP, they are charged for the slots they are allocated, whether or not partners attend.

GE has an extremely high level of buy-in for its CLD efforts. Crotonville has proved its worth time and time again, so the company has few qualms about investing in corporate training efforts.

To get LEAP off the ground, it was necessary for Shell corporate to fund the initial design and development of the program. LEAP needed to take strides toward the direction in which the organization wanted to go, not simply reflect the current needs of the businesses. Shell realized the initial costs would be considerable, but it believed strongly that creating leaders throughout the organization was essential to long-term success.

As LEAP has become more successful, being sought out by many of the businesses, it has moved to a joint funding process. If the CMD wants an addition to the LEAP offerings, it will fund it. The businesses pay for the regular offerings. However, Shell feels that the businesses should fund LEAP efforts, as this shows that they are truly deriving value from the process.

The World Bank realized that to foster a strategic cultural change and re-create a new language for leaders, the price would not be low. As Chairman Wolfensohn laid out the strategic compact to the board, he stated that creating real change would take a large investment. The World Bank has done just that with its EDP, as the initial investment for creating the program was approximately $20 million dollars. Maintaining the program is also not inexpensive. The cost-per-manager for EDP is approximately $22,000. It includes all travel, lodging, and business school fees for all three modules and the Grass Roots Immersion Program (GRIP). This fee is not charged back to the business groups but is funded centrally through the $12 million Executive Education budget.

Leadership Development Is Essential

Each of the leadership development efforts studied began with a commitment unique to the organization, and from that solid foundation the organization has built superb programs and processes. This excellence is based on two key pillars. First, an overall tone of quality is anchored to this commitment. Second-best is simply not acceptable. At the same time, good value for money expended is important. Second, the leadership development process is created to fit each organization. It is unthinkable that GE would spend as much time on measurement as does Andersen. Conversely, the senior partners at Andersen need more data to support the value of leadership development than is demanded of Crotonville, because of GE's long-standing success using education as a lever of strategic change.

The distilled experiences of these top practitioners of leadership development can provide a starting point for the development of a company program. None of these approaches will perfectly fit another organization, but they may suggest alternatives or stimulate new ideas that might fit specific business challenges.

2

Arthur Andersen

The Search for Qualification

Arthur Andersen (Andersen) helps clients find new ways to create, manage, and measure value in the rapidly changing global economy. With world-class skills in assurance, tax, consulting, and corporate finance, Andersen has more than 72,000 people in 385 locations in 84 countries who are united by a single worldwide operating structure that fosters inventiveness, knowledge sharing, and a focus on client success. The company competes in a realm in which knowledge is the key source of competitive advantage; therefore, it maintains a constant dedication to knowledge management, training and development, and performance enhancement.

A visit to Andersen's Center for Continuing Education in St. Charles, Illinois, demonstrates what can happen when an organization is fully committed to the knowledge development of its people. The sprawling campus, a former college, is one of the few pieces of land owned by the firm, and it serves as the entry point for all new employees.

Arthur Andersen Performance and Learning functions as an internal consulting service to Andersen by developing training and providing organizational, team, and individual performance enhancement strategies and interventions. A part of this group also provides similar services to clients.

Andersen's Role as an Education Leader

Andersen's outstanding leadership training program is exemplary in an arena in which all the players are good and getting better. The field of management and leadership training is enjoying a major resurgence since the early 1990s recession. Of U.S. companies with 100 or more employees, 72 percent sent managers to leadership training in 1995. The growth in expenditures for executive programs is a result of the increasing recognition that education and leadership development are powerful levers in communicating and implementing key strategic initiatives.

In a time when everyone has technology, and competitive advantage goes far beyond consistently delivering a product better, faster, and cheaper, business leaders know that their human resources are the ultimate source of their competitive advantage. In the "knowledge era," organizations have to be adaptable and flexible to respond to changes and developments that can make or break their products, services, and markets. Intellectual capital is the new key to success.

With more new information generated in the past 30 years than in the previous 5,000 years and with information now doubling every four years, the expectations, values, wants, and needs of today's knowledge workers are different from those who began their corporate lives 10, 20, or 30 years ago. The outstanding leaders in this new era will not likely be measured by their personal achievements, but rather by their ability to unleash other people's talents. As Marshall J. Gerber, a former partner-in-charge of Andersen's Partner Development Program (PDP), puts it, "Companies are finding that treading water is not enough. Now they have to run just to keep up. Our job is not to just help them keep up, but to provide what they need to lead the race."[1]

Andersen Zeroes in on Leadership Development

Executive development programs continue to exist in large numbers. They may be provided by vendors from educational institutions such as Harvard and Wharton, organizations such as the Center for Creative Leadership, or individuals such as Gary Hamel, Peter Senge, and others. A few consortiums of companies are working with "gurus" to create highly relevant satellite or Internet presentations that will help their executives stay current.

Not only are organizations spending more time and money on executive development, but they are targeting their time and money more specifically. Distinctions are being made between managers and executive leaders. It is no longer assumed that managers and leaders are two points on the same career path. They are now seen as different roles with "different, but parallel" career paths within an organization.

Andersen's belief is that tomorrow's leaders need to be identified early and then provided with appropriate opportunities and learning experiences to enhance their leadership capabilities

Andersen's Partner Development Program

PDP was created in 1994 to help provide its more than 4,000 partners with the competencies they needed to help the leaders of contemporary corporations succeed in a global market. Today, PDP works hard to complement its programs with those offered by the various service categories and other parts of the organization. PDP also makes a significant effort to communicate its benefits to the rest of the organization, so that everyone can understand where this program fits into the big picture.

One of PDP's challenges is the fact that Andersen is a company with so many owners! The target audience for PDP is all of the partners at Andersen. Andersen is not a corporation and its partners are more than executives. They are in fact the owners and operators of this professional service firm. Each partner falls into one of four service categories: economic financial consulting; business consulting, tax; legal and business advisory; and assurance and business advisory. To add to the challenge, Andersen partners are found in a wide variety of locations around the globe working on-site with their clients. Thus, communication and knowledge distribution among such a group can become a difficult but, nevertheless, essential task.

PDP continues to prove its ability to accomplish the challenging communication and education task. Not surprisingly, Andersen continues to pay the annual cost of its corporate education arm gladly.

Despite its initial successes, PDP continues to modify its measures and programs to stay one step ahead of business-unit needs. For example, instead of simply measuring the overall quality of its training courses, PDP has begun to declare its courses successes or failures according to the extent to which the course participants feel their job performance has been improved. This is, to be sure, a tougher measure to meet, but a much more relevant one for the business, and thus for PDP.

A Brief History

We will use this important part of Andersen's history of education programs to provide insight into how this organization approaches the challenges of developing leaders. The popular Arthur Andersen Executive Program was created in the early 1980s. It was the firm's first formal attempt to provide organization-wide executive development. In 1988, the Tax Division started what it called the Trusted Business Advisor initiative. This approach stretched the role and responsibilities of the partner, and it was so successful that it was eventually adopted by the rest of the organization. The idea led to a number of small pilot programs that endeavored to provide some of the new skills that these Trusted Business Advisors would need to do their jobs.

In 1992, Andersen conducted a partner satisfaction survey.

The findings made it clear that the partners wanted the program to:

1. Focus on the client
2. Help partners meet changing marketplace needs
3. Address specific challenges faced by CEOs and CFOs
4. Link to Andersen's strategic framework and measures
5. Be valuable to the partners

In its initial needs assessment for PDP, Andersen did a great deal of research beyond its own clients. It also went to business school faculties and executive search firms to seek input from those outside the firm who could advise about types of behaviors and skills that partners were likely to need in the future. A subsequent task force recommended the creation of PDP to fill the partner training need. By 1994, the program was in operation.

PDP's Initial Challenges

Some of the initial challenges the leadership development program faced are easy to guess for anyone who has lived under the umbrella of a large corporation. It took time and proof of results to obtain real and confident buy-in from the partners. There was a predictable short-term focus on revenues that made partners initially reluctant to "sacrifice" three-and-a-half days worth of work for a training program. There was the assumption by some partners that technical training in their specific service line would be far more valuable than generic leadership talk. There were natural complexities and roadblocks in trying to provide the training cost effectively and on a global basis. And last, but by no means least, there were unsuccessful training programs of the past whose reputations had to be overcome.

The global and multiple-owner nature of Andersen created an additional challenge. The firm made it clear that partners were free to contract locally with external trainers for their local needs. Thus, PDP was under pressure from its inception to compete for its own partners' training business. The program had to develop credibility and do it quickly. PDP made maximum use of the impact data from its first few years of operation. The partners who had been through the first PDP courses outperformed their counterparts. Soon, the program gained respectability and enrollment numbers increased. Overall, partner ratings, in terms of performance improvement on the job, make it clear that PDP has earned its place as the one of the most effective training methods for the partners' money.

PDP's Primary Job Is Executive Development

The focus of PDP is executive development. The program is not involved in developing people at lower levels, although the company does have programs for this lower-level leadership development. One of PDP's major objectives is to help its partners move toward leadership behaviors and styles (such as transformational leadership) that are more productive in the new economy.

The PDP mission statement is "to help Andersen partners worldwide acquire and build the knowledge, skills, and behaviors required to be valued and trusted business advisors in an ever-changing marketplace."[2]

Andersen believes that this goal will be accomplished by providing development opportunities that improve the partners' ability to:

* Address the wants and needs of their clients (particularly, CFOs and CEOs) using the full resources of the firm
* Work effectively and productively with their colleagues and direct reports
* Contribute to the achievement of Andersen's strategy, mission, vision, and goals.

The PDP Team

The PDP partner-in-charge reports directly to the partner-in-charge of worldwide human resources, who in turn reports to the CEO of Andersen. Reporting to the partner-in-charge are the program's director and three subunits:

1. Development and Research
2. Program Conduct
3. Allocation and Enrollment

The PDP team currently has five people who are full time. Beyond those five, there can be as many as twenty others who handle specific assignments relating to performance analysis and consulting, vendor searches, bringing new programs online, measurement, and evaluation research. And, of course, Arthur Andersen Performance and Learning is a part of the organization that is made up of the type of experts that PDP often needs. These internal experts include industrial/organizational psychologists, organizational development consultants, educational psychologists, and various other subject matter experts.

The objectives of the PDP team are to:

1. To obtain and maintain leadership's commitment to the program
2. To provide alignment with Andersen strategy
3. To offer world-class quality and design of instructional programs
4. To communicate up, down, and across the organization
5. To develop and maintain the role of local office coordinator
6. To develop, research, evaluate, and continuously improve the program

PDP's Funding and Course Offerings

PDP operates on a zero-based funding model, meaning it seeks only to deliver its services and recover its costs. All profits go back into the business. The smaller costs of program development are handled as overhead costs allocated to each of the offices; student tuition and housing are charged back to local offices; and transportation costs are adjusted to equalize costs across the globe. In all, the total cost of delivery is approximately $4,000 per attendee.

Each Andersen office is charged for the number of training slots allocated to it. An office can pay for more slots, but it cannot get a refund for using fewer slots than have been allocated to it. (If an office uses a local provider and the training goals can be demonstrated to be close to PDP goals, some exemption may be granted.) This system assures payment for the program's fixed costs and encourages offices to utilize the training. This budgeting approach is similar for other corporate services throughout Andersen and is not unique to PDP.

Course offerings are generated annually from a similar zero-based approach. To determine each year's offerings, PDP carefully analyzes past and projected attendance based on changing needs and strategies. Slots are then allocated to the local offices of various regions and service lines, based on their number of partners and the training history of the partners in that office. The offices use their knowledge of their partners and local client needs to determine which individuals will benefit most from which courses.

When PDP was first started, Andersen conducted a "partner validation" to identify specific gaps between partners' current skills and the skill sets they needed to possess. PDP then designed programs to bridge those specific gaps. This same gap analysis continues today. The organization realizes that programs that treat the weaknesses of the majority do not always address the needs of each individual. So, PDP builds in flexibility for individual partners, enabling them to select the particular courses they want. Furthermore, PDP will actually perform external searches for partners who have a specific skill they want to develop or enhance. It is this kind of flexibility that helps PDP operate an organization-wide program that is individually relevant.

PDP's Curriculum and Learning Activities

The goal of PDP is to make sure partners are given relevant training; therefore, PDP does not have a core curriculum. Instead, the group has a series of courses that are highly interrelated and build upon one another. The group feels that partners must be given a high degree of flexibility to pursue a personalized development plan. As a result, partners are encouraged to take responsibility for charting their own development path based on individual needs.

Courses last approximately three-and-a-half days. Some courses have follow-up activities, such as executive coaching, that vary in length based on the needs of the partners. Typical course offerings might include:

◆ People Side of Change
◆ Strategic Renewal
◆ Enhancing Client and Colleague Relationships
◆ Managing Innovation: From the CEO's Perspective
◆ Leadership and High-Performance Teams
◆ Dynamics of Market Leadership: From the CEO's Perspective
◆ Global Financial Management
◆ Strategic Management
◆ Strategic Renewal—Changing the Rules of the Game

Some PDP courses involve a modified action-learning approach with both pre- and post-work. Before such a course begins, partners are given criteria and protocol for selecting and interviewing a client that they will use as a case study during the course. During the course, learners work in a team to develop a set of recommendations to help the client improve the business performance. After the course is over, the team must work together to complete and deliver its presentation to the client.

PDP courses are delivered worldwide in order to promote a global perspective. This strategy also forces program participants to focus on the program and not on their work. If the programs were delivered only in the St. Charles facility, PDP would have a hard time prying people away from their jobs. As a result, all programs are held in hotels in major international cities. This makes it easy for participants to travel in and out but still gives them some of the isolation conducive to learning.

Each program delivered by PDP has a unique design. Generally, Andersen makes maximum use of small, problem-solving groups in its program activities. There are elements of lecture in each course, but this approach is not emphasized. Other activities include case methods, simulations, action learning, experiential learning, and executive coaching.

Andersen believes that the periods before and after the course are every bit as important as the training event itself. For this reason, its training programs attempt to help the partners prepare to enter a course and use what they have learned once the course is over. Course pre-work includes reading case studies and working with clients to discuss problems or roadblocks. Post-work is used to reinforce learning and includes peer and executive coaching.

Coaching and Mentoring

Coaching is used in two courses of PDP. These coaches typically have backgrounds in psychology, organizational psychology, organizational behavior, and similar fields. Participants work with a coach throughout the training event and may continue to work with their coach after the course.

Minimal Use of Learning Technologies

Since Andersen's partners spend a majority of their time on-site with clients, they have a limited number of chances to get to know each other. PDP's former director Michelle Miller points out that, "One of the key goals of the PDP program is to give partners the opportunity to network and build relationships, which is going to foster teamwork across the organization."

Therefore, although almost all communications are electronic, the focus has been on the face-to-face interaction associated with PDP's programs. This strategy continues to be revisited as the breadth of knowledge the partners need increases. In the future, most of the knowledge-building components of the program will be delivered to the partners via their computers.

Use of Vendors

PDP prefers using vendors, because outsiders infuse the organization with new ideas and ways of thinking. Vendors also bring their own experiences to the table. New experiences and viewpoints combine with Andersen's experiences to produce powerful learning.

PDP works with vendors to modify existing courses in order to achieve the stated performance objectives and to enhance the relevance to the culture and the partners' roles. The PDP team provides each vendor with a set of stated performance objectives before a course is designed and then collaborates closely with the vendor in the program design phase. Because PDP does not use 100 percent of anyone's off-the-shelf products, vendors must show a willingness to adapt their courses to specific Andersen needs before they will be hired. At times, Andersen asks two vendors to work on the development of one course. This helps create a final product with a richer and fuller range of content and experiences.

Oversight of PDP vendors does not end when the design phase is complete. To ensure consistent and quality delivery of each program, a PDP representative attends each of the program courses offered.

To select a vendor, Andersen has a set of selection criteria based on what PDP has learned is necessary to achieve results. Standard selection criteria include:

- Course content
- Length of course
- Instructional strategy
- Delivery options
- Appropriateness for target audience
- Ability of content to be customized
- Cost
- Course's fit with tested and accepted practices
- Adaptability of the course to cultural differences
- Testimonials from past program participants
- Reputation of the vendor

Once the selection criteria are clear, PDP researches vendors worldwide that might provide relevant programs. Using published information and initial conversations with these vendors, PDP narrows the field to about two or three vendors. It then tries to select one of the remaining vendors based on references. If there is still no clear distinction, Andersen sends a few partners to a vendor's open-enrollment class to observe. (If open enrollment is not an option, PDP will authorize a pilot class with a small group of partners.)

Through this process, PDP selects a vendor. Using participant feedback from the pilot class and an in-house designer, PDP will make an additional iteration and pilot the course again with partners. With feedback from this second pilot, PDP makes final changes.

Outside Faculty

PDP courses are delivered by outside faculty. Because Andersen partners place major emphasis on credentials in determining the true value of a course, the PDP team must make sure all its instructors are world-class caliber. The firm seeks teachers with experience in both the academic and business worlds. Andersen's practical and pragmatic culture requires theoretically grounded academics who can provide practical learnings from real business situations.

Contracting with a world-class faculty is an expensive task. Consequently, as the credibility of its program has grown, PDP has been able to hire more up-and-coming faculty members who are on the cutting edge. This helps keep participant costs in line with external executive development programs. Every attempt is made to ensure that program costs to the partners remain at or below the cost of similar external executive development programs.

Leadership Pools

PDP's focus remains on the 4,000-plus partners in Andersen's 72,000-person organization. Any of these partners can participate in PDP's offerings. Andersen also has committees in which younger partners and potential managers have the opportunity to enhance their own development.

Andersen has a tradition of promoting from within the firm. Recently however, in order to add certain skills sets, Andersen has recruited experienced personnel from outside the organization. These hires enter the organization at different personnel levels that are appropriate to their level of experience. Some even enter the organization directly as partners.

Andersen has specific local and centralized programs to integrate new hires. These orientation programs attempt to help new employees at all levels adjust to the Andersen culture and make them aware of local and global goals and strategies. As Sue Bumpass, director of the program, expressed it, "There is a distinct Andersen culture that is consistent around the world, regardless of the office's location. It is definitely something noticeable. It seems to just sit right on top of the local culture."

While PDP has no formal responsibility in the integration process, it does recognize that some of its courses deliver valuable information that helps new partners operate more successfully. Informal feedback confirms that new partner hires who have participated in PDP's courses have a better understanding of the organization and how to operate more effectively within it.

Generally speaking, Andersen is committed to a diverse workforce. The firm makes a concerted effort to turn over control of its global offices to nationals as quickly as possible. Within the program, each local office is allocated a spot for about 25 percent of its partners. This ensures a diverse group of program participants, both across cultures and geographic regions, as well as through the company's different practice areas.

Identifying Leadership Talent

With each passing year of successful corporate leadership training, Andersen becomes better at recognizing the traits and competencies that indicate strong leadership potential. It has more experience spotting the behaviors necessary to excel in any job or leadership task. The qualifying competencies include multiple skills, knowledge, traits, and attributes.

While Andersen has no official set of competencies, PDP has been able to develop its own list of competencies for partners based on its performance analyses, which include findings from a variety of Andersen and PDP studies (such as client and employee satisfaction). The program concentrates on nontechnical competencies that apply to any of the service lines of the business. Technical competency development remains the responsibility of the different service categories. There are three broad categories for the competencies:

1. Business acumen
2. Personnel development
3. Personal development

Research has shown that overlapping competencies in all three of these areas are required for effective leadership. According to PDP's refined observations, Andersen needs to build partners who are:

- Globally aware
- Agents of change
- Strategic planners
- Trusted business advisors
- Team leaders
- Developers of self and others
- Marketers
- Skilled communicators
- Builders of relationships
- Providers of integrated services
- Promoters of advanced knowledge

These PDP leadership competencies apply to both client and internal leadership responsibilities. As a result, each competency now has a behavioral statement to the client and to roles and responsibilities inside the organization. The competencies are interrelated and link back to the organization's Four Cornerstones, which are to be "simply the best" in:

1. People;
2. Market share/growth;
3. Exceeding client expectations; and
4. Quality/risk management.

Engaging Future Leaders

Andersen uses both internal and external data to discern the learning, development, and performance needs of its partners. Internal data comes from client-satisfaction surveys, employee-satisfaction surveys, Andersen service-category strategies, upward feedback, and analysis of 450-degree feedback" (360-degree feedback, plus client evaluations)[3] and other studies.

The evaluations are given to partners as prerequisites before a PDP course is offered. This data is sent in aggregate form to Andersen's assessment and measurement staff, who in turn identify organizational strengths and weaknesses, as well as general behaviors that lead to better performance. This information has proven helpful when PDP is deciding what courses to provide in the future.

External data comes from:

1. Market research
2. Business trends
3. Leading-edge thinking from universities and business gurus
4. Best practices

PDP relies heavily on the large amount of research the firm does for other purposes. Andersen will also talk to leading thinkers in the field, as well as to executive development groups, to identify emerging trends. Last, but not least, secondary research has proven to be a helpful tool.

PDP conducts its performance analyses on an annual basis. Andersen does a thorough job of course evaluation, and this information, along with the internal and external data, is stirred into the overall performance analysis of partners. Based on the assessment, Andersen reviews its competencies and makes appropriate changes. If the competencies are changing, PDP will either

1. Make changes to existing programs
2. Identify new courses
3. Make revisions to the entire PDP strategy and approach

PDP Links to Andersen's Business Strategy

To meet the needs of a business that continues to diversify and globalize, PDP constantly works to link closely to Andersen's business strategy and remain in sync with current objectives. When conducting performance or needs analyses, PDP reviews strategy documents from Andersen and from its four service categories. By linking its program efforts to Andersen strategy and its organizational and individual performance measures, PDP not only helps Andersen achieve its business strategy, but also aids partners in achieving their performance goals.

Andersen partners tend to believe more of what they hear from their peers than what they hear from leadership. So, PDP's best path to get support for its program has been simply to deliver learning interventions that work: a corporate leadership training program must deliver more capable leaders or it is finished. On the other hand, nothing succeeds like success. Positive feedback and word-of-mouth continue to be the most powerful tools for achieving buy-in from the program's customers and top executives within the organization.

The Proof of PDP's Value

The result of Andersen's total and sustained commitment to corporate education and knowledge growth has become obvious in Andersen's long-term personnel policies. The firm believes it has an adequate supply of top-quality leaders in the pipeline. Because of this, some Andersen locations have instituted mandatory retirement-age policies to ensure that up-and-comers have room to grow. This confidence about the supply and quality of future leadership is certainly an attitude toward which many global corporations aspire. It should be noted that many mandatorily retired Andersen partners leave financially secure and still young enough to enjoy applying their skills in a variety of settings, including contributions to the voluntary sector.

PDP is known within the company for its dedication to collecting learning and performance measures and for its support of the firm's overall business strategies. The Development and Research activity of PDP conducts impressive performance analyses and needs assessments to help reveal and meet the requirements of the company's diverse business units. Impact research has revealed evidence that partners who go through PDP's courses perform better in the exact areas that the business uses to measure performance. Its learning intervention efforts work, and they generate clear and measurable improvement in the arenas.

Andersen's evaluation system is composed of three components:

1. Performance analysis/need assessment efforts
2. Course evaluations
3. Performance evaluation/impact research

Evaluation forms are collected prior to, immediately after, and two to three months after the course. These evaluations go directly to the partners and include course evaluation, performance evaluation, and needs-assessment questions. After the course is completed, partners are asked to assess themselves in terms of knowledge and performance gained from the course. Andersen has found this type of self-assessment to be a comprehensive method to track changes in learning and performance.

Impact research compares the performance of partners who have attended specific PDP courses to those who have not. Comparisons are made to organizational benchmarks of performance. The results of this research demonstrate links between transfer of training efforts, client satisfaction, and per-hour-supervised net fees. Impact research is conducted in a three-year cycle, with information being gathered on partners a year before they enter the program and continuing into the year after they have completed the training.

Andersen has learned the importance of using both participant satisfaction and impact research. In one case, in which participant satisfaction ratings were not as high as those of other courses, impact analysis revealed that course attendance had a positive effect on participants' job performance. In this instance, student praise did not tell the whole story.

Regression analysis has shown that course content is a huge factor in determining participant-satisfaction scores. If participants think the course content did not apply to their geographic area, or that class activities do not reflect on-the-job tasks and activities, overall satisfaction scores will drop accordingly. On the other hand, if they feel course content was appropriate and relevant to their job responsibilities, overall satisfaction increases.

Andersen staff members report that the major lessons they have learned through the experience of running many successful PDP programs include the following:

PDP Lesson No. 1: Offer World-Class Program Quality

PDP's offerings are market driven. Yearly needs assessments and performance analyses focus on helping participants achieve their key performance measures. By tying PDP's work to the success of both participants and the business, PDP has repeatedly demonstrated its worth to the company.

Tying program efforts to business results is only a first step. PDP is a success because it has accomplished its mission. The program has found that the use of leading-edge research is critical to delivering a top-quality product. The organization has developed a broad network of external experts. PDP keeps close watch on the vendors who develop its courses. It shares its evaluation data with them and helps them to update the program continually both in terms of content and in delivery strategies. It demands that vendors be flexible enough to change programs to keep them current. PDP continues to experiment with new and more effective approaches to program delivery. Continuous experimentation and reevaluation is key to offering world-class quality.

Andersen's PDP understands that to deliver a best-practice program, it must focus on value and not cost. Cost is important, but it must not be the driving factor. If the program offered improves business results, those who are paying the bills will be more likely to continue their support. And, by constantly raising the bar for itself, PDP continues to meet customer needs and expectations. According to an old saying, "If it's cheap and not good, nobody will come a second time."

PDP Lesson No. 2: Generate Leadership Support

The PDP team acknowledges that sponsorship by the CEO is critical to its success. Furthermore, "sponsorship" must mean participation and not just a "blind endorsement." Andersen's CEO backed the pivotal funding model that was chosen and provided the necessary support for PDP's efforts. But when a new CEO was selected in the late 1990s, the program worked hard for his involvement and the involvement of his leadership team. In addition, the PDP team has wisely labored to develop its advocates and supporters across all of Andersen's geographical regions and service categories.

PDP Lesson No. 3: Feedback Is Critical

Andersen spends a significant amount of time ensuring that its evaluation system is robust and credible. Impact analyses and performance evaluations have shown PDP's positive effect over time, which has been absolutely necessary in generating support. In addition, PDP engages in frequent benchmarking efforts and does its best to learn from others in order to improve its strategy and program offerings continuously.

PDP Lesson No. 4: Communicate, Communicate, Communicate

Communication up, down, and across the organization is essential to generating support, and it is essential to PDP's success. The group not only has to prove its worth to senior management, but it must also build credibility in its customer base. Some of the communication tools used include newsletters sent to all program participants, executive summaries, face-to-face communication with senior executives, and internal trade fairs.

Andersen has found that internal marketing through booths set up during key executive gatherings is a great way to promote the program. Remember that PDP is not only in competition with outside vendors, but also with other internal offices offering development programs. Local offices have the option to use any and all means for their partners' development, and PDP must prove that it is the best option. Again, PDP's use of impact analyses and performance evaluations is helpful in promoting its case.

Externally, the PDP team conducts presentations and writes articles about its successes. The group also participates in benchmarking forums to share trade secrets with other highly effective organizations. PDP's leaders have found that external credentialization is effective for generating internal support.

Maintaining the Momentum

PDP capitalized early on its high level of senior-management support. It rode the wave of a company-wide initiative to prepare Andersen's personnel for a business that was undergoing rapid change. The program itself was started by a taskforce appointed by the CEO. As a result, PDP's founders had a high level of organizational buy-in. They created the positive funding model in which local Andersen offices paid for their partners' seats in PDP courses, whether those seats were used or not.

However, even "paid-for tickets" will not raise a crowd for a losing team. PDP had to prove its effect on Andersen's business results. It has done this through skillful impact analyses and through the same measures Andersen uses to determine the effectiveness of a partner—customer satisfaction and per-hour billing. PDP has shown its direct link to the bottom line.

Summary

In 1994, following some unsuccessful training programs, the Partner Development Program (PDP) was created to help provide partners with the competencies needed to function in a global market. Although there was initial skepticism and a reluctance to donate valuable time, the program has proved its value based on results and thus achieved buy-in from the partners.

PDP's focus is executive development, and its goal is to ensure that partners are given relevant training. Therefore, there isn't a core curriculum. Partners are encouraged to take responsibility for charting their own development paths. All PDP courses are delivered by outside faculty. Faculty members with experience in both academic and business arenas are highly regarded, because the partners prefer to learn from examples of real business situations.

Andersen bases its strategy on its Four Cornerstones model. By linking efforts to Andersen strategy and organizational and individual performance measures, PDP not only helps Andersen achieve its business strategy, but also aids partners in the achievement of individual performance goals.

By conducting an in-depth performance analysis and needs assessment, PDP has been able to reveal and meet the requirements of the company's diverse business units. Impact research and performance evaluations show that the program's learning intervention efforts are working, and that they are generating clear and measurable improvement in exactly the arenas they were chartered to impact.[4]

Notes

1. Susan Bumpass, Constance Filling, and Marshall Gerber, "Trends in Executive Development," *HR Director: The Arthur Andersen Guide to Human Capital* (London: Profile Pursuits, Inc., 1997), p. 3.
2. APQC Arthur Andersen Site Visit Summary, June 19, 1998, p. 8.
3. Many organizations use customer feedback as the fourth component of 360-degree feedback, but Andersen wanted to put special emphasis on information from clients.
4. For further information about Andersen's "Developing Tomorrow's Corporate Leaders Today," *HRDirector The Arthur Andersen Guide to Human Capital.* (London: Profile Pursuits, Inc., (1997).

3

General Electric

Staging Ground for Corporate Revolution

G eneral Electric (GE) could not be more appropriately named. *Generally* speaking, GE works with everything *electric*. The company is the modern-day result of the historic genius of Thomas Edison, the American inventor of the lightbulb, who also held patents on many devices and applications designed to put electricity to work for humans. The company that is today known as GE was initially formed to make the most of all those patents.

GE was so perfectly positioned at the outset of America's eventual total electrification that its early growth was nearly out of control. From original business targets that were limited to the tools of generating, distributing, and using electricity, GE's world domain eventually came to include divergent fields like computers, air and space products, nuclear power, the world of plastics, financial services, and, more recently, the National Broadcasting Company (NBC).

It is not surprising that GE's phenomenal herd of cash cows continued to create the capital and momentum required to sustain growth and repeatedly spin off successful ventures. GE also had the money required to constantly give attention to better ways of handling its own complexity. In almost every decade of American business history, GE leadership has been documented in both texts and journals, not simply because GE was a famous company, but also because of its great work. Generation after generation, its leaders have set the pace for methods and concepts that have worked for American business, particularly big business.

In the 1950s, CEO Ralph Cordiner introduced profit centers to change the emphasis from megalith to manageable points of diversification. Today, profit centers are as natural a part of corporate thought and language as cubicles and coffee breaks.

As American soldiers returned to their post-war jobs fully indoctrinated with military concepts of rank-and-file, GE again set the direction of world business by its divisionalization. The company was organized into more than 100 "armies," each a company in its own right. As one of these companies within the company struck its own gold and grew large with its own success, it was further subdivided. Once again, GE led the way into a world in which the holding company was a widely understood and accepted way of managing diversity and maintaining motivation.

In the 1960s and early 1970s, Fred Borch and his GE brain trust originated the idea of increasing the fodder for the cash cows that performed most admirably. Today, business people understand, and often live by, the concept of allocating resources on the basis of projected return on investment (ROI). Even the flaws of ROI thinking led GE to the development of a more effective system for evaluating businesses. Strategic business units (SBUs) entered the language and helped leaders focus on the factors most crucial to the success of their businesses.

In 1972, Reg Jones took over as CEO of GE's 10 groups, 46 divisions, and 190 departments. He had the company reorganized into 43 SBUs. But Jones and his vice chairmen quickly realized that there was no way for them to mentally grasp and process so much information on so many fronts. So Jones decided that the burden of review had to be carried on more shoulders.

In 1977, GE regrouped its "companies" and added a level

of management intended to oversee and guide the "industries" or "sectors" within its vast domain. Thus, the sector approach became another GE organizational success story.

The next GE legend was to become richly apparent because of the sector approach's ability to showcase the skills and prowess of sector leaders. A hot, young executive—who had broken all records in his leadership of GE's engineering plastics business—was promoted to sector executive over the GE world of home appliances. His continued success in this brand-new arena clearly demonstrated his fitness for the position of CEO upon the retirement of Reg Jones. That executive was Jack Welch.

The House that Jack Built

There may be no more influential executive in the business world than Jack Welch. Though the companies of Bill Gates and a few others have made phenomenal records, their results can often be attributed to being in the right place at the right time. On the other hand, Jack Welch is widely known, admired, and emulated because of what he has done to change an elephant into a pudgy gazelle. Welch is likely to be remembered in business history as the master of stating a business goal in words that anyone can immediately understand, remember, and obey.

Jack Welch's plan for GE has been widely reported, admired, and copied. His vision statement began with a sentence filled with the traditional words of such statements: "A decade from now, I would like General Electric to be perceived as a unique, high-spirited, entrepreneurial enterprise, a company known around the world for its unmatched level of excellence." It continued with another sentence that got even more down to business: "I want General Electric to be the most profitable, highly diversified company on earth, with world-quality leadership in every one of its product lines." But it was Jack Welch's explanation of the way to reach that goal that became so famous. In effect, he told his troops, "Either be number one or two in your industry, be in the process of becoming number one or two in your industry, or be in the process of selling your company."

Thus, Jack Welch gave GE's companies the choice of dominance or divestiture.

Jack Welch's other claim to fame is a practice that has come to be known as "destaffing." It was a new term for an old concept: people who are not necessary need to go. Welch earned the nickname "Neutron Jack," for producing results like the neutron bomb, which eliminates the people and leaves buildings standing. Under the destaffing practice, about 100,000 GE employees became former GE employees in a three- to four-year period. Welch's own corporate-planning staff was cut in half, from 200 to 100, in order to get "general managers talking to general managers about strategy, rather than planners talking to planners."

Leadership Wisdom from Chairman Jack

Jack Welch's genius for phrasing complex concepts in clear, concise, concrete statements has made him a much-quoted person. The following list of slightly universalized Welch-isms is ripe for global e-mail trips, as leaders try to inspire their people:

♦ "Good business leaders create a vision, articulate the vision, passionately own the vision, and relentlessly drive it to completion."

♦ "Good leaders are open. They go up, down, and around their organizations to reach people. They don't stick to established channels. They're informal. They're straight with people. They make a religion out of being accessible. They never get bored telling their story."

♦ "Real communication takes countless hours of eyeball-to-eyeball, back-and-forth. It means more listening than talking. It's not pronouncements on videotape or in newspapers. It is human beings coming to see and accept things through a constant, interactive process that is aimed at consensus. It must be absolutely relentless. That's a real challenge for us; there's still not enough candor in this company."

♦ "Candid managers—leaders—don't get paralyzed about the fragility of the organization. They tell people the truth. That doesn't scare them, because they realize their people know the truth anyway."

♦ "We've seen over and over again that businesses facing market downturns, tougher competition, and more demanding customers inevitably make forecasts that are much too optimistic. This means they don't take advantage of the opportunities change usually offers."

♦ "Change in the marketplace isn't something to fear; it's an enormous opportunity to shuffle the deck and replay the game."

♦ "Becoming faster is tied to becoming simpler. Our businesses, with tens of thousands of employees, will not respond to visions that have sub-paragraphs and footnotes. If we're not simple, we can't be fast. If we're not fast, we can't win."

♦ "Simplicity, to an engineer, means clean, functional, winning designs—no bells or whistles. In marketing, it might manifest itself as clear, unencumbered proposals. For manufacturing people, it would produce a logical process that makes sense to every individual on the line. And, on an individual, interpersonal level, it would take the form of plain-speaking, directness, and honesty."

♦ "People who are freed from the confines of their box on the organizational chart, whose status rests on real-world achievement, those are the people who develop the self-confidence to be simple; to share every bit of information available to them; to listen to those above; below, and around them; and then to move boldly."

♦ "You can't taste winning if you spend your days wandering in the muck of a self-absorbed bureaucracy."

♦ "Speed. Simplicity. Self-confidence. We have it in increasing measure. We know where it comes from, and we have plans to increase it."

♦ "A flat-reward system is a big anchor to incrementalism. We want to give big rewards to those who do things, but without going after the scalps of those who reach for the big win but fail. Punishing failure assures that no one dares."

♦ "My concept of loyalty is not *giving time* to some corporate entity and, in turn, being shielded and protected from the outside world. Loyalty is an affinity among people who want to grapple with the outside world and win."

Turning Quotes into Reality

Of course, impressive statements about methodology remain impressive only as long as the speaker delivers: Jack Welch delivered. To keep in close touch with his employees, he continued GE's traditional management development process known as "CI" and "CII" reviews (three-hour meetings between the CEO and each GE business, held in the spring and again in the fall). The specific focus of each three-hour discussion continues to be the human resource potential of the interviewee company and how it is being developed.

Welch also made important changes to GE's traditional personnel practices. He adjusted the way the company compensates its managers and other employees. The new system gives more recognition to individual contributors and higher rewards to those who produce superior results.

The Welch belief that employees at all levels of the company have to feel the risk-reward tension, caused him to speak out against and try to eliminate any assumptions of a job-for-life at GE. He dispelled assumptions that a worker is owed lifetime employment or care simply because he or she shows up faithfully for years. By doing so, he refocused GE workers on the fact that GE is living in a competitive world in which no business is a safe haven.

During the Welch years, GE has undergone a huge transition: The new GE is leaner, de-layered, more global, and more productive. Surviving this amount of change, however, is no easy task. Now, more than ever, the organization needs leaders who can operate in a global environment and delegate responsibility to people over whom they have no formal authority.

GE currently consists of 12 businesses, all of which operate on a global basis. They include Aircraft Engines, Appliances, Capital Services, Electrical Distribution and Control, Information Services, Lighting, Medical Systems, Motors and Industrial

Table 3.1   GE: A Brief Perspective

	1981	1997	1999
Revenues	$27.2 billion	$89.3 billion	$111.6 billion
Net income	$1.6 billion	$8.2 billion	$10.7 billion
Businesses	45 SBUs 350 product lines 2 global businesses	12 unique businesses all global	20 top businesses* all global
Worldwide employment	404,000	240,000	340,000*
Management layers	9–11	4–5	4–5

*20 top businesses as identified by GE out of more than 36 distinct businesses. The increase in businesses and employees from 1997 to 1999 is primarily due to over 100 acquisitions.

Systems, NBC, Plastics, Power Systems, and Transportation Systems.

Jack Welch's clearly stated goal, that each GE company be number one or two in its industry, has essentially become a reality. As early as 1989, the following victories were among GE's trophies:

- Aircraft engines = First in United States; first in the world
- Broadcasting (NBC) = First in United States; no world competition
- Circuit breakers = Three-way tie for first in United States (with Square D and Westinghouse), four-way tie worldwide (with Merlin Gerin, Siemens, Westinghouse)
- Defense electronics = Second in United States; second worldwide (behind GM's Hughes Electronics)
- Electric motors = First in United States; first worldwide
- Engineering plastics = Three-way tie for first in United States (with Square D and Westinghouse); first worldwide
- Factory automation = Second in United States (behind Allen-Bradley); third worldwide (behind Siemens and Allen-Bradley)
- Financial services = First in United States; first worldwide
- Industrial and power systems = First in United States, first worldwide

- Information services = First in United States; first worldwide
- Lighting = First in United States; second worldwide (behind Philips)
- Locomotives = First in United States; tied for second worldwide (with GM's Electro-Motive)
- Major appliances = First in United States; second worldwide (tied with Electrolux, behind Whirlpool)
- Medical diagnostic imaging = First in United States; first worldwide
- Plastics = First in United States; first worldwide

Crotonville: Boot Camp for Leaders

In his drive to spread his doctrine of leadership, Jack Welch has also made maximum use of the outstanding corporate education center he inherited at Crotonville, New York. He has focused the attention of GE's education center on specific company-related development activities. From a motto of the 1960s, "Progress is our most important product," Welch has made the new GE mantra, "Leaders are our most important product."

In operation since 1956, GE Crotonville is the original corporate university and is well positioned to develop the next generation of leaders. With the backing of the chairman and GE businesses, Crotonville has created a slate of development programs centered on action learning and dedicated to solving real business problems. The results have not been disappointing. When Welch sits down to consider filling the top 500 management positions in the organization, he has thousands of qualified candidates from whom to choose.

Corporate Leadership Development (CLD) at GE is a global function, with approximately 30 employees in the United States and 12 outside the country. For decades, all corporate leadership development was run solely out of the fabled Crotonville facility. In the last five or six years however, the organization has started putting employees in key geographic locations outside the United States. Today, these individuals deliver courses based on what they see happening in Europe, Asia, or Mexico, and the offerings can be quite different from those created in the United States. In addition, many of GE's leadership programs are conducted all over the world, and program managers in Crotonville work with people in other locations to deliver those programs.

Only about half the people at Crotonville are permanent training staff. The other half spends approximately two years in the training organization, before rotating back out to the front lines of GE businesses. Not only does this help to ground corporate's training in business realities, but it also provides a global perspective, as several CLD team members are brought in from outside the United States.

As Crotonville Sees Its Mission

The mission of CLD-Crotonville is to create, identify, and transfer organizational learning to enhance GE's growth and competitiveness worldwide. The following activities are listed to contribute to the accomplishment of that mission:

1. Educate employees—focusing on leadership, change, Six Sigma (a five-phase quality improvement process), and key corporate initiatives;
2. Communicate and strengthen commitment to GE and GE values;
3. Build bridges across boundaries by transmitting best practices from one GE location to another, and by providing a setting for people in which to interact across businesses, functions, and hierarchies; and
4. Improve relationships with strategic customers and other key constituencies.

From this list, it is apparent that GE Crotonville's mission is broader than the typical corporate training center. Even beyond leadership development, CLD is determined to tie in with business initiatives and to "communicate, share, and broadcast." For example, CLD staff intends that all NBC employees feel they are part of GE and are committed to GE values.

CLD also plays a key role in breaking down boundaries

throughout the organization—not just those boundaries between functions and levels, but also those between GE and its customers. CLD is also chartered to improve GE's relationships with strategic customers, key constituents, and suppliers.

Many of GE's 12 businesses have major training centers of their own. So, in addition to Crotonville, there are similar training functions in the key GE businesses. The roles of these groups are distinct. While CLD integrates the work of each business unit, training departments located in each GE business provide the training specific to their products and industry. Consequently, training at GE Capital is different from training at GE Power Systems. Crotonville provides the training that GE wants consistently applied across its businesses. And, of course, Crotonville has the perspective and clout to bring people from all of the businesses together to learn from each other.

Creating a Leadership Development Process

GE makes no formal distinction between leadership and management development. CLD feels that the term *leadership* implies that you have to influence those over whom you have no formal authority. In the past 20 years, this ability has become critical to the success of the organization.

From 1981 to 1999, GE has more than tripled its revenues, while decreasing its worldwide employment from 404,000 to 240,000. Naturally, this type of growth caused an enormous cultural shift within GE, including one at Crotonville. The central training function even changed its name from Corporate Management and Development to Corporate Leadership Development. This change was made in recognition of the fact that the new GE would be a de-layered organization in which there were fewer layers of management, individuals received relatively few formal promotions during their careers, and more people were forced to persuade others over whom they had no formal authority.

In such an environment, leadership skills are of the utmost importance. Persuading others is different from giving them orders, and it usually demands a different style. GE has wisely made sure that this cultural transition is reflected in the program course offerings at Crotonville and throughout the companies. The GE philosophy is that each employee is a leader from day one. Each employee leads with his or her thoughts, actions, and ideas. Even an entry-level person must work toward leadership, if he or she is to be successful at GE.

Training Links to Business Strategy

CLD's courses focus on GE's major themes (such as globalization) and key initiatives (such as Six Sigma). Though the organization "blew up" its formal strategic-planning process in the 1980s, today it relies on its corporate calendar for planning purposes. Key meetings on the calendar include:

♦ *BOCA*—The top 500 operating managers worldwide help set GE's tone and direction for the next 12 months. The meeting is held at the beginning of each year in Boca Raton, Florida.

♦ *Corporate Executive Council (CEC)*—Top business executives meet each quarter to discuss challenges faced and results achieved.

♦ Session "C"—In this human resources meeting, CLD identifies key personnel within the organization. Session "C" consists of an initial meeting in March and a wrap-up session in June or July. Candidates are chosen for attendance at top-level, executive development courses at Crotonville.

♦ *S1 Strategy and S2 Budget Sessions*—These two meetings are conducted in lieu of the old, formal, strategic-planning process.

The chairman is involved in each of these meetings. In terms of setting the corporation's key initiatives, the BOCA meeting is probably the most important. Major themes and initiatives almost always start here. The results of the BOCA meeting are quickly communicated to each employee throughout the organization. And, at the end of the year, all corporate functions are measured against whether or not they were able to support these current initiatives. According to one program manager, "It makes no difference if you are the Corporate Audit staff, Corporate Research and Development (R&D), one of the businesses, or Corporate Leadership Development; you are always looking to the key initiatives that have been established, because you know that, at the end of the year, you will be measured and rewarded depending on whether you support those initiatives."

Keeping Training in Step with Leadership

CLD finds itself constantly challenged by these meetings, and it often has to make drastic curriculum shifts to tie in with these initiatives. CLD has plenty of buy-in to its programs for a number of reasons. First, GE Crotonville has been in business since 1956, and it is naturally part of the fabric of GE. Second, the group has had Jack Welch's tremendous support. Third, CLD has found ways to get business leaders engaged in its work at an operational level, rather than just through verbal support. This is accomplished in a number of ways.

To make training connect with real business, CLD surveys GE leadership around the company and around the world to pinpoint what training is needed for leaders in the future. This important input step keeps executives involved, because they see the results of their feedback appearing in CLD curricula.

CLD also identifies and leverages "early adopters" of its efforts. When GE launched its now famous Work-Out™ program, some business leaders were much more excited than others. Businesses identified champions for the effort and leaned on their results and their successes using Work-Out. The influence of these early adopters proved to be extremely helpful in getting late bloomers on board. Similarly, when corporate launched the Change Acceleration Process (CAP), business leaders and their staffs went to Crotonville to learn about the program and how to apply CAP tools. Those who seemed more receptive were used early on in CAP's existence, and their successes with the program were communicated quickly by word of mouth.

Rewarding Leaders

To promote leadership in general, GE has taken a number of steps. In the early days, when the company was a more hierarchical organization, the few rewards were available only to management at a certain level. Today, bonuses and stock options are available to people at every level of the organization. GE has tried to make available a whole set of rewards that bring forth leaders, not just managers. One example is the Management Reward. This cash award for outstanding leadership can be presented by any manager to anyone in the organization.

Identifying the Leadership Pool

The following GE value statement also serves as a competency model for GE leaders.[1]

GE Leaders—always with unyielding integrity:

- Have a passion for excellence and hate bureaucracy
- Are open to ideas from anywhere and committed to Work-Out
- Live quality and drive cost and speed for competitive advantage
- Have the self-confidence to involve everyone and behave in a boundaryless fashion
- Create a clear, simple, reality-based vision and communicate it to all constituencies
- Have enormous energy and the ability to energize others
- Stretch, set aggressive goals, and reward progress, yet understand accountability and commitment
- See change as opportunity, not threat
- Have global brains and build diverse and global teams

GE has actualized its value statement. It is a close approximation to a typical competency model but was created quickly, simply, and with typical GE self-confidence. These value statements play a key role in determining individual performance.

Every GE employee discusses his or her performance and career goals during a review meeting with his or her manager.

The organization has a (now-famous) chart for rating people. An employee's performance (the "numbers") is rated on one axis and the employee's adherence to the values on the other axis. Those who make their numbers and demonstrate GE values are the most valued. Those who do not make their numbers but do adhere to GE values are given a second chance. Those who make the numbers but do not demonstrate the GE values are next to last. Those who do neither are least valued.

Leadership Pools

Philosophically, the organization feels that it should spend the majority of its time developing its best and brightest. So Crotonville's leadership development offerings are targeted at high-potential individuals, people the organization refers to as its "A Players." Each year Crotonville trains about 10,000 (4 percent) of its approximately 240,000 employees worldwide.

All students at Crotonville have been nominated by their business leaders or identified through the Session "C" process. Two of CLD's higher-level courses, the Business Management Course (BMC) and the Executive Development Course (EDC), fill slots according to the GE business they come from, to get as many businesses and cultures as possible in the same room.

Attracting Internal vs. External Talent

GE has a significant pool of talent within its companies. As a result, the majority of open positions are filled internally. However, the organization tries to seed each of its businesses with some outside talent to avoid stagnation and "inbreeding." External talent is sought when GE is pursuing a new initiative or needs to build competence rapidly. For example, over the past few years, the organization has hired a number of people from the outside to promote its Six Sigma quality effort.

The GE Management Development Institute at Crotonville makes its facilities available for the training sessions of non-GE companies. It is a 52-acre, private enclave with an ideal environment for concentration, inspiration, and professionalism. The centerpiece of Crotonville is a 140,000-square-foot former private residence that combines lodging, dining, recreation, and conference facilities.

Diversity and Cultural Issues

There are no quotas at GE. Diversity is part of the value statement. In addition, the chairman has placed an emphasis on developing diverse talent pools. He often asks businesses what they are doing to advance the careers of high-performing minorities. In addition, the chairman has also identified a number of support groups to promote diversity.

Currently, GE has the luxury of having more than enough employees who want to be recognized by the chairman as the organization's top 500 "game players." As a result, the company has not had to rigorously address work-life issues to the extent that some other organizations have. GE certainly gives people flexibility in this area, but sometimes this means putting one's career on hold for a time.

Needs Assessments

In addition to taking its cue from the annual BOCA managers' meeting, CLD does ad hoc curriculum reviews: CLD team members visit each business group and conduct interviews and focus groups. In these focus groups, senior managers throughout the organization are asked: "What are key opportunities for learning? Where do you see the business going? And, what knowledge and competencies will leaders need to succeed in this new environment?" The feedback received is helpful in designing courses that will benefit customers and the company.

The Session "C" meeting on the corporate calendar is also

a good opportunity for GE to identify trends in the marketplace and to develop programs that fit these trends. At a recent Session "C" meeting, one trend that surfaced was "dis-inflation." Therefore, the chairman called for a program that would bring in leaders to focus on this problem.

Staying on the Cutting Edge

How has Crotonville changed over the last two decades? In the early 1980s, the organization focused on developing individual awareness and cognitive understanding. Corporate training had a huge catalog of courses, and people could pick and choose the courses they wanted to attend. In short, there was no real corporate strategic direction for training efforts.

Over time, CLD has refocused its efforts and now has a much smaller set of offerings. Today, CLD has a sequence of courses that are tied to key transitional points in a person's career. Many of the advanced programs no longer have open enrollment, and selection is part of the annual management development process. The organization has also shifted its focus from training individuals to training teams and dealing with organizational change. Also in the early 1980s, CLD started to refocus on developing new problem-solving approaches for employees. Today, Crotonville's programs provide learners with real-world problems that they in turn have to solve.

GE's core leadership development curriculum consists of six courses that start with entry-level employees and go through to senior management:

- Leadership Course (LC)
- New Manager Development Course (NMDC)
- Experienced Manager Course (EMC)
- Manager Development Course (MDC)
- Business Management Course (BMC)
- Executive Development Course (EDC)

CLD is constantly trying to give its students real-world problems to solve. Rather than bringing cases into the classroom, they take the classroom out into the GE world. Many training efforts involve people working on programs and projects that are part of everyday life.

The higher-level courses are designed to help provide direction for GE from a regional and strategic standpoint, and from a worldwide company standpoint. For example, recently, students in the BMC went to Russia and developed a set of recommendations for GE's operations there. Those learners then shared their recommendations with top leadership, and they, in true "Work-Out fashion," decided on a course of action.

In general, few recommendations that students have come back with have been tabled. Jack Welch himself chooses the action-learning topics for each BMC (three per year) and EDC (one per year). As a result, when GE employees hear that a certain initiative was a recommendation from the BMC or EDC, they work hard to make sure it becomes a reality. One of the biggest changes that occurred in GE was due to a 1995 BMC quality report. This report opened the door for the Six Sigma initiative that is driving the organization today.

Work-Out™

Work-Out is not a traditional program course. It is "made-to-order" workshops developed by CLD. When a business or customer has a problem, CLD assembles a workshop that leverages tools and techniques developed internally. This enables those going through the workshop to hammer out a plan of action for a real business issue. As a result, most of the offerings under Work-Out are not planned in advance, because they must be constructed to fit a specific need. (Any of GE's 240,000 employees is eligible to participate in Work-Outs, and about 200,000 GE people have participated in one of these sessions.)

Before a Work-Out session is assembled, care is taken to identify clearly the issues, communicate the expectations, identify the participants, and prepare the business leader for his or her role.

Work-Out usually begins with a town meeting of the 40 to 100 participants. A typical meeting begins with a one- to three-day, business-specific workshop led by a business team and facilitated by internal or external consultants. The town meeting takes about two half-days. There are multifunctional, multilocational, and multilevel dialogues between the business leaders and the Work-Out participants. Every idea gets a response, as Work-Out is built on the basic GE principle "Give people a voice."

As the town meeting begins, the business leader(s) sets the challenge and defines the expectations. There are team-building, skill-building, and priority-setting activities. Facilitated problem-solving teams then proceed to develop recommendations and make presentations of their ideas. Responses to the presentations and discussions of the ideas begin the process of bringing the benefits of Work-Out to the real-world problem(s).

Following the Work-Out meeting, implementation and follow-up mechanisms are put into place and the necessary supports are provided. Some of the most important supports involve putting into action the various communication processes required to get the word out. These communications can range from internal announcements and explanations to press releases when the public needs to be aware of a new direction or approach.

The RAMMP Matrix

GE's RAMMP Matrix is a process that helps groups scrutinize existing reports, approvals, meetings, measures, policies, practices, and other traditions, in order to verify, simplify, or eliminate them. The following matrix chart assists discussion by graphically representing the items under consideration and depicting possible actions for improvement.

As participants use the RAMMP Matrix to consider each document or procedure, they ask themselves if it could be:

- Eliminated
- Partially eliminated
- Delegated downward
- Done less often

Table 3.2   Matrix Chart

Reports					
Approvals					
Meetings					
Measures					
Policies					
Practices					
Other					
	Under Team/Dept. Control	Under Business/ Div. Control	Under Corporate Control	Under Customer Control	Under Regulator Control

- Done in a less complicated or time-consuming manner
- Done with fewer people involved
- Done using more productive technology
- Other

Change Acceleration Process

CAP is another made-to-order training activity. Launched in 1992, it is complementary to the efforts started by Work-Out. CAP originally called for a team to go through three educational events over a 90-day period, while that group was leading a strategic change. Today, this process has been collapsed to a single, two-and-a-half-day event.

CAP came about when GE recognized that most organizations do not spend enough time dealing with the human component of change. Seeing that this is the reason many change efforts fail, GE designed CAP to give teams the tools necessary to address the "acceptance" side of change and to complement the technical side.

CAP begins with one of the most important (and frequently overlooked) truths of change: "A champion needs to sponsor and lead the change." Time after time, in all sorts of organizations, change efforts have failed when they were legislated, but not led. People only move willingly across the uncertain grounds of unfamiliar territory when they are following the confident encouragement and urging of a trusted leader. The success of any change effort is almost always directly proportional to the skill of its champion.

With its champion in place, the change process moves forward through the following essential stages (as described in the CAP outline):

♦ *Creating a shared need.* The reason to change, whether driven by threat or opportunity, must be instilled within the organization and widely shared through data, demonstration, demand, or diagnosis. The need for change must exceed the resistance to that change.

♦ *Sharing a vision.* The desired outcome of change is clear, legitimate, widely understood, and shared.

♦ *Mobilizing commitment.* There is a strong commitment from key constituents to invest in the change, make it work, and demand and receive management attention.

♦ *Making change last.* Once change is started, it endures and flourishes, and learnings are transferred throughout the organization.

♦ *Monitoring progress.* Progress is real, benchmarks set and realized, and indicators are established to guarantee accountability.

♦ *Changing systems and structures.* The management practices are used to complement and reinforce the change.

Both the Work-Out and CAP processes are now common throughout the organization and are considered part of the fabric of GE. Currently, the organization has thousands of CAP coaches who can lead a team through this process. These coaches do not necessarily need a human resources background, and they are selected for training only after nominating themselves. As a result, GE's businesses are no longer dependent on CLD to provide them with the tools necessary for CAP, because those skills are available within their own businesses.

Productivity Best Practices

GE has an on-going "Productivity Best Practices" study commissioned by its CEO. The study's objective is to transfer best practices for sustaining growth and productivity improvements across GE. The approach is for GE study teams to evaluate best practices both inside and outside GE. Operations personnel take the lead. There are up to 20 of these best-practice workshops per year, with up to 100 people in each one.

GE's emphasis on change is a healthy one. One frequently heard battle cry is "Make change the only constant." As one GE leader told site visitors, "People have to understand: What is the need for change? Is it an opportunity? Is it a threat? Where are we going? What is the vision? And, of course, you need to mobilize and get commitment. If you don't have individuals on board, if they don't understand the changes, you're going to be less successful."[2]

Relative Speeds of GE's Change Mechanisms

GE has been able to document the relative speed, simplicity, and self-confidence of change that can be expected when using each of its leadership training techniques. For example, GE knows that

1. Work-Out town meetings are an easy-going, low-intensity approach to changing the organization and therefore are likely to be slower in bringing about the change

2. Sharing of best practices is a little more intense and moves toward accomplishing a desired change a little faster

3. Process improvement and continuous emphasis on reengineering is what GE refers to as the "bullet-train approach"

4. CAP is much more intense and therefore moves participants more swiftly to accomplishment of change

5. A key strategic initiative is, of course, the speediest and most intense approach to accomplishing any organizational change. It occurs with marching orders from the general and all

lieutenants and usually has full financial and logistical support for reaching the change objective as fast as possible.

Six Sigma Quality

GE has embarked on a five-phase, quality-improvement process that is referred to as Six Sigma.[3] The company's Six Sigma GE Quality 2000 plan has been described to its leaders as "the biggest, most personally rewarding, and, in the end, most profitable undertaking in our history."

The five phases of the Six Sigma approach are:

1. *Define.* Define who your customers are and what their requirements are for your products and services—their expectations.

2. *Measure.* Identify the key internal processes that influence critical-to qualities (CTQ) and measure the defects generated relative to CTQs.

3. *Analyze.* Begin to understand why defects are generated.

4. *Improve.* Confirm the key variables and then quantify the effect of these variables on the CTQs, identify the maximum acceptable ranges of the key variables, make certain the measurement systems are capable of measuring the variation in the key variables, and modify the process to stay within the acceptable ranges.

5. *Control.* Ensure that the modified process now enables the key variables (xs) to stay within the maximum acceptable ranges using tools such as statistical process control (SPC) or simple checklists.

The Six Sigma roles within each business consist of:

1. *Champions.* Senior-management leaders who are responsible for the success of Six Sigma efforts. Champions approve and fund projects and alleviate roadblocks to project success.

2. *Black Belts.* Full-time leaders of teams responsible for measuring, analyzing, improving, and controlling key proc-

esses that influence customer satisfaction and/or productivity growth.

3. *Master Black Belts.* Full-time teachers, who also review and mentor Black Belts. Selection criteria for Master Black Belts are quantitative skills and the ability to teach and mentor.

4. *Green Belts.* Trained to a similar level as Black Belts, but staying in their operating assignments working on Six Sigma projects.

Funding of Leadership Development

Tuition from participants covers only part of CLD's program expenses. The funding also comes from a corporate assessment that is divided among the 12 business units. Because of the high level of buy-in for Crotonville's work, finding money is generally a straightforward proposition.

Some of business units have programs in which employees are sent to universities and other outside programs. GE also has a tuition-reimbursement program for those individuals who further their education and skills outside the organization. Basically, GE feels that if someone is a high-performer, then whatever training he or she needs will be supported by the company.

Learning Technologies

Various businesses at GE use learning technologies to different extents in their leadership development efforts. At the corporate level, CLD does not do much electronic training. Currently, the organization is reviewing the curriculum, trying to assess in which areas it can effectively use learning technologies. But CLD has some philosophical problems with technology-based training, since its mission is to promote "boundary-less-ness," networking, and best-practice sharing. The organization still has some reservations as to whether this objective can be accomplished fully with learning technologies. Says one GE representative, "Bringing people from 12 businesses together into the

Crotonville classroom and residence environment is a huge part of the whole leadership development process."

Even while preparing for retirement, Chairman Welch emphasizes that a major part of any leader's role is to teach others. As a result, CLD readily finds senior executives inside the company who are ready and willing to help teach leadership courses. With that kind of star power available, it is hard to get excited about off-the-shelf training packages.

Training the Trainers

Generally, CLD feels that when anyone (even a corporate star) participates in adult education, a lecture format is not the most effective way to transfer learning. So leaders who are asked to teach high-level executives (as in the EDC) usually arrive with a representative problem that they have personally encountered. They then ask class participants to work through the problem. The leader facilitates an open discussion that works toward a written set of recommendations.

GE provides training to employees who are going to teach. One course deals with the basics (such as don't jiggle the change in your pocket and don't use red pens to write because people in the back can't see). The other course deals with issues such as creating lesson plans and facilitating breakout sessions. Both courses are handled primarily by vendors. CLD places a great deal of emphasis on this type of training, because it not only helps the students in the classroom, but it also gives the teacher additional skills that can be put to effective use on the job (such as when he or she interacts with the media, customers, or direct reports).

While GE has both coaching and mentoring efforts throughout the organization, most are not formalized programs at the corporate level. Nonetheless, GE is a mentor-seeking environment. For example, the chairman recently had a luncheon to which each of the officers had to bring a minority mentee along. At the business-unit level, some units have formalized programs, while others do mentoring on an ad hoc basis. Coaching is handled primarily at the business-unit level as well.

Crotonville makes sure its programs fit the current needs of the businesses. Once the kind of training and the target audience are identified, CLD will work with outside contacts. The organization has no instructional designers in house. Instead, Crotonville relies on a variety of academics and consultants to develop its courses. CLD adds the GE flavor to the design by either citing company-specific examples or tailoring the course to the GE executives who will be teaching.

Through the years, CLD has developed a good relationship with a number of academics who help design the courses. For example, there are finance professors who understand the GE financial model as well as the company. These professors also bring an external, academic view to the table that might otherwise be ignored.

Even in GE's EDC, which is taught solely by GE's top business and corporate leaders, the organization relies on key consultants to design the program. They use their expertise to help create an action-learning environment, and GE's leaders share their experiences and help learners work through real-life problems.

Succession Planning

Every year, each manager at GE participates in a mandatory, annual performance review with all of his or her employees. This review includes discussion about both performance and adherence to GE values. The performance review is then interpreted by a higher management level to make sure it is fair and accurate.

As part of GE's corporate-wide, human resources, planning process, Session "C," every individual is placed in a nine-block rating system (see Figure 3.1). On the vertical axis, GE measures potential through three categories: A Player, B Player, and C Player. A Players are those of highest potential. On the horizontal axis, the organization measures performance by assigning a numerical rating from one to five. One and two indicate exceptional performance; five indicates that significant improvement is needed. These ratings are determined in part by 360-degree feedback from managers, co-workers, and even customers.

From those individuals rated "A1" or "A2," the chairman identifies the top 500 people in the company. He takes a personal interest in promoting the education and development of each of these people—not just from a particular business-unit standpoint, but from a corporate standpoint as well. Welch himself likes to say, "Corporate owns the top 500 people in the company; we just rent them out to the businesses."

The system is effective, because it is hard for the businesses to hide their top performers, rather than share their talents with the entire company. To prevent the further hoarding of talent, GE has mechanisms built into its values that result in negative reviews for managers who hold back talented individuals.

Each manager decides whether or not to disclose how each of his or her direct reports has been rated. Corporate training encourages individuals to ask their managers to disclose their ratings, and any individual who asks will be told.

The Effect of Leadership on the Bottom Line

GE's leadership development process is not driven by typical measures, such as cost and ROI. Instead, the organization relies on feedback from a number of sources to make sure it stays on the right track. For example, more than half of the senior executive development courses at the company are run by the leaders

Figure 3.1   Nine-Block Rating System

	1	2	3	4	5
A Player	Top notch—those who are sent to Crotonville				
B Player	Doing fine				
C Player	Need improvement				

of the corporation. They are a great source of feedback as to whether or not the course design is effective. The organization also relies heavily on student feedback.

GE relies primarily on participant evaluations for its courses. To establish a model that may be used across all courses, the organization is piloting analysis in one of its programs, using perceived behavioral change (Level Three). The organization uses 360-degree feedback before the training, after the training, and six months later to see what the long-term effect of the course is.

As for courses centered on action-learning topics, GE occasionally reviews the effects of recommendations made by BMC courses. A group goes back to the region the BMC group studied and makes a report on which recommendations were implemented and how the initiatives have improved business results.

Maintaining the Momentum

The costs of education are up front and tangible. The benefits are downstream and intangible. GE's culture is wired for change: Employees generally have the attitude that there are infinite possibilities to improve everything. CLD has been able to play an integral role in promoting this atmosphere through programs like Work-Out and CAP.

In an environment in which training and development are given such a high level of importance, maintaining the momentum is a relatively easy thing to do. But, the situation at GE underscores the fact that to have buy-in, one must start at the top. If the leadership development program is not sold to the top person, then, more often than not, the enthusiasm will not filter through the organization, and change quickly becomes unlikely.

GE after Jack Welch

As this book goes to press, the media attention to Jack Welch's choice of his own successor is intense. In the chairman's own unique style, he continues to hold his cards close to his chest and deftly moves his princes around the GE chessboard of companies. As much as teasing the media, Welch is wisely working to avoid the political infighting that might naturally break out among the heirs apparent. Welch and the GE board wisely promised top dollar (but time-sensitive) stock options to each of the princes-in-waiting, with the intended result that those prime targets of executive recruiters are priced out of the market until the new king is chosen.

Headhunters looking for CEOs for the world's top companies know that GE is a gold mine. It is one of the richest sources for any large firm looking for an outside chief executive. Corporations want the specific kind of leader that GE goes after and never stops developing: non-Ivy League; usually with military experience; and strong on confidence, competitiveness, hard work, machismo, and humility. As *The Economist* of London observed, "Soft handshakes are rare" at GE."[4]

Whoever is chosen will be stepping into one of the most challenging leadership positions of all time, leading one of the world's most complex entities into the most complex global business climate ever. The anticipated procedure has been that shortly before his retirement at the end of 2000, Welch will name a pair of vice chairmen to join him in the corporate executive office.[5] This approach would ease the transition by giving Welch time to confirm his decision before it becomes final, and by letting off some of the pressure on those highly competitive CEOs who are not chosen. It is the chairman's objective to pass the scepter as skillfully as he has run the company, and no one doubts that he will achieve his objective. As Noel Tichy (who has written several books about GE) says of the company's depth of management talent, "It's the most powerful bench in the world."[6]

Summary

General Electric (GE) was formed to make the most of Thomas Edison's many patents. Now, the company includes not only the tools of generating, distributing, and using electricity, but also such divergent fields as computers, air and space products, nuclear power, the world of plastics, and financial services.

Former Chairman Jack Welch made maximum use of the corporate education center he inherited at Crotonville, New York. The company's Corporate Leadership Development (CLD) arm at Crotonville exists to create, identify, and transfer organizational learning. Welch also emphasized that a major part of any leader's role is to teach others. As a result, GE's executives are often asked to teach leadership courses.

CLD has a sequence of courses, training, and workshops that are tied to key transitional points in a person's career. These include Work-Out, RAMMP Matrix, the Change Acceleration Process, Productivity Best Practices, and Six Sigma GE Quality 2000.

GE's culture is set up for change, but without high-level support for a leadership development program, it is unlikely that enthusiasm for the program will filter through the organization. As a result, change quickly becomes improbable.

Notes

1. GE Web site, "Inside GE," http://www.ge.com.au/insidege/ogc _values.html, 4/7/00. (The original reference material with the value statement is from a GE confidential presentation document. The Web site version is identical and in the public access domain.)
2. Information based on research interviews.
3. Sigma is a metric that tells how many defects are likely to occur from or in a process. The higher the sigma value, the lower the number of defects. Six Sigma refers to a rate of 3.4 defects per million opportunities—or near-perfect quality. From the GE Website: www. crd.ge.com/whatwedo/sixsigma.html
4. Anonymous, "General Electric: The House That Jack Built," *The Economist*, (Sept. 18, 1999), p. 3.
5. John A. Byrne, with Jennifer Reingold, "Who Will Step into Jack Welch's Shoes?" *Business Week*, (Dec. 21, 1998), p. 2.
6. Anonymous, "General Electric," p. 6.

4

Hewlett-Packard

Diversity and Development through Decentralization

I f you are one of those people who believe that all companies should start in a garage or a basement, you should love Hewlett-Packard (HP). If you favor the good old American practice of putting the owner's name over the door, then the company Bill Hewlett and Dave Packard started in 1939 could be your favorite. Beginning in a one-car garage in Palo Alto, California, Bill and Dave turned a new type of audio oscillator for testing sound equipment into an American dream company.

By 1979, the two employees had grown to 52,000 employees, the garage had spawned multiple facilities and plants, and a line of over 4,000 products for electronic measurement, analysis, and computation was creating over $2 billion in annual sales.

Today, more people worldwide probably know the initials "HP" than could tell you the names behind the letters. The company designs, manufactures, and services electronic products and systems for measurement, computing, and communication. Its products are used by people in business, engineering, science, medicine, and education.

HP has grown into a world leader in the computer industry, with more than 29,000 catalog products and revenues of $42 billion in 1999. HP provides sales and service in approximately 600 offices throughout more than 120 countries and has manufacturing, research, and development operations in 59 cities in 18 countries around the world. To maintain these operations, HP has 83,200 employees in the United States and internationally.

But HP's history just became ancient history. In early 2000, as this book goes to press, HP is reinventing itself and redefining what is meant by the phrase "The HP Way." HP today is not the same organization that was envisioned by its founders, Bill and Dave, and HP's new CEO may make the HP of tomorrow completely unrecognizable by those who loved the two-engineers-in-a-garage concept.

Under new CEO Carly Fiorina, HP is rushing to reclaim its status as a top high-tech innovator. A star executive from Lucent Technologies Inc., Fiorina arrived at the Palo Alto headquarters with quite a task ahead of her. Her role is to convince the public and HP employees that HP is the hottest new company of the Internet era, and to do so without losing contact with the old-time commitment to quality and integrity that made the HP name so trusted. In effect, she must teach a bunch of stodgy engineers to break dance without losing all the pens out of their pocket protectors! Carly's comment on the familiar and trusted HP logis: "We have to make sure it represents the next century, rather than the last one."

Fiorina has begun her HP tenure with the bold steps the job requires. On the day that departing CEO Lew Platt introduced HP's new CEO to the world, he also announced the spin-off of HP's $8 billion test-and-measurement division. The spin-off, now called Agilent, had little to do with HP's faster-growing computer and printer businesses. It was a clear example of things to come under The Carly Way. HP is now filling key positions from outside the firm and is considering an expansion of a pay-for-performance policy that was recently introduced for 90 of its top executives.

Fiorina sees her number-one job as "craft[ing] a compelling vision of HP as an Internet company that can stitch together a vast range of products—from $25 inkjet cartridges to $1 million supercomputers—for any customer who has to compete in the online and offline worlds."[1]

The Carly Way is certainly a mirrored universe from The HP Way, on which the corporation had long prided itself, but which was gradually dragging it downward.

HP continues to use the development initiative to gain diversity as it prepares a new generation of leaders. Lew Platt recognized that a series of retirements were coming up—of people who actually grew up with Bill and Dave—and that those retiring and their immediate successors tended to look a little too much like each other. As the company globalizes, it must create more diversity in gender, ethnicity, and geographic dispersion. It has therefore begun an all-out program to accelerate the development of new leaders and speed up the development of people who are underrepresented in the organization. A narrow gene pool tends to foster inbreeding and lack of creativity, and innovation is the key to long-term viability.

The HP Way

As might be expected with such a red-white-and-blue history, HP employees look back to the personal ethics and strong beliefs of Mr. Hewlett and Mr. Packard as foundational. The original partners unquestionably shaped the direction and approaches of the company through personal example and plain words on paper. In the early days of the venture, Dave Packard grasped the concept of clearly stated objectives: ". . . I kept getting back to one concept: If we could simply get everybody to agree on what our objectives were and to understand what we were trying to do, then we could turn everybody loose, and they would move along in a common direction."

The HP Objectives were put into writing in the late 1950s and needed only minor tweaks and adjustments to remain relevant, guiding forces for a global HP. These HP Corporate Objectives reduce to a few words the intricate activities of a worldwide enterprise (see Figure 4.1).

Underlying HP's Corporate Objectives are HP's Corporate Values (see Figure 4.2). These beliefs about employee behavior

Figure 4.1   HP Objectives

HP Corporate Objectives

* *Profit.* To achieve sufficient profit to finance our company growth and to provide the resources we need to achieve our other corporate objectives.
* *Customers.* To provide products and services of the highest quality and the greatest possible value to our customers, thereby gaining and holding their respect and loyalty.
* *Fields of Interest.* To participate in those fields of interest that build upon our technology and customer base, that offer opportunities for continuing growth, and that enable us to make a needed and profitable contribution.
* *Growth.* To let our growth be limited only by our profits and our ability to develop and produce innovative products that satisfy real customer needs.
* *Our People.* To help HP people share in the company's success, which they make possible; to provide employment security based on performance; to ensure them a safe and pleasant work environment; to recognize their individual achievements; to value their diversity; and to help them gain a sense of satisfaction and accomplishment from their work.
* *Management.* To foster initiative and creativity by allowing the individual great freedom of action in attaining well-defined objectives.
* *Citizenship.* To honor our obligations to society by being an economic, intellectual, and social asset to each nation and each community in which we operate.

and interaction with colleagues, customers, and shareholders have truly been able to go from paper and into a unique HP business style. These values and objectives are clearly connected to HP's growth and level of employee loyalty and satisfaction.

Participative Management

From the first, one of the mainstays of The HP Way has been a participative management style. Even while maintaining its emphasis on teamwork, the company has encouraged individual freedom and initiative. HP makes sure that directions are clearly stated and effectively communicated and then expects its em-

Figure 4.2   The HP Way

HP Corporate Values

We have trust and respect for individuals.
We focus on a high level of achievement and contribution.
We conduct our business with uncompromising integrity.
We achieve our common objectives through teamwork.
We encourage flexibility and innovation.

ployees to find their own best ways to accomplish those directions.

Participative management has helped HP maintain the closeness and personal involvement of a small company, even as it has grown into a giant enterprise. It manages to communicate a basic faith in people to use their discretion, and there is an understanding that people to must make mistakes in order to make contributions. HP sees that its people buy into the underlying objectives and then turns them loose to follow their own individual paths to a creative solution. As one HP employee put it, "There's an inherent feeling that you just have to do the right thing for the company, the people, and the customer."

Organizational Structure

In the past, HP maintained a decentralized organization and worked constantly to keep a flat, hierarchical structure. An executive committee made up of nine people managed the two large business organizations: computers and measurement. Now, this committee will be concentrating on computers. Within the organization are business units known as "groups." Before the spin-off of Agilent, HP had 156 business units that ran like individual companies. These units provided a great opportunity for individuals to gain critical profit-and-loss experience.

At HP, activities are guided by a comprehensive system of management by objectives (MBO). Long- and short-range objectives are based on both company and profit-and-loss group objectives. The company communicates that these objectives are goals, not assignments, and encourages employees to find the best ways to attain the unit's goals. MBO is initiated from the top, but adjusted down through the organization to allow for individual initiative and influence.

In the words of co-founder Bill Hewlett: ". . . a manager, a supervisor, a foreman, given the proper support and guidance (that is, the objectives), is probably better able to make decisions about the problems he/she is directly concerned with than some executive way up the line, no matter how smart or able that executive may be. This system places great responsibility on the individuals concerned, but it also makes their work more interesting and challenging. It makes them feel that they are a part of the company and can have a direct effect on its performance."[2]

In the midst of encouraging individualism, HP equally emphasizes teamwork. Since the beginning of the company, there has been an attitude that openness, trust, and cooperation keep tension between individualism and team play in a proper and productive relationship. Speaking in the late 1970s, Dave Packard said, "One of the things we have tried to achieve, and I think have achieved thus far, is this concept of teamwork. The only way this company is going to run successfully is if we can ensure that there is a maximum flow of information and cooperation between all the elements of it and this is a very tricky situation."[3]

Leadership Development at HP

HP's decentralized culture is especially evident in the way it educates employees. HP strongly believes that the primary place for learning and development is on the job and on the line. Off-line education has always competed with the day-to-day demands of the business and "real-time" learning opportunities. To help employees learn within this culture and provide education on the job, education organizations exist within each individual business. Currently, HP has more than 1,300 educators worldwide and more than 100 education groups.

In addition to these training organizations, HP has a Corporate Education group with a 36-member staff. Since its inception, Corporate Education has been housed within human resources.

Corporate Education currently reports to the vice president of human resources, who in turn reports to the CFO of the company.

Within Corporate Education is the Business Leadership Development (BLD) team. This group focuses on executive development and overall leadership development, and it is responsible for all training specific to leadership. BLD also provides a resource referral system for personnel to go outside of HP to receive training. Figure 4.3 provides an illustration of the team's structure.

Prior to the formation of the BLD team, many businesses within HP used their own preferred leadership models. Through benchmarking, working with small focus groups, and internal process mapping, BLD realized that there was significant overlap in what the separate business units were using. BLD looked for the convergence and then put together what it calls The High Performance Leadership Model.

BLD has used this model to create a number of programs for the businesses but does not intend to employ it to handle all development needs. The businesses still handle needs specific to their organizations. They rely primarily on BLD for the management and leadership development, but there are a few instances of leadership programs within the businesses. For example, the growth of the Sales and Services Group (SSG) in HP is resulting in the addition of a large number of general managers. At the same time, the group is facing the rapidly approaching retirement of several general managers. To address these specific needs, SSG created the New GM Boot Camp, a one-day event hosted by SSG's vice president to clarify leadership expectations for general managers in sales and services.

Creating the HP Leadership Development Process

HP makes a distinction between leadership and management in its formal program and through senior management. Management is about measurement and results; leadership is how you get there. Top executives speak about "pervasive leadership"—

Figure 4.3 HP Leadership Development Organization

Business Leadership Development

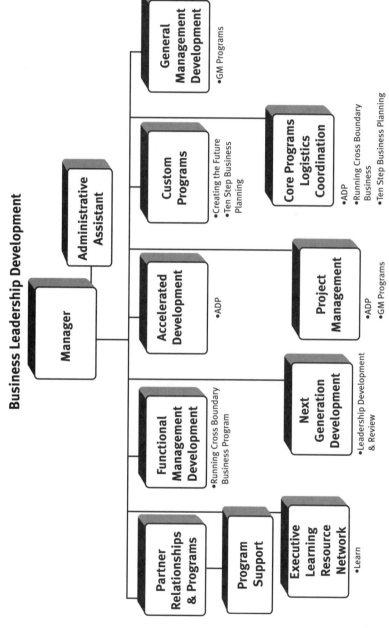

instead of hierarchical leadership—and about needing leadership at every level within the organization.

HP is determined that its leadership process is computer-based or "tools-driven." Leadership tools can be used if asked for, but the system is not to be dependent on any uniform set of training hardware or software. This distinction is important, as it reveals a company determined to have an "HP program," not just another training program.

Business Leadership Development looks for systematic ways to build the capabilities of HP's business leaders. The emphasis of the BLD process is to provide development opportunities at key transition points in individuals' careers. To accomplish this goal, the curriculum is designed and operated under several principles:

- Based on real business problems and strategic initiatives
- Linked to business objectives and company values
- Segmented by customer needs, such as executive roles, business models, and business life cycle
- Sponsored by CEO and senior executives
- Comprised of global content and delivered worldwide
- Based on validated competencies for success

To fund the development of business leaders, HP businesses pay for the participation of their managers on a charge-back basis. This keeps BLD providing programs that are in line with the objectives of the businesses. An annual budget that includes the BLD employee's salaries must be approved by each of the HP businesses.

Facing the Need to Change

Before HP could become more than a company dealing with tests and measurement instrumentation, required a necessary shift in company strategy was required. HP leaders, their thinking, and their management systems needed to be re-examined. Furthermore, a system had to be developed to turn out leaders prepped and tuned for the new context.

HP's entry into the printer business is an excellent example of the company's ability to adapt to and train for a brand new set of challenges and market realities. Though the company did not introduce its first personal computer (PC) printer until 1984, it was able to dominate the market by 1990. Having gained success almost overnight, HP leaders knew that their position of strength could also go away just as quickly. This kept them focused on customer satisfaction.

Listening to customers led to HP's ahead-of-the-pack introduction of inexpensive, high-quality, ink-jet technology. The ink-jet printers actually competed against HP's already highly successful laser printers. It took some deliberation to understand the value and ultimate importance of introducing these new products, which would compete with HP's existing ones. The company realized, before its competitors, the need to sacrifice some current business to lead the way into new opportunities. As a result, more than half of HP's orders are for products introduced or revamped within the past two years.

To shift gears from being a test-and-measurement champion to becoming a major competitor in computers required company-wide adaptation. It also gave HP a clear look at its future. HP had little of the required knowledge about computer workstations. So the company with a lifelong tradition of avoiding acquisitions and partnerships had to go shopping. In 1989, it purchased Apollo Computer to gain Apollo's expertise in workstations and its broad customer base. Interestingly enough, some old-line principles were not negotiable, and longtime pay-as-you-go HP made its Apollo acquisition completely "out of pocket."

The sharper competition in the PC business forced HP to sacrifice other traditions as well. It began to do contract work and was forced to begin using forward pricing. The company that had been synonymous with independence had to learn to consolidate and outsource. These changes created feelings among HP employees that the solidarity of the company was being compromised. But change was not an option—it was a necessity. Some of the old pride had to be traded for new profits. A representative example was highlighted in the HP company magazine. It explained that, at one time, HP even made its own screws. These screws were the best in the world, but the company decided that making screws was not a core competency it had to have.

Downsizing and redeployment have also entered this former workplace utopia. So far, HP has never had to institute a company-wide layoff. But there have been cases in which a company was acquired by HP, and not all the employees of the acquired company could be placed within the HP organization. HP's positive relationship with its employees has clearly been eroded by this. The question is whether a lurking mistrust of the company is simply the way business must be done today, or whether the feeling that one has lost membership in the "good, old HP family" will eventually cripple one of the world's great companies.

In order to take an even more strategic look at its business, HP has organized an HR Strategic Council, made up of the heads of human resources from each HP business organization. This council is perfectly connected to gather data directly from the "customers." BLD views this group as a partner and an opportunity to eventually sell its programs and services to HP businesses.

One real challenge that BLD faces in linking its initiatives to business strategy is that it has people in so many diverse business models. BLD has tried to respond by offering customized programs to meet the needs of each different situation. For example, one general management program, called "Creating the Future," provides reconfigurable components or modules that can translate from one program to another.

Leaders Leading Leaders

HP's senior executives sponsor and actively participate in leadership development. Examples include Carly Fiorina's involvement in management conferences and Lew Platt's opening and closing of every Accelerated Development Program (ADP) with a dialogue session. CFO Bob Wayman was the sponsor of a planned worldwide broadcast. Wayman played an active role as facilitator of a "Challenging the Growth Barrier" panel discussion during the broadcast. Senior executives also serve as faculty in some part of every core program. Carly Fiorina has indicated a commitment to continue this tradition and is expected to use leadership development as a "bully pulpit" for strategic change within the organization.

BLD has identified a set of competencies to distinguish its leaders. There are six broad categories of characteristics that potential leaders need to possess, and under each category there are specific behaviors. (See Fig. 4.4.)

1. *Practice The HP Way*—build trust and respect, focus on achievement, demonstrate integrity, be innovative with customers, contribute to the community, and develop organizational decision-making.

2. *Lead change and learning*—recognize and act on signals for change, lead organizational change, learn from organization experience, remove barriers to change, develop self, and challenge and develop others.

3. *Know the internal and external environment*—anticipate global trends, act on trends, and learn from others.

4. *Lead strategy setting*—inspire breakthrough business strategy, lead the strategy-making process, commit to business vision, create long-range strategies, build financial strategies, and define a business-planning system.

5. *Align the organization*—work across boundaries, implement competitive cost structures, develop alliances and partnerships, plan and manage core business, and help design the organization.

6. *Achieve results*—build a track record, establish accountability, support calculated risks, make tough individual decisions, and resolve performance problems.

These competencies are used as criteria to identify, evaluate, and develop high-potential performers in HP's Leadership Development and Review (LD&R) process. They provide content for the leadership and management assessment processes, through activities like self-assessment, multisource feedback, and assessment simulations. They help identify and qualify ex-

Figure 4.4   HP Competencies Model

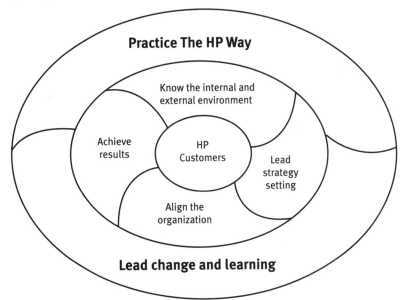

ternal executive development resources. Finally, the competencies serve as de facto objectives for all BLD development programs and processes.

To create these competencies, BLD took each of the organization's 32 existing competency statements and put them on individual cards. These cards were then sent out with three envelopes to the top 1,800 group managers and their staffs. The managers were instructed to sort these competencies into three categories:

1. Those that are considered mission-critical and would make or break success within the business
2. Those that are important, but not critical
3. Those that are fundamental to the job

In addition, the managers were asked to add any invalid or missing competencies.

With a response rate of 78 percent, BLD was excited by the results. Even with the varying cultures and measurements among the different businesses, there was a phenomenal alignment and convergence across the businesses in regard to what was considered mission-critical. Five key, relationship-based competencies surfaced and cut across roles and businesses. These competencies demonstrate how HP businesses relate to one another in areas such as customer respect, respect for the individual, and uncompromising integrity.

Leadership Pools

HP has different levels of leadership pools and tries to create leadership modules that are appropriate for functional and general managers. When the company hires, it seeks those with the highest demonstrated skills in technical, interpersonal, cultural, and adaptability areas. Not only does this give the company a top work force, it also gives any employee a measure of pride for having been chosen.

With a basic commitment to promoting from within and growing its own managers, supervisors, and technical people, HP looks for those with growth potential. Instead of relying heavily on standard tests, applicants go through progressive interviews in which they are asked how they would approach a problem. A relevant Dave Packard quote is still revered: "Now there are some who say that a person is a good manager who has mastered managerial techniques; he can manage anything. Well, maybe he can. But, I hold very strongly that he can manage it a hell of a lot better if he really knows the territory."[4]

In all the years BC (Before Carly), it was almost unheard of for anyone to be hired for a management position from outside HP. The hiring of Carly Fiorina from the outside was an incredibly controversial move for the organization that prides itself on developing its own leaders. However, there was a general feeling that someone who had grown up in the organization might not be able to see the challenges with enough objectivity to make the kinds of changes required. There was criticism of Fiorina's initial speeches to the group, because she stood in front of the garage where the organization began. Many of the old-timers in the organization felt that she had not yet "earned the right" to stand there. With the advancement of the HP stock price, however, complaints were significantly less frequent. In February 2000, Fiorina delivered an important speech to the top management. It proved to be a masterful integration of how HP was to reinvent itself and, at the same time, remain true to the core values that had been introduced by the founders.

Everyone at HP knows that it takes time to learn the system and for the system to learn them. New employees at all levels go through a period of adaptation that is sometimes characterized by frustration with the HP style. As one employee said, "Instead of your being told point by point what you're supposed to do, your boss is relying on you to be able to use your head. I think maybe that's sort of frightening to some people."[5]

As The Carly Way began and continues at present, HP watchers are encouraged about the future of the company. The selection of a woman to be the most powerful female CEO in the country is an indication of HP's commitment to build a new and different management team.

Telling the Company Stories

As in any culture, newcomers learn by hearing the stories from the past. The favorite "Bill and Dave" stories are part of company speeches and internal publications and can be called upon to make specific points. As more "new people" are added to the HP family, it becomes harder to pass the legends along. So these stories have been incorporated into orientation and management-training course work. Some of the more popular HP company stories are:

- Bill and Dave starting the company with $538 in the garage behind Packard's rented house
- Dave smashing up an instrument in a laboratory, because he thought it was poorly designed, unreliable, and generally a "hunk of junk"
- Bill challenging his labs to build a scientific calculator he could put in his shirt pocket, which led to the first small scientific calculator and an important business segment

♦ Avoiding the need to borrow $100 million in 1973 by imposing a tough program of asset management

Today at HP, stories about Bill and Dave are supplemented with new examples of people who demonstrate The HP Way. Already, Carly stories are making the rounds at HP facilities, but, of course, the passage of time is required for a simple story to grow into a corporate legend.

Selecting Participants

All of HP's profit-and-loss organizations run like individual companies. This means that someone new to HP or someone searching for a first promotion is searching for opportunities within a small company (not the $42 billion conglomerate). This makes it easier for the result and impact of an individual's efforts to be visible and for rewards to be more direct.

High performers at HP frequently do not have a master career plan. They simply get tapped on the shoulder for each subsequent job within the company. Managers within the HP family of companies frequently take lateral moves, demotions, and moves to other jobs in order to develop their professional careers and round out their internal HP resumes.

This natural process has worked well for HP. Only recently has a more systematic growth of leaders started to take place at the company. BLD has created the Accelerated Development Program to provide an opportunity for leaders to develop skills that will help them take on new challenges. The nominating process for ADP is a once-a-year undertaking. Nominations must be made by a manager and supported by his or her business unit.

The HP businesses send the BLD team a prioritized list of nominees for ADP. There are usually over 100 applicants for the 48 ADP slots. People are selected by a cross-functional, cross-business group of ADP alumni who serve as a collaborative review team. Performance criteria and diversity goals also drive the acceptance process. The annual ADP class, which consists of 48 students from around the world, is balanced according to culture, ethnicity, race, and gender. Classes are intentionally kept small to allow participants access to HP's senior executives serving as mentors.

Beyond ADP, most other programs in the BLD portfolio are open. Employees are allowed to self-select into them or they may be nominated by their managers.

Addressing Diversity Issues

Creating a diverse executive team was one of the drivers for HP's increased emphasis on leadership development. The company did not feel it had a handle on the positions of its top women and minority talent within the organization and recognized the need to find that handle quickly. As HP became more dominant in consumer markets, its customer base grew in diversity, and so did a strong need for its staff to reflect these changes.

This need for diversity drove the Leadership Development and Review (LD&R) process used for succession planning and found its way into other programs that BLD offers. ADP was designed in 1991 in conjunction with the Corporate Work Force Diversity to meet HP's diversity objectives within the United States. Each ADP class brings in a varied group of participants. The result of this effort has been bringing worldwide representation into the HP leadership process. World-wide representation goes far beyond simple U.S. representation, which can be accomplished by achieving a balance of one-third women, one-third minorities, and one-third white men.

Teaching Leadership Down the Line

For HP programs like ADP, only about one percent of the entire corporate population is eligible. But for those programs that are open to everyone, HP works hard to make its offerings inclusive. There are even some programs being developed specifically for those who do not make it into the accelerated programs.

HP also makes every effort to identify low performers who

have been put the wrong job slots. If a person is found to be in a position that is not going to maximizing his or her potential, HP tries to help locate the right job within the company. The intent is to make it clear to competent, but unhappy, employees that there are lots of opportunities within the organization.

Engaging Future Leaders

The team created to validate and prioritize HP's competency model also began the process of designing and developing a leadership curriculum. This team consists of six people, including both general managers and functional managers. To begin the process, the BLD manager and a program manager put out a Request for Proposal (RFP), which was reviewed and edited by the six-member team. Building on this RFP, the executive team and BLD met often to develop criteria, assess the proposals, and select a provider. Not surprisingly, the most popular proposal was the one that included a computer-based business simulation.

When the development of simulation content began, the executive team and BLD found it necessary to take an assertive role as curriculum advisers to the third-party developer. The HP team did not do any of the hands-on design work but was actively involved in the phase-review portion and also participated in the pilot of the program. The trend developing at HP is to be actively involved in the customization of outside packages rather than do the core development.

As a curriculum is created, the challenge is to ensure that the presentation of The HP Way remains accurate and complete. There must be a clear understanding of how the unique corporate culture affects values, business objectives, and management practices. Developers had some concern that descriptions of The HP Way might be reduced to only those values and relationships that occurred inside the company. They felt that the proper emphasis would be lost if the language of The HP Way did not also apply to corporate objectives that are more business driven. BLD continues to work to create programs that consider business-driven objectives and demonstrate the role that The HP Way plays in achieving them.

Key Components of LeaRN

In delivering its services, BLD focuses on several categories that make up the Business Leadership Development Portfolio. This portfolio addresses next-generation talent, the executive core, strategic initiatives, and a host of development resources. Referred to as LeaRN (the Learning Resource Network), the system seeks to be a "one-stop shopping" site (at *learn.corp.hp.com*) for locating and acquiring executive development solutions. It has a reference database in place, so that searches for solutions by topics are linked to available and approved university programs. LeaRN also provides consulting services designed to accelerate the match between a development need and a pre-qualified learning solution.

LeaRN is a Web-based database for locating pre-qualified development resources. These resources are either recommended by HP employees, or identified by BLD staff. The criteria for both is whether or not employees would recommend it to peers as being worth the time spent away from work and whether it is informative about tools that might be applied on the job. One person within BLD focuses on what is referred to as "value-added brokering" and is a liaison between employees and external education providers.

The reference is listed within the Web site database. Employees drive their own education, but BLD has made it possible to search for solutions by topic with links to competencies. This has helped tremendously, as BLD has also marketed the concept of career self-reliance. The LeaRN system enables HP employees to identify learning solutions that will help them develop the competencies HP has identified as critical to their success.

Accelerated Development Program

The Accelerated Development Program is a one-year program for high-performing HP middle managers. These high-performance managers are identified through the use of the yearly development plan and the performance evaluation process. In order to meet a specific profile required for participation, nominees must:

- Be ready for a functional manager position
- Have potential for higher-level, senior-management positions
- Be highly motivated to accept increasing demands of senior-leadership positions
- Have five to seven successful years of experience as a manager inside and/or outside HP
- Have experience in two different functions, geographies, or sectors

ADP begins with an orientation week. The general manager sponsoring the program kicks off each session. He or she talks about expectations for the participants and for leaders within the HP organization. After this setting of the tone, feedback is shared with the participants from a 360-degree survey done prior to the meeting. The remaining time is spent assessing the current skills of the participants and creating a focused development plan for each participant.

As the program continues, participants receive individual career coaching based on assessments using the Meyers-Briggs and Brikman tools. Participants are assisted in evaluating their career paths and identifying potential assignments that will hone individual development needs. Two workshops on timely business leadership topics are also included.

One of the most valuable outcomes of the process has been the creation of an active network of alumni. This group provides informal mentoring to those in the program and shares experiences and lessons gained through their past participation.

A structured, internal, mentor relationship is created when participants are matched with a group general manager or more senior officer in HP. But participants are also matched with external executive education programs specific to their development needs.

To wrap up ADP, a dinner is held with the CEO, members

of the executive committee of HP, and the BLD staff. An executive panel is put together for the participants, and each participant leaves with a structured career plan.

Running Cross-Boundary Business Program

Running Cross-Boundary Business was an existing program that was rebuilt for new functional managers. A third-party group was brought in to accomplish the rebuilding.

This seven-day program addresses the challenges of working across organizational and cultural boundaries to lead a successful HP business. A core piece of this program is a simulation in which the participant gets to select the role he or she wants to play within a business scenario. Key components of this new curriculum are:

♦ Strategic thinking
♦ Value delivery system
♦ Organizational alignment
♦ Alignment change
♦ Leadership across boundaries
♦ Team dynamics

Involvement of University Programs

Another program similar to ADP is being developed for general managers. This program maximizes HP's interactive relationships with university programs. It is the starting point for new general managers, and it will be delivered in the field worldwide.

These programs work to bring new managers comfortably into the HP culture. People brought in at senior levels often struggle with the new culture, trying to find their place in the organization. BLD has learned that assimilation is most effectively accomplished through sharing HP stories and experiences. So BLD is building such sharing into these programs and creating additional programs that help to ease the transition into the organization.

As BLD began its efforts, a number of executives were attending university programs. The problem was that BLD did not know what impact the programs were having, and the offerings were not centralized, so it was difficult to determine how much HP was spending. To address this issue, BLD took the University Consortium for Executive Education (UNICON) list of universities and prioritized it with *Business Week's* list of top ten business schools. From this list, BLD identified those employees from HP who had attended classes at these schools and how much the programs had cost. It found that 116 managers had attended university programs during a recent academic year. About $4 million was spent on this education. The average cost of the programs came out to about $15,000–20,000 dollars each.

BLD is now trying to determine the relative value of each offering. It is also following up with the people who attended last year's university programs and assessing the programs with a set of questions. Right now, at universities such as Harvard, HP has a number of seats available for managers on a first-come, first-serve basis. In the future, BLD wants to be more strategic about those attending university programs.

Customized Programs

The decentralized nature of HP and the autonomy of its business units also requires BLD to arrange custom programs. One person within BLD works with intact business schemes, events, and programs customized to meet specific business needs and accelerate change. BLD pulls together external resources that can speak to business units concerning particular issues.

"Power of One—Best of Many" Series

"Power of One—Best of Many" is a series of events delivered over multiple years to build business-team capabilities and accelerate the enterprise-wide goal of unprecedented value growth. For example, BLD hosted a videoconference called "Challenging the Growth Barrier" for HP's worldwide general manager population. This was the first videoconference called for this audience, and it enabled an impressive and productive global-panel conversation and interaction.

Leadership Development and Review

The Leadership Development & Review (LD&R) is HP's succession-planning process. It is designed to review all managers, and its major driver is diversity. HP's previous, informal process for identifying talent to fill senior-management positions often overlooked talented women, minorities, and white men in nontraditional jobs. The business imperatives for this process are to:

- Identify and retain high-potential HP people for senior-management positions
- Increase diversity in HP's senior management positions
- Accelerate the readiness of high-potential people for future senior-management roles through development experiences

LD&R was first implemented at the executive level to look at the candidates for the next group of general managers and vice presidents. It was an immediate success, finding people who had not been identified prior to the process. Two good examples are a salesman in the United Kingdom and a software division manager in India (who has since been promoted to business-unit manager). The fact that this practice was not formally being done across boundaries prior to LD&R, kept people from being recognized.

LD&R helps reviewers identify high-potential people for senior-management positions. Equally important, it insures that HP puts development opportunities in place to keep those valuable resources. BLD, along with an executive vice president sponsor, the heads of Human Resources, and a few line managers made up the design, development, and implementation team.

The real value here is in giving people an opportunity to discuss talent. Enough structure is provided to get the development conversation on the agenda of the management team at the group level. The team discusses future needs, in terms of talent; the capabilities, given their business challenges; and diversity. The reviewees create an online profile of themselves, which includes background information, strengths, development areas, and career aspirations. In other words, they self-assess against the competency model and then meet with their direct manager to talk about this process. Finally, senior management reviews each profile. The self-assessment profile is not being administered in the 360-degree fashion.

LD&R is not mandatory, but it is becoming an institutionalized process across HP. It works because it provides a tool for, and is managed by, the business. The business reviews talent at the level it deems appropriate, given its business challenges.

There are two ways BLD helps management reach its goals through the LD&R process. First, it provides stretch assignments for the best people in the company. Second, it makes ADPs available for individual contributors, first-level managers, and mid-level managers.

Prior to LD&R, employees often referred to "the career maze" at HP. It was not a surprising description given the difficulty of getting known and getting transferred across functions, divisions, and even international borders. The lack of any organizational, career-development map made it nearly impossible for an individual to plan his or her personal progression. Promotions and additional responsibilities occurred independently of each other. HP liked the constant cross-function fertilization of this system, but, as the HP domain grew and expanded, it became obvious that the method for spotting and engaging rising talent had to be systematized.

Though the career map was confusing, there were not many complaints about the reward system, because it favored those who did well. Performance was judged by immediate supervisors, and individuals who ranked in the top quartile by performance were given larger and more frequent raises. Since this ranking was based on sustained contribution, sudden, dramatic changes in performance position were rare. If performance declined, there were smaller or no increases. The results were predictable: HP people did well or they looked for other work.

Up Next for BLD

In addition to its current offerings, BLD has outlined three initiatives. It intends to:

1. Develop a "Leadership Development Program" for general managers that supports the HP enterprise goal of achieving unprecedented growth

2. Expand the LeaRN Web site into a central information site for locating qualified development resources for HP's business leaders

3. Define and implement a succession-planning process that identifies and develops business leadership talent across HP's diverse businesses

Senior managers' roles in leadership development involve serving as mentors, faculty members, and sponsors in the design of BLD and its programs. In ADP, the CEO is the program sponsor, and he or she kicks off the program and closes it. At these meetings, the CEO discusses The HP Way and expectations for those participating in ADP.

In addition to the support of the CEO, the support of other senior leaders is applied in a more formalized mentor program. Each person in the ADP program works individually with a mentor, with each participant providing BLD with a mentor wish list. BLD looks at the participants' development plan and the mentor pool and then tries to match them with mentors that are best suited for them. Some mentors have been in the ADP program, and all are familiar with its goals. BLD also provides a videotape and custom workbook to aid them in their roles as mentors. It is such a part of HP's culture to develop people that finding mentors is not at all difficult. The current mentor pool consists of approximately 70 people.

The development of the participant's plan drives the mentorship, and the mentor aims to understand quickly the goals that the participant has set for the year. HP encourages structured shadowing as a way of providing the mentoring the participants need. Mentors lead participants into situations appropriate to developing the objective that they seek. Mentors will sit with the participants in advance of a particular event and talk about such things as what they hope to accomplish, what the obstacles are, and what their role needs to be. They then go to the event. And, after the event, they meet to debrief and discuss what they heard, what worked, and what did not.

The Effect of Leadership on the Bottom Line

HP has a performance rating system that drives salaries and differentiates people. Their performances are compared to those of their peers and against their performance contract, and a rating is assigned. These performance ratings are called "bands."

The performance evaluation process contains substantial variation, but the system is always used in one way or another. For example, in some production areas a PC-based, peer feedback system exists. In addition, there are several efforts that are either driven by the business or BLD efforts—including 360-degree surveys, which are purposeful in that they focus on a particular change that is about to occur. For example, the computer systems organization was trying to make some specific changes to accurately upgrade the skill level of management in its organization. Pervasive 360-degree surveys were done and specific development plans were created. The 360-degree surveys were readministered 18 months later.

Tracking

Today, each employee at HP has an individual development plan with two components: a business plan and a personal development plan. The business plan consists of what the employee says he or she will commit to completing in the next year. The personal plan includes what that employee would like to do to promote continued personal and professional growth. The personal plan might include such things as identifying a mentor outside the business unit or an external educational opportunity.

In the following year, the evaluation is based on the results achieved and whether or not improvements in that employee can be seen. In other words, it is based on whether or not that employee produced what he or she was looking to produce. This kind of subjectivity is protected in order to give the individual more discretion in the process. This is a solid procedure that happens consistently for every employee. Managers are measured on whether or not they are on schedule with this process for every employee.

Communicating the Results

BLD distributes program evaluation results to participants and sponsoring managers. In the case in which 360-degree assessments are used, reports are provided to the participants and a copy is sent to their immediate managers.

Key Lessons for BLD

The first key lesson that BLD has learned in its process of creating leaders is the importance of alignment and integration. Keeping learning distinct from an employee's daily work simply is not as effective as integrating the learning into the job. The tolerance for learning "off-line" is shrinking, so the role that BLD must play is helping to shift the mindsets of employees to acknowledging and reflecting upon the learning that takes place during the course of work.

A second key lesson that almost sounds like a dichotomy in this fast-paced, high-tech world is the importance of conversation and relationships. It is necessary to build in time for leaders to network with one another. For this reason, the design of events that BLD organizes has to have an increased percentage of time that allows for people to simply talk with each other. This time is loosely structured to allow leaders the opportunity to step back and see how their experiences have contributed to their growth and development and then share those insights with each other.

The third is that BLD has realized the need to create more strategic initiatives at the business-unit level. Involving the human resources community and human resources managers with those in the business in a learning capacity will increase the awareness for their efforts and will make the learning more relevant.

Finally, as HP rolls into the next generation of managers, the level of technical savvy and comfort will continue to increase. Acceptance of alternative models with easy access to the information they want when they want it will increase.

The New HP Way

Some of the new characteristics of The HP Wway may seem like natural progressions today, but they would have been hard to believe years ago and, in fact, still pose problems in some parts of HP's global empire. For example, the informality that is so much a part of the HP system, such as calling the founders by their first names, has to be modified in cultures like that of Korea, where informality is viewed as disrespectful and inappropriate. As a result, HP attempts to adapt its culture to fit each context in which it is operating.

As HP's environment has shifted, some of its traditional ways have been forced to change. In the past, teamwork meant decision by consensus. Today, there is no longer time for consensus. The new HP cannot be limited to consensus decision-making. In the past, a bell would signal that coffee and donuts were served: Employees would gather around to talk with one another. This doesn't work in the world of flex-time. Coffee is available all day long, and occasional "coffee talks" are scheduled for employees to hear about current HP issues.

Management by Wandering Around (MBWA) is one of the practices most affected by the newer, higher-pressure environment. There is no longer time to dedicate to MBWA. Many managers have turned to e-mail or teleconferencing to practice MBWA, especially to reach international employees.

The personal nature of division reviews has necessarily changed. In the past, divisions would be reviewed with Bill Hewlett and Dave Packard sitting in. Today's large number of divisions preclude this kind of attention. Now, many divisions are reviewed in groups. The era of the personal touch as practiced by Bill and Dave is over.

Summary

Hewlett-Packard has had to update The HP Way to maintain its operations. The most obvious symbol of this updating is new CEO Carly Fiorina, who has the opportunity to move HP into a new world.

HP maintains a decentralized organization, and constantly strives for a flat hierarchical structure. Within the organization, business units known as "groups" are operated as separate profit-and-loss organizations.

To help employees learn within this culture and to provide education on the job, HP has a Corporate Education group. Within Corporate Education, the group that focuses on executive development and overall leadership development is the Business Leadership Development (BLD) team.

The Accelerated Development Program (ADP) was created by BLD to provide leaders the opportunity to develop skills that will help them take on new challenges. Other programs in the BLD portfolio include the Leadership Development & Review process, the LeaRN system, and Running Cross-Boundary Business. BLD also hosts videoconferences for HP's worldwide general-management population.

The company's new leadership development effort is helping reviewers identify high-potential people for senior-management positions, thereby using its good sense and innovative thinking skills to build a profitable future on the legacy of the successful and respected old Hewlett-Packard.

Notes

1. Peter Burrows, "The Boss," *Business Week,* (Aug. 2, 1999), p. 2.
2. G.C. Rogers, "Human Resources at Hewlett-Packard (A)," Harvard Business School, Case 9-495-051, Nov. 1, 1995, p. 6.
3. G.C. Rogers, *op. cit.,* p. 10.
4. Based on research interviews.
5. G. C. Rogers, *op. cit.,* p. 10.

5

Johnson & Johnson

FrameworkS of Leadership

C hairman Robert Wood Johnson was ahead of his time when he wrote the Johnson & Johnson (J&J) Company Credo in the 1940s. At the time J&J was about to go public, the chairman framed the basics upon which the company had been built for those who would continue his vision.

The Credo took the unusual step of declaring that the organization's primary responsibility was to "the doctors, nurses, and patients, to mothers and fathers, and all others who use our products and services." This customer-driven focus had been the basis of J&J's success to that point, and it continues to pervade the company today, serving as common ground for the organization's 190 operating companies.

Johnson & Johnson Credo[1]

We believe our first responsibility is to the doctors, nurses, and patients, to mothers and fathers and all others who use our products and services. In meeting their needs everything we do must be of high quality. We must constantly strive to reduce our costs in order to maintain reasonable prices. Customers' orders must be serviced promptly and accurately. Our suppliers and distributors must have an opportunity to make a fair profit.

We are responsible to our employees, the men and women who work with us throughout the world. Everyone must be considered as an individual. We must respect their dignity and recognize their merit. They must have a sense of security in their jobs. Compensation must be fair and adequate, and working conditions clean, orderly, and safe. We must be mindful of ways to help our employees fulfill their family responsibilities. Employees must feel free to make suggestions and complaints. There must be equal opportunity for employment, development, and advancement for those qualified. We must provide competent management, and their actions must be just and ethical.

We are responsible to the communities where we live and work and to the world community as well. We must be good citizens—support good works and charities and bear our fair share of taxes. We must encourage civic improvements and better health and education. We must maintain in good order the property we are privileged to use, protecting the environment and natural resources.

Our final responsibility is to our stockholders. Business must make a sound profit. We must experiment with new ideas. Research must be carried on, innovative programs developed, and mistakes paid for. New equipment must be purchased, new facilities provided, and new products launched. Reserves must be created for adverse times. When we operate according to these principles, the stockholders should realize a fair return.

Three Basic Commitments

Today, J&J ties its business to three basic principles:

1. *Commitment to the Credo*—The Credo acts as the driver for behavior at all levels within the organization, from J&J's re-

sponse during the Tylenol crisis to its decision to give away a disease-curing drug at no cost when the organization could not find a profitable market for the product.

2. *Commitment to decentralized management*—To create a competitive, innovative environment, J&J's 190 companies remain fiercely independent of each other.

3. *Commitment to the long term*—J&J invests heavily in research and development, and avoids short-term decisions that will hurt long-term results.

Within this framework, J&J strives to be an innovator in its field. One of the organization's key measures of performance is its percentage of sales from products introduced in the last five years. In the 1980s this measure was around 30 percent; today, it is closer to 35 percent. As a result of this level of innovation, the organization has increased its sales by more than $3 billion since 1995, while adding more than 8,000 new employees.

In an organization that is growing so quickly, leadership development is an issue of tremendous importance. Without a sufficient pipeline (sufficient leaders coming up through the development ranks), J&J would be unable to sustain its consistently high rate of growth.

Without the proper bench strength for J&J coaches to call on at all levels, the company would be unable to sustain its consistent double-digit rate of growth. In the words of Ralph S. Larsen, J&J's current chairman and CEO, "As you look at our growth projections over time, we're going to need more and more leaders. Leadership is the biggest single constraint to growth at J&J, and it is the most critical business issue we face."[2]

Organized for Leadership Development

The company is highly committed to executive development, from the chairman all the way down through the ranks. Today, programs like Executive Conference III, the Executive Development Program, and the Leadership Challenge continue to pay large dividends for the current and future leaders of the organization.

J&J has three major business groups:

1. *The consumer and personal care business group,* which focuses on infant and child care products, wound care, oral care, women's sanitary protection products, vision care, and adult skin and hair care.

2. *The consumer pharmaceutical and professional business group,* which markets over-the-counter medications to consumers.

3. *The pharmaceuticals and diagnostics business group,* which conducts research into medicine's newest frontiers.

All three businesses are served by Corporate Education and Development (CED). CED, an organization of about 50 people, is headed by the vice president of education and development and has the following structural components:

+ *Educational Technology and Research*—responsible for coordinating J&J's corporate, technology-based, training efforts

+ *Management Education and Development*—supplies customers with worldwide programs for development

+ *Geographic Directors of Education and Development*—responsible for interfacing with J&J's companies in each respective region

+ *Learning Services*—performance consulting (organizational development) group that serves the United States and Puerto Rico

With the help of the global human resources vice presidents, CED revised its mission statement in the late 1990s. The current mission is to "strengthen J&J's leadership and organizational capabilities needed to win in the global marketplace. We will achieve this mission through world-class education, development and performance consulting services."[3] Figure 5.1 shows the CED organization.

Figure 5.1 The CED Organization

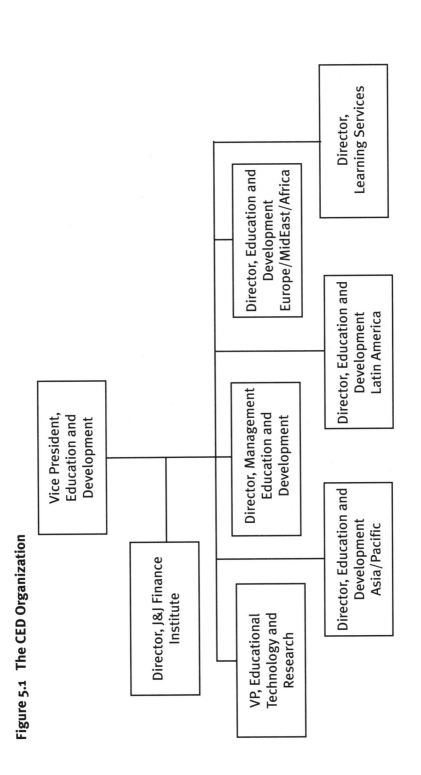

Cooperation between Corporate and Business Units

Within the J&J organization, leadership development and teaching the company's core values are a responsibility of the corporate development function. Management development falls into the hands of the operating business units. J&J believes that the expertise for management development in a particular operating company lies within that company. But because leadership development needs to be consistent across the company, it makes sense to have a central group take the lead on this issue.

J&J divides the training assignment as follows: management development deals with the basics (the "blocking and tackling" issues), and leadership skills build upon those basics. For example, the J&J course catalog offers programs that concentrate primarily on management development issues (such as conflict management, problem-solving, and decision-making), while programs like Executive Conference III and Executive Development Program focus on building the organization's future leaders. These programs internalize J&J values, using them as a base to spur innovation and activity within the organization.

Currently, CED is responsible for the design and delivery of three major executive development courses: Executive Conference III, Executive Development Program, and the Leadership Challenge. In addition, J&J has a shared services model for a number of training courses. Employees sign up for these courses through a course catalog; in 1999, the company had over 10,000 registrations for these corporate training events.

Creating a Leadership Development Process

Where does such an exemplary program come from, and how did it get started? Ten years ago, J&J had no centralized executive development function. Senior executives at J&J decided that the organization had to change its culture. The company had over 100 years of success operating in a decentralized manner, but decentralization was becoming a roadblock in the corporation's move into the global marketplace.

The organization had to teach its 190 companies to partner with each other. If they did not, J&J would be at the mercy of more centralized (and tightly organized) competitors. Leadership development was seen as a vehicle to bring together top leaders from the various J&J companies, giving them a new view of their business and of each other.

Thus began the corporate development function. The organization's first formal corporate development programs, Executive Conferences I and II,[4] were focused on developing individual leaders and getting leaders from across the corporation to meet and understand each other. The goal was to force communication and appreciation among executives of J&J as a whole, not just within a particular J&J company.

Fueled by the demise of other once-powerful companies, J&J took the initiative to determine how its customers and its competitors viewed the organization. With the help of a major consulting firm (McKinsey), J&J developed a process called FrameworkS to help the executive committee, which included the chairman, tackle issues and develop strategies for important topics. FrameworkS topics included innovation and information management. In 1997, a FrameworkS discussion about people development and leadership revealed a critical shortage. Indicators from the J&J succession-planning process raised significant concerns that the company's team did not have enough bench strength in the leadership area. If something wasn't done, future growth was likely to be limited by an inability to fill new positions.

Through the FrameworkS process, J&J identified seven principles of leadership development:

1. Leadership development is a key business strategy.
2. Leadership excellence is a definable set of standards.
3. People are responsible for their own development.
4. J&J's executives are accountable for developing leaders.
5. Leaders are developed primarily on the job.
6. People are an asset of the corporation; leadership development is a collaborative, corporation-wide process.
7. Human resources is vital to the success of leadership development.

J&J proceeded to use these seven principles as a base to create its Standards of Leadership model. Once the Standards of Leadership model was unveiled in 1996, CED had a window of opportunity to put the model into action. Corporate found the operating units hungry for direction and in need of some sort of leadership program. The three-part result was Executive Conference III, the Executive Development Program, and the Leadership Challenge.

J&J did a good job of creating buy-in from the top of the organization. CED had the go-ahead to develop the first Executive Conference under the previous chairman, James Burke. By the time the program was developed, however, a new chairman, Ralph Larsen, had come in and CED had to convince him on the benefits of the program. The eventual success of the program did sell the new chairman on Executive Conference program. Today, the chairman or a member of the executive committee spends a day at Executive Conference III talking with the conference participants about the J&J Credo and its application in the business.

To create support at all levels, CED continues to market its successes internally. The organization is doing follow-up studies to determine the results of the programs on the business. This information will in turn be used to help sell the success of programs like Executive Conference III. CED will also be launching an Education and Development home page on the company's Intranet to better communicate successes.

J&J's Current Model for Leadership Standards

After the FrameworkS meeting on people development and the creation of the Standards of Leadership model, J&J felt that it needed competencies unique to J&J's culture, not those that were generic in nature and application. The J&J Standards of Leadership were developed by line management and tested by senior executives across the company. The objectives of the model were to:

- Be built on J&J core strengths
- Be globally applicable

- Be situationally adaptable
- Be simple, but not simplistic
- Be positive influences on behavior of current and future leaders
- Be central to J&J leadership development.

Based on these objectives, the organization created its current model for leadership standards. Each of the following five key standards is interrelated and driven by J&J's focus on the Credo and desired business results.

1. *Customer/Marketplace Focus*—to create value for customers and an external focus for J&J leaders
2. *Innovation Focus*—to forge a vision for the future, fuel business growth, and promote innovation and continuous learning
3. *Interdependent Partnering Focus*—to build interdependent partnerships
4. *Masters Complexity Focus*—to manage complexity and implement positive change
5. *Organizational and People Development Focus*—to create an achievement environment and develop people for optimal performance

Executive Conference III is targeted to senior executives and management boards, and the Executive Development Program is tailored to advanced managers. Each program participant is nominated by those in charge of their operating company. The J&J Leadership Challenge is for new managers at all levels, from first-line managers to presidents and managing directors.

The focus at J&J is clearly on developing leaders, especially senior executives, from within the organization. J&J does bring people from outside but knows this method is almost always more costly and generally less effective. To promote hiring at lower levels, J&J makes no charge to its companies for training new hires who are undergraduates or M.B.A. grads. It does, however, automatically charge its companies for training experienced hires.

Diversity at J&J

Diversity is a consideration in J&J's succession-planning process. The company tracks the number of minorities and females at different levels within the organization. In addition, it has a philosophy of letting nationals take the lead within their respective countries.

J&J has also made a concerted effort to address work and family issues, and this has had a positive effect on diversity within the companies. For example, corporate headquarters and many of the operating companies have day care centers, and employees are subsidized for day care costs based on salary. The company acknowledges that taking care of families is not only a social responsibility but it is also good business. J&J's efforts in this regard help to keep good people and to attract prospective new hires.

When the Standards of Leadership model was created, groups were sent throughout the world to validate the effectiveness of the model with various cultures. What those evaluative groups discovered was that the broad-based characteristics of the model, with minor exceptions, were acceptable across the organization. The only major issue was translating the standards so that the wording was consistent across cultures.

To promote worldwide interchange and movement, J&J is now encouraging its people to work in global assignments much earlier in their careers. The belief is that it's easier for younger people to move about, and that the valuable learnings from their multicultural experiences are of use to the company for a longer time. Some of the programs helping to achieve this end are:

• *International Service Employee Program.* This program currently involves about 100 people. It takes them primarily from the United States and seeks to place them in positions abroad. These employees get a base-compensation package comparable to their pay in the United States, along with other potential perks, such as a cost-of-living allowance, company car, and private education for their children. The goal is to promote cross-cultural management experience without making a person suffer unduly.

♦ *International Recruiting Program.* J&J hires 50 to 75 M.B.A.s from foreign countries and places them in the United States or some place other than their home country. After an 18-month assignment, these individuals return to their home countries. This program helps develop managers with global perspectives.

Focusing on the Future

CED is in the process of laying down a leadership development strategy for the next three to five years. To this end, the group has identified organizational sponsors in the business and is working with these people to test new ideas and pilot new products and services. J&J is currently testing the proposition that there should be a strategic plan for leadership development in the business plan (just like a marketing plan).

CED has teams working on leadership development for the next generation and leadership development platforms for individuals. CED's goal is to see an integrated system for leadership development that is embedded in the needs of the business.

There is no core curriculum for leadership development. Instead, through the succession-planning process, each senior or high-potential manager at J&J creates an individual development plan. The plan is based on 360-degree feedback, crafted in part by the individual's supervisor, and on the Standards of Leadership model. (360-degree feedback is used solely for development purposes as part of the executive development programs and for the succession-planning process. Companies that want to use 360-degree feedback for their own purposes must go through a certification process to make sure that the data is collected and used in a proper manner.)

J&J's Education at the Core

Currently, J&J has three major corporate programs for leadership development:

1. Executive Conference III
2. Executive Development Program
3. Leadership Challenge

Executive Conference III is designed specifically for senior executives and management board members.[5] Executive Conferences I and II, which brought individuals and management teams together to discuss strategic issues with the senior leadership team, were so helpful that Executive Conference III was launched with senior executives and company group chairmen as the key customers.

The core of the conference has participants discuss how to bring about transformational change in their mini-organizations. Participants discuss how to infuse Credo values into developing leadership standards, principles, and interdependent leadership. From this core, each group experiences its own conference, tailored to its operations. Education and Development (E&D) assembles the meeting participants according to natural work groups and executive committee involvement, and the meetings are then delivered in various regions.

The following highlights the three goals of the conference: (The first two goals demand follow-up meetings with supervisors and action plans that ensure long-term fulfillment of the goals.)

- *Goal 1*—Leadership development on a personal level. Develops a personal improvement plan vis-à-vis gaps against the leadership model.
- *Goal 2*—Leadership development on an organizational level, both leading "my" management team and leading across organizational boundaries. Practices personal leadership in a business context.
- *Goal 3*—Leadership development through Credo values and culture. Supports today's new realities of doing business across boundaries.

During the pre-session, which is approximately two months prior to the "In-Region" session, E&D ensures overall commitment; creates teams to start studying the issues at hand; and gives the teams a chance to find information, data, and a change model from which to work.

As a sponsor, one must be involved across the total effort and remain accountable for the team results. In addition to selecting the team and determining its issues, the sponsor participates in pre-session activities, remains an active voice throughout the session, and makes presentations during the follow-up session.

The five-day session consists of the following:

♦ The first two days focus on personal leadership and the main issues at hand for the specific teams. Topics of discussion usually include 360-degree feedback, personal change, personal improvement, and leading with the Credo values.

♦ During days three and four, the chairman facilitates the session and presents historical J&J cases that capture a business-project issue. Breakout groups then discuss the assigned case, apply it to their own organization, and report back to the group on day five. To ensure that the team will implement their business plan, the entire group meets after 90 days in a follow-up session. J&J does not expect managers to have the ability to implement all points of their plan but instead encourages steady change by tackling problems in smaller parts.

♦ On the last day, program participants recommend to senior executive sponsors of the conference which actions should be taken surrounding the critical business issue. Ninety to 120 days after the program, participants reconvene for one day to report implementation results and to discuss further opportunities for improvement.

J&J knows that action learning has been crucial to the program's success. Using real business issues has brought high-potential leaders together to learn collaboratively and to innovate. The program has serviced about 2,500 people in the organization, from top management to the operating boards within the operating companies. Executive Conference IV will probably be launched in 2001.

Executive Development Program

The EDP focuses on future leaders, that is, advanced managers who would normally report to the functional head of the operating company. Through the EDP, J&J intends to develop bench strength and future leaders who can work effectively across global, functional, and operating company boundaries.

The program itself is a three-week course involving approximately 25 high achievers per session. It is conducted in the part of the world in which the business issue resides. Course specifics include:

♦ *Week one*—Participants are brought up to speed on the issues of teamwork and leadership capabilities. In addition, participants are briefed on the business problem they will study.

♦ *Week two*—The group is broken up into teams and sent to various markets to do research. For example, a team was sent to Germany, Sweden, and Poland to assess the local market for a program that focused on introducing a new product. The participants research and interview clients, government officials, competitors, and best-practice organizations.

♦ *Week three*—Teams create a set of business recommendations based on their market research. Participants also debrief on team effectiveness. This is important, since program participants do not know each other, come from different cultures and backgrounds, and are forced to study a market with which they are not familiar.

Over a three-week period, the EDP focuses on leadership, teamwork, and change through business-issue, specific, action learning. The operating committee supplies the business issue, and then the EDP runs highly customized interventions for each business group. A large part of the three-week program involves site interviews with companies in the region. For instance, teams of two interview J&J businesses, best-practice companies, current and potential customers, government officials, and health care experts to draw data and recommendations for their report on the business issue.

Participants gather after the interviews, then synthesize and present their findings. The experience is very intensive, but probably the best developmental experience they have in their time at J&J. The program helps develop people without the expense of placing participants in another country to live and work. The "issue" becomes their business, so the participants have to work diligently to make it work. The process mimics a McKinsey consulting engagement, except that "the reports are simpler, information is better and more focused, and the talent is your own and stays." The program charges the participant's department $15,000–$20,000 per head. The main difficulty in the program lies in formulating a crisp issue. One group focuses on defining the issue, and another coordinates the country logistics to determine the contacts and details for that section.

An EDP takes four to six months to set up. Sponsors often resist the program initially, because they don't like the idea of having 25 of their best performers out-of-pocket for three weeks. However, the feedback for the program has been positive. Senior executives feel that the reports from their own people are much better than anything they can get from a consulting firm, and participants take the skills they have learned from the experience back to the organization.

The Challenge for Mid-Managers

The Leadership Challenge (LC) began in 1996 to create awareness and understanding of the Leadership Standards, to teach and discuss the ethical decision-making model, and test the 360-degree feedback model. Feedback and quality control are crucial for the individuals involved in the LC.

The initial target audience for the LC was newly advanced managers. However, CED received feedback that all advanced managers should be put through this course. So, the current focus of the program is on bringing the Credo and Standards of Leadership to life. Senior executives are brought in to teach the programs and to help make the standards real for participants.

To actualize the Standards of Leadership, the LC involves discussion of how to incorporate Credo values into the organization. The LC also addresses role expectations to implement leaders' plans. J&J presents the LC on a regional level, in which the executives act as faculty members. Over the course of four days, the LC covers the six Standards of Leadership and concludes with summary action planning. Of the three main corporate leadership development programs, the LC stands as the only one that does not incorporate action learning.

Selection Process for Developing Leaders

On a broad scale, J&J wants to find people who can accelerate change. Each of the programs noted above cater to different groups, based on seniority, position, and performance in the company.

The Executive Conferences serve key people who head up different operating groups (such as Acuvue and Ortho-Denmark) focused on communicating and reviewing Standards of Leadership, individual leadership development, and company action plans.

The EDP focuses on future leaders who are considered "advanced" managers. These leaders normally report to the functional head of the operating company. Two company chairpersons sponsor the EDP and facilitate the learning teams of 20 to 25 participants, who are nominated by company chairpersons. Participants for EDP are not chosen based upon content expertise, but rather on talent. The multi-company EDP participants are global and diverse.

The LC course was designed for advanced managers from around the world. It looks to develop new leaders at key transition points in their careers. Initially, the program targeted only new directors, but it evolved to include all directors—a change that took its target from 1,500 to 5,000 people. J&J assigned coordinators in four regions of the world—Europe, Asia, South America, and North America—to gather participants and manage the complex logistical issues involved with the program.

For succession-planning purposes, competencies have been used to select leaders. Officially, succession planning results in placements for the board level at every operating company. At lower levels, J&J designed two major endeavors to develop the next generation of leadership. The process is not yet fully integrated, and J&J recognizes that this aspect of leadership development is an area that it must continue to improve.

Since the organization plans on continued high growth, J&J will need to increase its leadership pipeline, both in numbers of people and in skills. To increase that pipeline, J&J regularly observes current presidents and managing directors to learn the ways they manage a business. The organization can then capture and disseminate this knowledge to people preparing to assume these positions. J&J excels at identifying people, but does not do as well at preparing people to run the diverse businesses. The corporation has been working with an outside consultant to find a way to better determine who those employees are and to improve the methods used to develop them. The goal is to start developing someone six months before he or she assumes a new position and stay with the employee for six months on the job. J&J recognizes that this concept is a lofty goal.

Diversity among Leadership Candidates

A critical aspect of the EDP is its emphasis on an interdependent partnering mix. When the program heads send out nomination forms, they must be cognizant of the need to build a diverse participant mix—in culture, country, and gender. As teams are assigned, the coordinators make sure that the Americans, for instance, disperse among teams and visit other countries.

J&J formally tracks diversity from the corporate level and holds a debriefing session at the end of the program to see if the program met the goal of a "diverse participant mix." The authors have noted that J&J has found it difficult to ensure a proper mix of "career mom" diversity in the EDP courses, because the program requires participants to leave the country for three weeks. No easy solution has been found, but executive development is always looking for ways to improve its diversity.

Communication with Potential Leaders

Employees at J&J view their jobs on a defined path and will often realize who is and who is not moving along that path. Employees can usually determine whether or not they will make it to the senior-management ranks. If they perceive themselves as "on the wrong path," they will often leave because they feel undervalued.

The MacNeil subsidiary of J&J, in particular, defines and communicates its career paths well. It provides its employees with a map of where they are and development tracks that will help them achieve the highest level for which they are capable. However, many of the operating companies still need improvement in that arena. Each operating company's human resources department drives the succession-planning process. The fierce independence of the operating companies often causes inter-business communication difficulties and subsequently diminishes the organizations' ability to recognize talent. The New Brunswick office, for instance, often fails to identify talent outside the New Brunswick area, because it lacks information from other parts of J&J. The decentralized nature of the company can hamper efforts to share such information extensively.

J&J currently believes that on-the-job training is its most valuable tool in leadership development. Within the various higher-level leadership programs, action learning is considered the best way to foster development. Employees are encouraged to explore jobs in other operating companies and regions to broaden their perspectives and increase their skills. Each of the three distinct leadership development experiences relies heavily on a combination of action learning, 360-degree feedback, and executive involvement to promote teamwork, leadership, and communication among those considered to be "high potential."

Mentoring, Coaching, and 360-Degree Feedback

J&J does provide some coaching for its high-level employees. Informal mentoring has proven helpful as well, but again, each operating company determines the best method for itself. Some operating companies have formal programs, while some emphasize that mentoring should be strictly voluntary. If a mentor's sponsor is strong, employees tend to move into key developmental assignments. J&J is in the process of evaluating systems in place among the operating companies, to determine what practices can be promoted throughout. J&J has identified key areas that affect career success for its employees, and, much like other organizations, these include mentoring, coaching, and feedback.

The Executive Conference, Executive Development, and Management Conference participants receive coaching on their action plans. J&J will offer coaching based on the participant's 360-degree feedback report. In North America, the advanced manager receives one-on-one coaching.

In the LC, one faculty member offers leadership, coaching, and teamwork advice for the participating teams. The coach assists in conflict resolution, teamwork, and the like. In terms of 360-degree feedback, J&J uses three different forms, one for the executive level, one for the management level, and one for the individual contributor level.

J&J looks at trends of succession planning, business results, and position breakdowns to track its success. Each manager who takes part in the LC, EDP, or Executive Conference receives feedback from peers and bosses that factors into a development and job strategy. This is used to help employees move into positions that will help them grow, while also benefiting the company. However, the results of the 360-degree feedback remain confidential and separate from the compensation or evaluation process.

Executive Involvement in Leadership Development

As part of the EDP, employees repeatedly touted the importance of executive faculty involvement. Program participants clamored for executive participation, because top leadership constantly promoted leadership as all important, and they wanted to see leadership "put their money where their mouth is." This became a mutually beneficial arrangement and even a privilege for the executives. The movement began with SBU presidents, then moved down to vice presidents. Informally, this structure spread throughout each group. For the executives, J&J provided some coaching and feedback and used shadowing to help the executive faculty be more effective.

The J&J Course Catalog

In addition to the courses described above, J&J also has an elaborate system for delivering other management development programs at the corporate level. Originally, each J&J operating company in the United States had its own training and development department, and each would contract with outside vendors to do its training. About ten years ago, the organization created a consortium for corporate-sponsored training. In 1998, the director of the consortium had over 10,000 registrations for corporate training events.

A late-1990s catalog offers training in 13 different locations across the United States. Course offerings run from technical training to issues such as conflict management and improving communication. Ninety-eight percent of the courses are given by outside vendors, and the cost is allocated back to the businesses on a per-head basis. This service is not yet available internationally, and the company hopes to use learning technologies in the future to help fill this void.

J&J contracts with a different vendor to deliver the action-learning components of its two corporate executive development programs (Executive Conference III and Executive Development Program). The downside of the action-learning approach is that people who participate in Executive Conference or the EDP almost always create additional work for themselves. While this causes the issues of prioritization and focus to become critical, it is completely in line with J&J leadership development philosophy. As Al Andersen, former vice president of education and development, said, "We believe that 85 to 90 percent of leadership capabilities are developed on the job."[6]

The Role of Educational Technology

J&J is a complex organization with 190 operating companies around the world (130 of which are outside the United States). Educational technology gives the company the opportunity to offer resources to employees globally. Part of J&J's development strategy is to have 90,000 leaders within the company. This can become a reality only through the use of learning technology. And, at J&J, leadership development must include business results. Its Educational Technology and Research function knows that its job is "to utilize educational technologies to leverage learning across J&J worldwide in order to enhance business growth."[7]

The business benefits of using learning technologies include improved global access, speedy dissemination of knowledge, electronic distribution of learning materials, and self-managed learning at one's own pace. Most important, education technologies enable J&J employees to take personal development into their own hands. This is, of course, one of the company's leadership development priorities. When employees feel the need or the desire, the material will be there waiting for them.

J&J has a four-point strategy for implementing learning technologies:

1. *100 Percent Access*—Every employee worldwide should have access to whatever that employee needs to know to be effective on the job.

2. *Experiment*—Since it is not clear what the best educational technologies are, J&J must experiment with various design and delivery modes.

3. *Benchmark & Partner*—Internally, CED partners with Information Technology and the Advanced Communication group[8] to leverage resources and figure out the best strategies for using educational technology. Externally, the organization does a significant amount of benchmarking to keep up-to-date.

4. *Business Value*—Learning and experience must always be connected to compelling and critical performance issues.

Nontraditional Methods of Leadership Development

To keep pace with the rapidly changing nature of technology, J&J adopted an overarching strategy in education technology to guide its work. With three regional professionals, J&J researches and plans to "invest in technology for global access." These three focus on their region and deliver products to their area. Worldwide, J&J intends to use technologies to leverage learning across the entire organization, in order to enhance business growth. J&J takes advantage of existing technology to distribute knowledge throughout the organization.

Electronic distribution of learning materials eases costs and speeds distribution. J&J desires 100 percent access for its employees and a common platform that provides opportunity for self-managed learning worldwide (for instance, browser access). J&J prides itself on providing the tools to those who have ambition to achieve their goals.

The education technology group enjoys experimenting with new technologies. Its mission is to identify, experiment, and facilitate their introduction into the organization. To improve, the group benchmarks against quality organizations. J&J also leverages its E&D experience and partners with other organizations that are similarly engaged.

The E&D home page links to the Learning Navigator and J&J InfoNet, an orientation Web site. The E&D Web site provides the available products and services, consulting services, leadership development, and an E&D conference center. The Learning Navigator catalogs the 400-plus, traditional, J&J-sponsored courseware. It also provides 350-plus performance tools, such as job aids from vendors including PDI and CCL, Web-based training (on such topics as personal skills and conflict management), and information on the organization. Employees can take traditional courses, use the online tools, or study from paper programs. To ensure quality, J&J will not post a course unless a business group sponsors it. The Web site has greatly improved access for the individual.

To assimilate new hires into the J&J culture, an Intranet site known as InfoNet provides three applications to orient new hires and continually educate long-term employees. The first application allows the user to hear the J&J story, along with the values, history, and structure of the organization. Interviews with executives play a large role on this part of the site as well. The second application allows the user to explore the other 190 operating company Web sites, with their history, market, products, and management teams. The last section supplies new hires with orientation action planning. J&J sets forth six major goals for new hires and then gives them action plans that can be customized based on the new hires' thoughts. Access to this framework on the Intranet allows new hires to accelerate their learning processes.

Organizing to Maximize Learning

J&J's Education Technology Task Force is chaired by the vice president of Educational Research and Technology. It has representatives from Information Technology, Advanced Communications, and CED. This group works together to integrate technology with the J&J learning agenda, including projects that require J&J to partner with a vendor.

The Education and Development group is composed of 54 people, employs 20 consultants, 8 U.S. professionals, 7 U.S. support personnel, and regional counterparts. E&D reaches customers at every level of the organization. Due to the extremely decentralized nature of the organization, E&D's interaction with each group is different. The E&D group's customers include:

Chairman and CEO Executive Committee Product Groups

- Consumer
- Pharmaceutical
- Professional
- Consumer pharmaceutical

Worldwide Franchises/Umbrellas such as

- Skin and hair care
- Wound care
- Endosurgery

190 Operating Companies Worldwide such as

- Advanced sterilization products
- Cordis corporation
- Ortho biotech

Under the supervision of the Management Education and Development committee, J&J "develops leaders through innovative, high-impact, business-driven products and services." In order to achieve this mission, E&D began developing its leadership programs with a comprehensive look at other organizations' leadership models. J&J benchmarked both U.S. and international companies to enhance and strengthen its efforts. J&J studied companies with widely recognized management strength, including Coca-Cola, Philips, 3M, 3Com, Hewlett-Packard, Owens-Corning, Yamanouchi, and KAO. The benchmarking study intended to build on the core strengths of J&J, make leadership development globally applicable and situationally adaptable, design the program to be simple but not simplistic, and change the behavior of current and future leaders. E&D specifically did not want to study those traits that had made leaders successful at J&J, but instead focused on what would be needed for leaders to be successful in the future.

The FrameworkS 6 taskforce realized that J&J needed to build leadership development experiences to actualize core concepts and leadership principles. This initiative gave birth to the Executive Conference III, Executive Development Program, and J&J Leadership Challenge. These programs have given J&J a framework by which to infuse core concepts into the day-to-day culture of the organization.

To evaluate participants in the programs, E&D integrated its own brand of 360-degree feedback to be used as a developmental tool, rather than as an evaluation instrument.

Executive coaching and mentoring at J&J is decentralized and is handled within each of the 190 companies. As a result, some companies have formal programs, while others do nothing at all. Centrally, J&J does have the Standards of Leadership on its Intranet, and these are accompanied by a coaching section for each one of the five standards. This coaching section suggests specific actions that might be helpful to improve one's performance and resources along the way.

J&J spends a significant amount of time with people who are going to teach in the LC program. CED works extensively with these organizational leaders to help them fit their experiences into the framework of the class. These leaders also observe other faculty members teaching and can have someone from CED cofacilitate their sessions, if necessary. At any one time, corporate has about 45 to 60 executives in North America qualified to teach the LC.

In its search for leadership teachers, J&J only goes after people within the organization who passionately want to be involved in the development process. Faculty members have either stepped forward on their own or have been nominated by others in the business. In order to generate support for this process, J&J has published a list of "leaders who develop leaders" and distributes this information on a worldwide basis.

With regard to outside trainers, J&J's policy is that the fewer vendors used, the better. The company looks for those who mesh well with J&J's culture and seeks to develop long-term relationships with them. J&J also looks for vendors who have content knowledge and are willing to go the extra mile to meet J&J's specific needs. Says Al Andersen, "No matter who the vendor is [business schools or independent consulting firms], there has to be a degree of flexibility and customer focus."[9]

The few vendors who do mesh with the J&J culture are used for tasks ranging from the design and development of executive development programs to the actual delivery of these programs. With two J&J directors responsible for managing twenty-six Executive Conferences worldwide, it is obvious that vendor help is needed to accomplish all the necessary logistics and delivery.

Succession Planning

There is no succession-planning department at J&J. Instead, the process is the part-time responsibility of a number of people across the organization. Succession planning fits into the selection, appraisal, development, and compensation/reward processes of the organization. All are woven into the Standards of Leadership, and all play a part in identifying future talent. It is these processes, along with J&J's "bubble-up" philosophy, that keep the organization's leadership engine in high gear.

The objective of the succession-planning process is "to provide senior management with an assessment of management talent for succession planning, to identify highly promising future leaders, and to create appropriate action plans." The intent is to create a "snapshot" of the organization each year, so that the chairman can see whether or not there is a dearth of leaders coming down the pipeline.

The key challenges for the J&J succession-planning process include:

+ Early identification of sufficient numbers of future leaders
+ Developmental planning across three distinct business groups
+ Creation of leaders with a global perspective

The evaluation of the succession-planning process takes a balanced-scorecard approach. It considers one's values, business results, organization results, and process skills. Measurement criteria fall into three key areas:

1. *Performance*—focus on business results
2. *Potential*—ability to live the standards of leadership
3. *People development*—performance as both a developer and a supplier of talent

A 360-degree evaluation focused on leadership standards is used to ensure multiple feedback channels. By the 360-degree evaluation process, J&J reviews all business unit heads, management board personnel, direct reports to the management board, and all other high potentials for leadership positions. Starting at the department level in January, managers must go through their organization and identify high-potential talent, and identify people in trouble and work on development plans. After this process is completed at the department level, it is done at the company, corporate, and operating group level. At the Group Operating Committee Review, senior executives identify the following: critical positions; world-class business leaders; world-class functional leaders; and gaps in the succession, developmental, and recruiting plans.

In the final step of the 360-degree review, the Executive Committee identifies and agrees upon high-potential, senior-management candidates; action plans; and timetables. Perhaps the most critical part of this meeting (and succession-planning meetings at all levels) is the sharing of talent across business lines. Since J&J has such a decentralized philosophy, it is often hard to get people to move around within the organization. Even so, the company has realized that this type of movement is critical to leadership development. As a result, J&J has moved more to a "corporate-property" approach to leadership development in order to make sure that its high-potential, senior-management candidates get all the developmental experiences they need to move up within the organization.

Lastly, there is no formal policy as to whether an employee should know where he or she stands in the succession plan. Instead, it is left up to the discretion of the supervisor.

FOLIOMAP Presentations

In order to provide a snapshot of people at a particular level, J&J relies on the use of FOLIOMAPs. FOLIOMAPs plot each person's position relative to performance and potential on a five-point scale. In addition, individuals are given "people development" codes—five colors that plot their behavior in this area— outstanding, superior, competent, needs improvement, or unacceptable. Figure 5.2 is a sample FOLIOMAP.

Understanding the Effect of Leadership on the Bottom Line

J&J's executive development programs are fueled by a general belief that "the process is working." As a result, the organization does not stress the need for metric information on the results of its corporate development programs. In the two programs with action-learning components (Executive Conference III and EDP), participants are brought back 90 to 120 days after the main session to discuss the implementation of the action plans that were created during the program. The organization is beginning to

Figure 5.2   Sample Johnson & Johnson FOLIOMAP

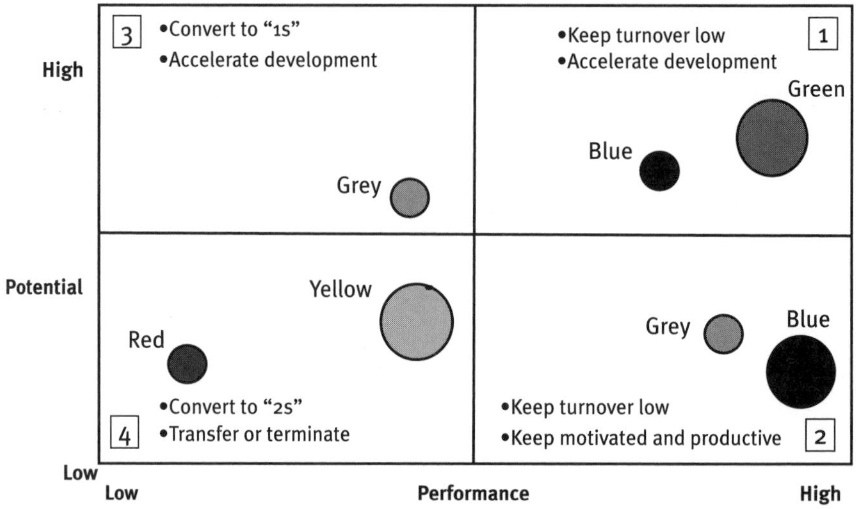

PEOPLE DEVELOPMENT CODES—J&J FOLIOMAP

Green	Outstanding	4.3−5.0
Blue	Superior	4.3−5.0
Grey	Competent	4.3−5.0
Yellow	Needs Imprpvement	4.3−5.0
Red	Unacceptable	= 1.5

*Note that the size of the circle indicates the individual's amount of responsibility.

go back and track some of the results of these action-learning initiatives to better market these programs internally. Even so, there is still a general consensus from the business side that these programs have positive impacts on business results.

Communicating the success of the executive development function is an opportunity for improvement at J&J. The corporate education function has a Web site to communicate projects on which it is currently working. Generally, though, the high level of senior executive support for the programs, along with word of mouth, has made communication of results a moot point. In the words of Al Andersen, "You can drive yourself crazy with measurements. If you want, you can hire three people to measure everything. There must be a balance between quantitative and qualitative data."[10]

Summary

Johnson & Johnson's (J&J) business is tied to three basic principles: commitment to the J&J Credo, commitment to decentralized management, and commitment to the long term.

Corporate Education & Development (CED), an organization of about 50 people is devoted to "strengthen[ing] J&J's leadership and organizational capabilities needed to win in the global marketplace. [They] will achieve this mission through world-class education, development, and performance consulting services." This commitment is evidenced through the company's three corporate programs for leadership development: the Executive Conferences, the Executive Development Program, and the Leadership Challenge.

Part of J&J's development strategy is to have 90,000 leaders within the company. Electronic distribution of learning materials eases costs and speeds distribution. The Education & Development homepage links to the Learning Navigator and J&J InfoNet, an orientation Web site. Employees can take traditional courses, use the online tools, or study from paper programs.

Although there is a general consensus from the business that these programs have positive impacts on business results, communicating the success of the executive-development function remains an opportunity for improvement at J&J.

Notes

1. 1999 Johnson & Johnson Annual Report (http://www.johnsonand johnson.com/whoisjnj/crusa.html)
2. "Johnson & Johnson Site Visit Summary," *Leadership Development Consortium Benchmarking Study*, APQC, June 25, 1998, p. 6.
3. "Johnson & Johnson Site Visit Summary," *Leadership Development Consortium Benchmarking Study*, APQC, June 25, 1998, p. 6.
4. Executive Conference I: Setting the Competitive Standard gathered the top 750 executives of the organization to New Brunswick, N.J., for this program. Executive Conference II: Creating Our Future

used the Merlin Exercise to look at where J&J should be ten years from now.

5. Management boards are the direct reports of the presidents or managing directors of the individual operating companies.
6. "Johnson & Johnson Site Visit Summary," Leadership Development Consortium Benchmarking Study, APQC, June 25, 1998, p. 17.
7. Ibid.
8. The Advanced Communication group is an internal group that focuses on the commercial benefits of the Internet for J&J's business.
9. "Johnson & Johnson Site Visit Summary," Leadership Development Consortium Benchmarking Study, APQC, June 25, 1998, p. 19.
10. "Johnson & Johnson Site Visit Summary," Leadership Development Consortium Benchmarking Study, APQC, June 25, 1998, p. 21.

6

Royal Dutch Shell

LEAP to Remain a Living Company

R oyal Dutch Shell/Shell International (Shell) is one of the most successful, long-lived companies in the business world. Its kingdom is built on top-performing businesses in oil, gas, petrochemicals, and other allied fields. The group has more than 102,000 employees, 300,000 full-time contractors, and operations in 130 countries around the world. With a current market capitalization of $115 billion and $56 billion in annual revenues, Shell is often cited as one of the world's strongest living companies.

Arie de Geus, who was in charge of strategic planning for Shell for several years, observes in his book *The Living Company*[1] that the average life expectancy of a multinational Fortune 500 company (or the equivalent in other nations) is only between 40 and 50 years. To establish that, de Geus directed a study that found that a third of the companies listed in the Fortune 500 disappeared within ten years. They were acquired, merged, spun-off in pieces, or otherwise no longer had their identity.

Where human beings have an average life expectancy of around 75 years or more, relatively few corporations are that old and still flourishing. A subsequent study of successful long-time survivors like Shell identified the following characteristics:

♦ They were sensitive to the environment in order to learn and adapt. They were cohesive with a strong sense of identity.
♦ They were tolerant of unconventional thinking and experimentation.
♦ They were conservative in financial policy to retain the resources that allowed them to be flexible.

It might seem that a company that has done so well for so long would have been especially adept at the flexibility and change ethic required for staying atop the global totem pole. Actually, the opposite is true. With a long tradition of excellence in developing and applying technology and engineering, Shell found the impetus for change had become hard to find. But change began to germinate at a meeting called by Cor Herkstroter, the (now retired) chairman of Shell. In that meeting, the top 50 to 60 leaders in the organization gathered to address the return on average capital employed, which was not what it should have been. As these leaders looked across the businesses and at the relationship between the central offices and the operating units, it became clear that change was essential. Even so, they did not discuss an overall transformation. They chose rather to initiate a restructuring at the central offices and undertook a service-company review.

In his article in *Executive Excellence*,[2] Maarten Van Den Bergh, a senior executive with Shell, clarifies the threefold challenge his company faced, a challenge shared by most global operations today. Van Den Bergh lists:

1. *The impact of globalization*—as worldwide markets cool as a result of the poor judgment of past decision-makers, forcing businesses to fight to maintain profitability through cost-cutting and technological development.

2. *New expectations of business*—as society presses diverse, and sometimes conflicting, demands with regard to human rights, rights of workers, environmental controls, and others.

3. *Need for new structures, new management methods, new internal cultures*—geared to expecting the unexpected and dealing with it quickly and effectively.

Shell's service-company review showed that to continue as an industry leader, the firm would have to undergo a restructuring. The matrix governance structure that had been in place for 30 years was minimized and shifted from a function and region (geography) focus to a line of business focus. The national boundary structure changed, and the operating companies became a cluster of operating units either in or among different countries. Processes that supported the old structure were changed or abolished. These changes began the transformation, but to truly change the organization and address the challenges of a new global economy, the people of Shell needed to change the way they worked and did business.

Making the LEAP

In the mid-1990s, the Leadership and Performance program (LEAP) was created to be a major enabler of the required transformation. An institution of global business was setting out to learn new ways. The change, however, was not seen as a luxury, but as a necessity for continued success. Previous efforts at creating leaders had often been lost in an unfocused management development program run through human resources. The Committee of Managing Directors (CMD) decided that LEAP was too important to fall through the corporate cracks. In the words of Steve Miller, managing director of Shell, "The company that wins is the one that has the most best-leaders."

LEAP was not dropped into the organization as a finished product. It began as a white paper that gave few details about how the new leadership process might look. A director was brought in from one of the business lines. He worked with the CMD to select the small group that would create the program. The strategy for LEAP was to "get on the playing field" and start delivering results. LEAP used this approach to build its overall strategy as things progressed. Instead of devoting a large amount of time to building theoretical structures up front, the LEAP team wisely decided to start something and then work at improving it.

LEAP's challenge was to create leaders at every level

throughout the organization. There was a further requirement that the new leadership training program would blend the hard skills and the harder skills (traditionally known as the "soft skills"). And finally, LEAP's assignment was to be completed quickly and on a large scale, which the assignment givers recognized as the only way to cause a true transformation.

Organizing for a Giant LEAP

Initially, the LEAP development team consisted of the eight individuals selected by the CMD. This group reported directly to the CMD, and its simple, but difficult, charter was to create the kind of leaders that could guide Shell through critical transformation and reinvent the business. The CMD provided limited input, but no directives about the appearance or characteristics of the new super leader.

From the beginning, the LEAP staff was given a two-part charge, to assist in the company's leadership transformation process, and simultaneously, to accelerate the process. LEAP was not only to "make it up as they went along," it was to make it up, learn quicker, and be smarter.

Once this group of eight determined the components that would make up the LEAP process, it recognized the large amount of time required to sell their new concepts properly throughout the monolith that was Shell. This selling time, referred to by the LEAP team as the "contracting process," became a critical focus of the team's work. Contracting meant sitting down in protracted meetings with the leaders of different Shell business lines and negotiating contracts that specified exactly when, where, and how their staffs would participate in LEAP. LEAP representatives not only had to explain what they had to offer, but they had to make the executives want it. These executives had to be shown enough value in LEAP to support their employees during the training and in the critical follow-up to LEAP training.

To date, thousands of Shell employees have completed LEAP training. The more employees that have completed the training, the more obvious it has become that the contracting and follow-up stages are of paramount importance to the success of the training. As a result, LEAP has grown from its original 8 members to a staff of 48 in the last two years. The majority of those added to the staff come from other business units within Shell and are on two-year contracts with LEAP. They will return to their business units at the end of the two years.

Of particular interest is the fact that the growth of the LEAP organization has occurred without the creation of a hierarchy. LEAP has made every effort to maintain a flat structure, practicing what it preaches and allowing everyone on the staff to be a leader. For the sake of working with the various Shell businesses, the LEAP staff is divided into three overlapping key teams: product, business, and logistics. None of them is deemed more important than another.

LEAP tries to use Shell's existing assets to keep its costs of doing business to a minimum. While most of the learning activities take place within the operating units, Shell does have a learning center in Holland, which can be used by LEAP for workshops or follow-up meetings. In addition, LEAP students have access to Shell's New Product Development group for research. And, as the students turn up useful new concepts, the company's existing knowledge-management and distribution systems help spread the learnings across the organization. This keeps LEAP's learning processes integrated with Shell's ongoing business and gives LEAP a "think tank" reputation that is more than one of "corporate academia."

Leading vs. Managing

Shell sees a significant difference between management skills and leadership skills, yet feels strongly that the latter can be taught.

Shell's Definition of Leadership: Everyone has the capacity to be a leader.

Shell believes in the concept of the servant leader, which is someone who helps to create the conditions that enable others to realize and develop their potential in the workplace. It means recognizing that, as an individual, you do not have all the answers, and being able to demonstrate a sense of humility and vulnerability. Far from a weakness or character flaw, these qualities help foster trust in a leader, and that is critical to any leader's success.[3]

Shell believes that effective leaders are those who advance their own transformation, the personal transformation of others, and the transformation of the company; produce superior results; and build the capacity of the organization and of the people in it.

What Makes a Corporate Giant Choose Change?

It remains somewhat amazing that a global organization with so many entrenched habits it might have defended would choose to think change. A review of history may be helpful. Remember that the LEAP initiative evolved amid a transformation that Shell was undergoing. The company had realized that it needed to become the top performer of first choice through energized leadership, a strong focus on customers, and the unleashing of talent at all levels.

One of the foundational concepts of LEAP was that leaders would need to be created at all levels of the organization. An initial step evaluated all current management and leadership training offerings. The evaluation revealed that most of these offerings were focused on management skills, were informal and inconsistent across operating units, and had small attendance. Wisely, the company began the process of minimizing, and eventually eliminating, these programs.

Even though every Shell company wanted the best training possible, something more substantive and related to the bottom line was necessary to occasion a top-to-bottom change. Shell needed something more than small-class attendance to embark upon a total renovation of itself. It needed something that all of its businesses would buy into.

Consequently, LEAP began a journey with an undefined destination. Shell knew that it needed a transformation to remain competitive in the constantly changing global economy and that it had to make a habit of breakthrough performance that could routinely capture the full potential of emerging new opportunities. However, it could not describe the future leaders it wanted to emerge from its reinvention process.

LEAP began from the company's unquestioned and long-standing organizational values of integrity, professionalism, respect for people, long-term focus, and pride without arrogance. As Steve Miller said, "I think it is important to understand that, when we talk about growth, it puts another dimension in how we are trying to grow the business; it does not change the core values of the business. In fact, throughout the transformation process, we went back and looked at the core values of the group—honesty, integrity, and respect for people—and we reaffirmed them. It's not about changing value systems; it's about changing how we work."[4]

Very Few Givens

There were a few things Shell's top leadership knew about the new style of leadership that they were asking LEAP to create and spread throughout the organization. The enterprise needed to be less controlled from the top and more from the businesses. Leaders in the various operating units needed freedom and flexibility to develop and create change. Shell was aware that it needed to "walk the walk," not just "talk the talk," of empowered leadership.

LEAP had to accomplish this goal, while simultaneously fostering an understanding of, and a response to, the new competitive realities. Shell leaders would need the ability to understand current market realities, anticipate future realities, and create innovative business strategies in response. Lastly, for the LEAP program to be successful, it needed the wholehearted participation of everyone at Shell.

LEAP realized it could not, on its own, accomplish the task of developing leaders at all levels of the gigantic Shell pyramid, since the organization could not even be led by one entity. LEAP knew it had to sell the leaders of each of the various businesses on the concept of shifting the focus to business improvement, bottom-line results, and the necessary soft skills for energizing the organization.

With all of this in mind, corporate funded the initial design and delivery. This was necessary to get the right program off the ground, not just the program that the businesses wanted. As LEAP has become more successful and is even sought out by many of the businesses, it has moved to a joint funding process. If the CMD wants an addition to LEAP offerings, then it will fund it. The businesses pay for the regular offerings. At the end of the day, however, Shell feels that the businesses should fund the program, as that shows that they derive value from the process.

Links to Business Strategy

Alignment with the business units comes from the primary meetings of the LEAP staff and the business operations leaders. These contracting sessions set clear goals for participation and anticipated achievements. LEAP's use of team projects, instead of traditional classroom sessions, heightens interest and allows LEAP to tailor its offerings to specific business needs. LEAP gathers this information from its contracting sessions, and every successful training session reveals a need for further programs.

Achieving Buy-In

The chairman of Shell's CMD initiated the service-company review that led to the transformation process and the formation of LEAP. With such a beginning, senior-level support was already established. Shell leadership knows that this level of support must continue. Senior-level support must go beyond gestures—it must sincerely believe that LEAP is the agent of change that will save the company. If current leaders do not reinforce what employees are learning in the programs, the learnings will be lost and no real change will happen.

To facilitate the active participation of the current leadership, the CMD and other leaders take personal responsibility for projects. Each work team reports to a leader within its group, or, if the project is cross-functional, one of the leaders within Shell champions the project's efforts. In the case of the Value Creation program, one of the managing directors leads each of the teams.

Identifying Leadership Candidates

Defining competencies is an ongoing process, but Shell has identified four competencies for successful leaders:

1. Ability to build a shared vision
2. In-depth knowledge of the business
3. Ability to think systemically
4. Ability to communicate through open and honest dialogue

In addition to these defined competencies, Shell values integrity, vision, coaching skills, and willingness to reveal vulnerability. These characteristics, combined with entrepreneurial and engagement skills, make strong leaders at Shell.

With its emphasis on transforming the entire organization, LEAP is open to leaders from anywhere within Shell. The process has created a new language of leadership and individual empowerment at all levels throughout the organization. Employees are nominated by their managers, and they are part of the contracting process that determines their projects.

The majority of participants come from managerial ranks. Currently, the top 5,000 managers are being monitored in an informal succession plan. LEAP staff and the CMD believe that 10 to 20 percent of managers must complete the LEAP process before organizational change begins in earnest. In addition, talented employees in their thirties are being leap-frogged into senior positions, and it is important that these fast-rising individuals attend LEAP.

Instead of selecting only from the executive ranks, Shell wants to ensure that it creates leaders at all levels. Therefore, it begins its efforts of appraising leaders from the moment their employment begins. From the time Shell recruits new employees on college campuses, and continuing throughout their careers, the company uses a model to examine three key qualities in each candidate. This model, encapsulated by the acronym CAR, evaluates the following:

 ◆ *Capacity*—Ability to analyze data quickly and learn fast; ability to make judgments on fact instead of sentiment; ability to identify all implications and learn from others; creativity to propose innovative and workable solutions; and ability to manage uncertainty in complex environments.

 ◆ *Achievement*—Drive and enthusiasm; ability to set ambitious targets for self and others; ability to deliver results; resilience; courage to go against the crowd.

 ◆ *Relationships*—Genuine respect for people of all cultures and status; honesty and integrity; open and direct communication; ability to inspire sensitive and clear vision; clear means of communication and decision.

CAR qualities are not limited to leadership or LEAP; they are baseline characteristics desired of all Shell employees. Theoretically, each of the three CAR elements has the same weight. But, since Shell is such a large and diverse organization, it is not surprising that each operating unit places its own unique emphasis on the various aspects of the CAR assessment. For example, the upstream business, which is mostly engineers, may place the most weight on capacity, while the downstream retail focuses more on relationships, the primary arena of sales and marketing. The key to the entire process is to remain flexible and to realize that there is no absolute formula.

Ninety-five percent of current Shell executives come from within the organization. With this hiring record, and the recent shift from a closed sourcing system to a more self-directed, open system, the importance of a program like LEAP becomes even more critical to the future of the organization. Transforming the organization means retraining and redefining skills and characteristics that have been, for so long, engrained within the corporate culture. Constantly evaluating employees' capacity, achievement, and relationship skills and addressing any gaps ensures that the transformation Shell desires will occur.

There is a ranking system that correlates to potential within the organization. As with all organizations that have ratings and ranking systems for employees, Shell must deal with those individuals who are not ranked as highly. If an individual does not show the potential to move up within Shell, that message is communicated to the individual. It is hard to do and takes coaching for the managers to convey it in the right way, but Shell believes it is the fairest thing for the employee.

Addressing Diversity Issues

Building a diverse leadership team has been a challenge for Shell. Currently, senior management is 80 percent Anglo-Dutch white, and 96 percent male. This demographic reflects the fact that Shell's major offices have been in England, the Netherlands, and the United States. However, with the new global economy and operating companies all over the world, diversity has become an important issue that Shell needs to address when looking at its future leaders.

In fact, the CMD recently asked one of the value creation teams to address the issue of diversity as its project. The team found that Shell did have a diverse workforce, but it needed to create more diversity in senior management, and so it recommended finding local nationals to replace current leaders in each country in which Shell has an operating company. In addition, a goal has been set to have women make up 20 percent of the top leaders within the next ten years. This means a comprehensive look at how talent is assessed, as well as investigating the recruiting patterns in countries with assessment centers, and with those doing the assessing. Many assessors have been Anglo-Dutch white and have tended to choose those similar to themselves.

Needs Assessments

Shell conducts formal surveys to determine the needs of its businesses every six to twelve months. In comparison, the majority of the needs-assessment work that the LEAP staff does is on a just-in-time basis and occurs during the contracting process.

The contracting process takes place each time a business wants to participate in a LEAP program. When a business shows interest in sending a potential candidate or team to LEAP, a staff member meets with the leader of that business. The LEAP staff member listens to the specific needs of the leader and explains in detail the offerings of LEAP and which offerings will be most effective to meet the need.

The initial meeting provides LEAP staff members with insight about the specific needs of the businesses. It also opens up an opportunity to discuss LEAP strategy in detail. The LEAP staff member clarifies the role that the business leader must play while his or her employees are in LEAP programs. Together, the staff member and the business leader create a contract for the program, set budgets for the team project, and set time expectations, goals, and outcomes for the process.

LEAP's contracting process is the make-or-break session that determines the success of the effort. It lets businesses know exactly what they are getting into, and it provides trainers with valuable goal-setting information about the specific needs of the business. Wisely, all of this occurs at the beginning of the process, so that time, money, and opportunities are not wasted because of misunderstood responsibilities. The LEAP staff does a great deal of follow-up throughout the contract, which can be for one program or for many. Sometimes, initial training steps reveal subsequent training needs.

Leadership Research

LEAP constantly discusses whether it should be a customer-focused agent first and a change agent second, or vice-versa. In essence, it needs to be both. To ensure that this happens, and that LEAP does not simply react to the immediate needs of its business customers, it maintains a continuing conversation with the CMD about the transformation of the company. It also stays alert and informed regarding the latest in leadership research.

Shell is a member of the Global Research Consortium, which is made up of 12 companies and a worldwide faculty that constantly explore and discuss the latest information and knowledge about leadership and learning.

Shell also works with outside learning consultants and university professors to stay abreast of the latest in leadership research. LEAP is committed to maintaining these research and educational connections, in order to constantly test the boundaries of its current leadership process.

Design and Development of LEAP Programs

Before Shell focused on creating its transformation, the company had to rely heavily on consultants to create knowledge and solve business issues. The problem with this method is that it is usually the consultants who have the greatest learning experience, and, once the problem is solved, the consultants leave, taking the tacit knowledge with them.

To remedy this problem and to ensure that it will not happen in the future, LEAP emphasizes compressed action learning that empowers its own teams and forces them to resolve issues for themselves.

The four programs that make up LEAP build teams that create real solutions to real issues. Shell personnel own the solution and keep the learning experience for future use. This hands-on philosophy enables LEAP to empower Shell people to perform effectively; coach instead of carry out work for clients; remain a catalyst and follow up frequently; continue research and update tools and techniques as needed; and assist in creating tools and techniques and transfer all of them to its Shell clients.

LEAP's Core Curriculum

The LEAP process currently encompasses four programs. Each of the four programs fits one of Shell's core values and is tied directly to the goals for transforming the organization.

1. *Business Framework Implementation* (BFI) takes an intense, vertical look at the business, to reinvent business methods, using Shell's new, proprietary business model. The bottom line of this model is to increase the profitability and growth of Shell. BFI uses a six-month process, which puts a natural work team through three workshops. In addition, there is a 120-day work period, during which the team members continue with their jobs but have additional work assignments to complete. Approximately 1,500 leaders attend this program each year.

2. *Focused Results Delivery* is another program in LEAP's core curriculum. It is used to stimulate learning and change on a specific topic of leadership and on a specific project worked by the team. The results of this program are amplified even more because, as a part of the process, each team leader must complete a workshop with his or her direct reports. This leaders-developing-leaders process reaches approximately 10,000 leaders a year and has three workshops and a 90-day work period.

3. The *Value Creation program* brings together a small group of high-potential staff members to work on a specific group-wide issue and recommend how Shell should address the issue to add value to the shareholder. Value Creation introduces high-potential individuals to each other and to the managing directors. (A managing director always serves as a champion for each project in this program.) Value Creation has three workshops and a 120-day work period. Approximately 25 leaders attend per year.

4. The *Shell Leadership Challenge* is aimed at developing systemic thinking, helping leaders understand their mental models, and improving their engagement skills. Listening, people, and engagement skills have been identified as areas in which Shell leaders need improvement. So, this program addresses these specific issues for approximately 2,500 leaders per year.

Mix of Activities

Each of LEAP's core curriculum programs mixes classroom days and team-based projects during periods of 90 to 120 days. LEAP strongly believes in the benefits of mixing its activities. It brings teams together for the purposes of discussing certain leadership or business issues, reporting results, and building cohesiveness among the group members.

There are approximately 11 classroom days for each program. Each day is challenging, well-planned, and ideal for networking and best-practice sharing. However, everyone agrees that the most valuable learnings take place during the team-based projects. No more than nine teams participate in a program at one time. Depending on the program, a team may come from a single business or consist of individuals across diverse businesses and functions.

The team project for BFI is already set, but the projects for the other courses are determined during the contracting process. This ensures that the team members will solve real business issues or create new products that will improve their companies' performance. Measurable outcomes and goals are set so that team members are not simply running through a simulation, but trying to create value for the organization as they learn.

Each team has a LEAP member assigned to work with it and coach the members on content and process. Team behavior dictates success or failure and acts as a motivating factor. And, of course, none of these high-performing participants is willing to let down the team. During the 120-day program, participants spend an average of 50 percent more than their normal working time on the project. Feedback has indicated that the programs have placed a strain on the participants' personal and business lives, but that the programs do facilitate tremendous learnings about values, teamwork, and leadership.

Learning Technologies

To circumvent cost and time constraints, LEAP has made use of some existing technologies but still does not use technology extensively. Laptop computers, e-mail, and Internet forums are used by the teams throughout the 120-day period, but no efforts have been made (or are anticipated) to replace the face-to-face workshops with distance learning. At the heart of each LEAP program are the invaluable networking and interaction that takes place among the leaders. Face-to-face interaction is, therefore, a key component of every LEAP experience.

In one success story, the knowledge generated by LEAP participants resulted in a knowledge-management system that is now used throughout the entire Shell organization. An Internet forum called *Silent Dialogue* is an electronic magazine that discusses what LEAP is doing and also highlights best practices discovered by the project teams. *Silent Dialogue*'s 70,000 hits a month help market the LEAP program and provide solutions for Shell employees.

The Role of Current Leaders

Leaders play a major role in the LEAP process. First, they must buy into the process enough to be willing to send their employees to the programs. Their involvement is further solicited during the contracting process, since they must ensure that their participants are fully supported throughout the LEAP process.

Last, and probably most important, they must champion the project their reports are working on and ensure that learnings are supported and reinforced on the job. It is this last step that sets Shell apart from other leadership trainers and enables those at Shell to take maximum business advantage of the LEAP. Shell's leadership training is serious about the corporate transformation the LEAP process was created to facilitate.

Mentoring is also an important aspect of current leader involvement. At this stage, mentoring remains an informal process in LEAP but is still emphasized from the contracting negotiations all the way through the program. Some Shell businesses have created formal mentoring processes, and the learnings from their results are being used to create a pilot program for the rest of the organization.

LEAPing to Outside Vendors

In addition to the external consultants and universities involved in the development of LEAP programs, more outside players were also needed. The LEAP staff completed an extensive train-the-trainer program to get its trainers well versed in the programs and philosophies.

Of course, starting a program is tough, but the real challenge occurs in maintaining the momentum as demand for the program grows. LEAP faces the question of whether or not to bring in outside vendors to run the programs. Another option is to outsource to universities. LEAP generally feels it should continue to offer programs with the same regularity. This allows Shell to maintain the heart of the efforts with the internal LEAP staff and keep the programs unique to Shell.

Succession Planning

To keep an organization of Shell's magnitude running, 200 senior executives manage the 100,000-plus full-time employees, as well as the 300,000 full-time contractors. That 200-person senior cadre needs to be refreshed constantly. To ensure that this happens, the CMD meets twice a month to address the issues surrounding the talent base of the organization. With the support of the human resources staff and the watchful eye of the outside board of directors, the CMD has a process that deals with budget strategy and personnel.

It is understandably difficult to keep abreast of the organization's many leaders beyond the top 200. Shell attempts to cross-check the operating companies every six months and to move individuals across the companies whenever possible. Within this new process, Shell also focuses on providing continuous knowledge of the top talent-base to allow for a more informed discussion and, ultimately, a more informed selection.

Shell is shifting from a closed model of sourcing to an open resourcing model. In an open resourcing model, the individual drives his or her career path with input, as opposed to directives from the line and from human resources. Thus, the approach to succession planning has changed from dictating moves to employees to career road maps to guide managers as they work with assessment centers to choose their career paths.

LEAP is heavily involved with the leadership development process and coordinates strategic projects that expose young, high-potential employees to senior management. Projects that employees undertake in LEAP must be relevant and tied to actual results, so that managers can confidently recommend their employees for leadership positions within their own organizations or across the various operating companies. Overall, the transformation within Shell relies on having a great deal of knowledge about the skills of its employees. LEAP plays a leadership role in shaping those leadership skills.

Measuring Outputs

The outcomes of LEAP programs are determined during the contracting process in meetings between LEAP staff members and Shell's business leaders. During this discussion, the business leader expresses his or her objectives for sending a candidate to the program. In many cases, that objective defines the program and the problem that the candidate and his or her team members will address.

Specific goals are tracked by LEAP staff, and the results are reported to the business leader throughout the 120-day period. In addition, LEAP looks at the financials at the beginning and at the end of the program to identify any changes and to scan for factors that may have played a role in those changes.

LEAP works with each business unit by sending a trainee to gauge LEAP's progress during the first 90 days, during the first year, and after the second year. Traditional "smile sheets" (participant reaction forms that ask "Did you like the program?") are not often used, but surveys are employed to gather qualitative data on the benefits of the process to employees. LEAP also uses 360-degree feedback before and after the program to share information with the participants.

Much of this has been specified in the contracting process

as described earlier. Businesses set expectations for what they hope to accomplish during the process, and the results are measured against those expectations. LEAP sets high standards for itself. Its members do not feel they are adding value, unless the projects generate revenues at least 25 times the project costs.

Tracking Leaders

Shell uses a standardized profile to track all candidates, giving the CMD a clear way to compare the talent. The manager and the employee share the responsibility for updating a Career Assignment Summary (CAS), which provides a current snapshot of the employee's skills, key characteristics, and abilities. The CAS contains the following:

♦ *Current Assignment History*—Job title, job dimensions, the competence acquired, the learning gained, and the languages in which the employee is proficient

♦ *Performance Narrative/Ranking*—Comments on performance relative to expectations and peers.

♦ *Own Views and Wishes*—Goals for short-term development, long-term development, mobility, and other general comments

♦ *Resourcing Aspects*—Personal portrait, list of short-term development needs, potential next assignment, ideas about longer-term career direction, and an estimated end-of-current-assignment date

♦ *Potential Ranking*—Ranking that reflects each employee's potential to move into a leadership position (This ranking is derived by the employee's manager, based on annual reviews and 360-degree discussions and is shared with the employee.)

Employees are encouraged to work with their managers to address career goals and explore ways to achieve them. In addition, Shell has set up a number of assessment centers to help employees self-direct their careers. These centers can help put employees in touch with the type of learning experience or job assignment that will advance their careers.

Maintaining Momentum

Shell has a unique situation in that all LEAP programs have goals and quantifiable deliverables. The first team to go through one of the programs had actual deliverables, and this helped create management excitement about the bottom-line evidence that LEAP training was worthwhile.

In addition, two annual surveys have assessed customer attitude toward LEAP. The responses to these surveys run the spectrum, indicating that participants and those sending participants have varied feelings about the process. However, the main measure used to judge success is the repeat business that LEAP encounters. The "proof of the pudding" is that LEAP programs are adding enough value that managers keep sending more students!

Communication

As LEAP was launched, the small staff did not have much time to market the process. By default, the team decided that the best advertising it could get would be by word-of-mouth. By building successful programs, pushing them out to many leaders, and documenting the results, LEAP expected more students would be nominated to participate in the process. That expectation has proved to be true.

The program has grown greatly. It has become well known throughout the organization, and credibility has increased with the continuing delivery of hard results. LEAP staff comes from, and returns to, the business units. It spends most of its time in the field, spreading the word about its efforts. In addition to the increased size of the LEAP organization, technology has been a major enabler for communicating what LEAP has and will accomplish. The *Silent Dialogue* online magazine has tremendously increased the awareness of LEAP's efforts within Shell.

It has now become a badge of honor within Shell to be in, or a graduate of, LEAP. And it is becoming more difficult to get into the programs, even though it is common knowledge that enrolling means a lot of extra work. This notoriety is helpful as more Shell employees are motivated to investigate and involve themselves with LEAP.

Key Lessons from the LEAP Success

1. *The importance of the contracting process.* Shell's governance structure includes six managing directors, each with his or her own sphere of influence. Unlike GE, where one person can give the order to begin an initiative, LEAP must contract with each of the company's internal businesses and secure their buy-in of the process. Before any business unit takes part in a LEAP program, a LEAP staff member meets with that business unit's leader and contracts the work. The staff must secure not only buy-in for the program, but also the support of those leaders. They must contract to make the time and work with LEAP teams to ensure their success. This contracting process is the make-or-break situation that determines the success of LEAP efforts. It is a process that LEAP constantly strives to improve. LEAP failures can, in almost every case, be traced back to an inadequate job of communicating the importance of the process in the contracting phase.

2. *Senior leadership.* Senior leadership's visible support for LEAP has been key to its success. The program has to reside with the CMD, or it simply will not have the credibility it needs. This does not mean simply funding LEAP. Senior leaders must actively participate in this new emphasis on leadership. They must use the new language and actively promote the new leadership styles that LEAP teaches. Only if they model what LEAP teaches will employees follow and any type of real transformation take place. The first eight people that made up LEAP were selected by the managing directors, and this brought ownership for them and the participants.

3. *Follow-up is critical.* LEAP started with 8 people and now employs 48. In many respects, this growth happened because

of the early success of LEAP programs and a resulting call to accelerate the transformation process. Most LEAP employees spend 70 percent of their time on the road, coaching the participants in the process. To assist with this process, most LEAP employees come from the business on a two-year contract. Their Shell background is essential to their role in LEAP, and, after they leave, they become agents of change for the program within the businesses. It has become a very selective process to work for LEAP, which ensures that the group does not get any problem employees.

4. *Quality.* To do its work effectively, LEAP must maintain quality. This seems like a given, but it is difficult to maintain quality when the majority of LEAP employees are on two-year assignments from other parts of the business. Regular training and follow-up ensure a constant of strong service and maintain the quality focus necessary to build strong leaders.

5. *Knowledge management.* As LEAP programs began, there was a great deal of discussion about the journey of discovery. Initially, it was felt that each team should make 100 percent of the discovery to truly build its leadership capabilities. However, this became too time consuming, and the teams began to learn from the findings of prior classes and teams on their own. By using the templates of others, they were able to innovate beyond the start-up teams. This caused a shift to a balance between discovery and using the successes of others. Additionally, in the second of the three workshops for each of the four programs, participants were encouraged to share what they had learned and applied to their job.

Summary

Royal Dutch Shell/Shell International (Shell) created LEAP in the mid-90s to energize and unleash its leadership talent. Its challenge was to create leaders at every level throughout the organization, and for the program to be successful, it needed the wholehearted participation of everyone at Shell.

The LEAP staff and the Committee of Managing Directors

(CMD) believe that 10 to 20 percent of employees must complete a LEAP process before organizational change begins in earnest.

The LEAP team's "contracting process" became a critical focus of the team's work. When a business shows interest in sending a candidate or team to a program, a LEAP staff member meets with the leader of that business to clarify the role that he or she must play during the LEAP process. Staff members must show executives the value of LEAP if they want the executives to support their employees during and after the training.

LEAP's learning processes are integrated with Shell's ongoing business. The use of team projects rather than traditional classroom sessions makes the process more interesting and allows individual tailoring of LEAP offerings to specific business needs.

The LEAP process has created a new language of leadership and individual empowerment at all levels throughout the organization.

Notes

1. Boston: Harvard Business School Press, 1997.
2. "Redrawing Boundaries," *Executive Excellence* 16 (Feb. 1999), pp. 3–4.
3. APQC Shell International Site Visit Summary, July 8, 1998, p. 5.
4. "Shell International: Site Visit Summary," Leadership Development Consortium Benchmarking Study, APQC, July 8, 1998, p. 6.

7

The World Bank

Its Most Important Investment

F or 50 years, the World Bank (the Bank) has been committed to helping its borrowers reduce poverty and improve living standards through sustainable growth and investment in people. To promote sustainable development, the Bank has supported more than 6,000 development projects in more than 140 countries with more than $300 billion in financing. With growing poverty and public concern of "economic imperialism," the future is more challenging than the past for the Bank. If change generates the need for leadership development, the Bank is in a world of need, because the global environment in which it operates is changing at warp speed.

By sheer numbers, poverty in the world remains the rule rather than the exception. And this discouraging situation continues today, 40 years after the Bank set up its International Development Association (IDA) to work on the problem. Jessica Einhorn, a former managing director at the Bank, has commented, " 'If that's the most celebrated initiative to usher in the new millennium, we'd better have some humility about the complexity and challenge of this enterprise.' "[1]

The task is overwhelming. Approximately half of the

world's six billion people are living on less than $2 a day, and nearly half of them on less than $1 a day. Furthermore, that world population of six billion is expected to become eight billion soon, with half or more still living in poverty.[2]

The process of development is being revolutionized by two major trends, the decline in official development aid, and the dramatic increase in the flow of private capital. As the appetite of the wealthy nations for handing out foreign aid continues to wane, corporate investment is bringing about major transformations in parts of the developing world.

Foreign aid by private, corporate entities has nearly quadrupled since 1990, reaching approximately $170 billion in the late 1990s. With such an explosion of private investment transforming countries, particularly in East Asia and Latin America, the Bank is under pressure to identify, learn, and implement techniques of responding to the demands of this radically transformed, global economic situation. The Bank has to encourage multilateral institutions to continue playing their role of effectively promoting development and eradicating poverty. But, at the same time, the Bank cannot abandon its benevolent conscience and sworn responsibility for the unexploitive development of world populations in need.

Within the Bank itself, intense discussion is under way about its most appropriate long-term, business strategy. There is deep debate about the scope of Bank efforts to fight poverty and the range of services it can best provide. The Bank's internal debaters know, for example, that private development capital is extremely uneven, with more than 80 percent of it going to 10 or 12 of the most economically promising countries. And, even in those countries receiving a high level of private capital, the Bank foots the bill to develop essential assistance of health and education systems and social safety nets.

The need for a global development agency has never been more apparent. Even with world capital flow mushrooming, conflict and poverty continue to increase. More riches are flowing into formerly poor countries, yet the benefits do not seem to be filtering down to everyone. There needs to be an entity that provides leadership to developing countries on how to develop wisely. Someone must show them how to integrate into the new global economy, transfer cross-regional experience, and manage global and regional initiatives to fight poverty and environmental degradation.

The World Bank Group is well placed to play this important role of catalyst. However, such a role is out of step with the approaches and procedures it has established in its first half-century of service. To meet the need that confronts it, the Bank knows it must change. It cannot simply change mission statements and written commitments. It must create a new kind of organizational culture that is open to continual change. It must accept that its future influence and accomplishment will be gained through partnership and leverage instead of acting alone with a shrinking portion of world capital.

Who Makes Up the Group?

The official name of the World Bank is the International Bank for Reconstruction and Development (IBRD). Founded at the end of World War II, IBRD provides loans to developing countries that have relatively high per-capita income and to those undergoing economic transition. The loans are used for development projects, such as building highways, schools, and hospitals, and for programs to help governments change the way they manage their economies. The World Bank Group is made up of IBRD and the following three entities:

1. *The International Finance Corporation (IFC)*—created in 1956 to help strengthen the private sector by providing long-term loans, equity investments, guarantees, "standby financing," risk management, and "quasi-equity instruments," such as subordinated loans, preferred stock, and income notes

2. *The International Development Association (IDA)*—established in 1960. It provides cheaper loans to developing countries that cannot afford to borrow from the IBRD. IDA "credits" go mainly to countries with annual per-capita incomes of $925 or less. About 70 countries fall into this category. IDA helps them

to finance the same kind of development projects that IBRD finances for richer countries.

3. *The Multilateral Investment Guarantee Agency (MIGA)*— the most recently created entity of the Bank. MIGA was created in 1988 to help developing countries attract foreign investment by providing investment guarantees against "noncommercial risk," such as expropriation and war.

IBRD, IFC, IDA, and MIGA make up the World Bank Group, or, simply, the World Bank. They work in conjunction with the International Monetary Fund (IMF).

Shifting Focus in a Changing World

The Bank and the IMF were created as World War II ended and have since been joined by regional development banks, such as the Inter-American Development Bank, the African Development Bank, the Asian Development Bank, and, most recently, the European Bank for Reconstruction and Development (EBRD), formed for the post-socialist economies of Central Europe and the former Soviet Union. All of these international financial institutions (IFIs), as well as UN organizations, such as the United Nations Development Program (UNDP), are international development institutions that are increasingly turning to knowledge-based development strategies.[3]

In the years after World War II, when development economics was first being developed as a separate discipline, the emphasis was on the accumulation of capital goods or hardware. The assumption was that using development loans to build modern factories in shattered countries was the surest way to launch those countries on the path to success. Unfortunately, reality was not so simple. Decades of painful experience showed that the emphasis needed to shift from hardware to software. Countries did not just need producing factories. They needed the knowledge to figure out what to produce and how to get it competitively to market. Germany and Japan rebuilt themselves into world economic powers, not by being given factories, but by adopting sound institutional habits and knowledge.

Technological and institutional learning is key to economic growth. That is why the Bank, international development institutions, and regional development banks are trying to retool their thinking. They have to stop financing projects that result in structures and start financing projects that result in human expertise. If this can be done, the structures will take care of themselves.

The recent addition of knowledge management efforts at the Bank have been exemplary in the modeling of this essential transition. The Bank is working hard to make itself a knowledge bank that can address knowledge-based development. This added capability complements the Bank's traditional role of providing infrastructure financing to developing countries—a role that is increasingly being assumed by the private financial sector.

Handwriting on the Wall

At its annual meeting in 1994, as the Bank celebrated its 50th anniversary, there was concern that the world had changed so much in those 50 years that the Bank needed a change, too. External customers and nongovernment groups had started to criticize the efforts of the Bank. Member governments were questioning why they should contribute money to the Bank. Increasing private-development capital seemed to be reducing the need for official aid.

Had it chosen to bury its head in the sand and ignore the handwriting on the wall, the Bank could have held its course for another 15 years. To its credit, the Bank was led by persons of character, who were unwilling to hold out for personal retirement while their organization died a slow death of irrelevance.

At the same time, internal barriers were becoming more evident within the Bank. The workforce was among the most qualified in the world. Yet employees entering the organization with very specific skills were being forced to become generalists. Their specialized skills were being organizationally and systematically dulled. The Bank's employees were also losing touch with their customers, becoming obsessed with the processes rather than with the results of their efforts.

Project 66 (Nice Try, but No Cigar)

The Bank put together a pilot leadership program called "Project 66," in which the Bank went through a very rigorous selection process and ended up choosing 66 people for an intense, high-cost, in-house leadership program. Unfortunately, this selective approach did not mesh with the organization's team-oriented culture. The Bank had always been an open environment, and the exclusivity of this program was simply not appropriate.

As the Bank began to recreate itself, the realization became clear that a much broader executive education program was needed to reach all managers and top officers within the organization. This goal and the lessons learned in Project 66 became the basis for the current Executive Development Program (EDP). The Bank's leadership wanted to create a program that:

+ Shows the Bank's willingness to learn from other organizations
+ Underscores the fundamental importance of client focus, results, and partnership
+ Illustrates the powerful impetus to change in large organizations, particularly those in the public sector
+ Demonstrates the importance of leadership and accountability as a force for change
+ Links the ability to build a learning organization to gain a competitive edge

In contrast to Project 66, EDP is a massive and inclusive program designed to make an investment in all employees who are in leadership positions. EDP puts managers of all levels in touch with the latest thinking on leadership, management, and organizational change, and in touch with one another. The programs are action-oriented and strongly tied to organizational goals. Managing directors sometimes sit in on sessions to discuss solutions to business problems. The end goal is to create a new language, a new culture, and a new team spirit among leaders—a spirit that transcends the managerial level and helps promote organizational change.

Enter a "Leadership Leader"

With the need for change apparent, investment banker James Wolfensohn joined the Bank as president in 1995. Acknowledging both the internal and external challenges, Wolfensohn also focused on a number of great opportunities at the Bank. The fall of the Berlin Wall meant that many new clients and potential funders could join, and the information revolution meant that knowledge could be transferred at a much more rapid pace, both with the member countries and the clients of the Bank. Lastly, while Wolfensohn realized the need to hone the specialized skills of the staff, he also knew that he still had a workforce that was extremely committed to the Bank's mission.

Wolfensohn came to the Bank with an impressive résumé, having been an officer in the Royal Australian Air Force, an Olympic fencer, a Harvard M.B.A., and a senior banker at Salomon Brothers and Schoders. However, his appointment (and his reappointment in 1999 for another five-year term) was no courtesy gesture by an old-boy network. James Wolfensohn quite clearly took the job to try and make a change in the world, and he has certainly made a change in the Bank.[4]

Wolfensohn has had an uneven path at the Bank that had many predicting he would not last through his initial appointment. He disputed historic Bank procedure, alienated many influential people, and locked horns on several occasions with the IMF and the U.S. Treasury.[5] Says James Smalhout, "Complex and mercurial, Jim Wolfensohn exudes a passion for the job. He considers his half-decade at the International Bank for Reconstruction and Development, more simply known as the Bank, to be the most important task that he has tackled."[6]

Feeling strongly that change needed to start at the top, Wolfensohn disbanded the old leadership development program and created the EDP. This program was based on the Advanced Management Degree program at Harvard. It is a comprehensive, five-week, residential program designed and delivered by five partnering graduate schools: Harvard Business School, INSEAD (France), Stanford Business School, John F. Kennedy School of Government, and IESE (Spain). EDP is presented in three modules. All Bank managers attend the program to hone and develop the leadership skills, characteristics, and qualities needed to create a more effective Bank.

As the Bank created the EDP, it first looked to Harvard to develop the entire program, simply because it felt that Harvard was the premier business school. But, since the contract for the EDP would well exceed $100,000, Bank policy required that global providers be used to create the programs. After working with many different universities, the Bank settled on the current five to get a good mix of vendors according to the changing needs of the Bank's program. The five specific vendors were chosen because they fit the specific needs of the Bank; the Bank wanted a mix of theory, case studies, and projects for their leaders to work with, and this group of vendors provided the right mix.

The Bank's mission statement also received the Wolfensohn interpretation and revision, and it came to emphasize the ultimate goal of poverty-reduction as much as it did knowledge and financial resources. Whereas the old mission statement had emphasized the importance of the Bank's role in providing financial assistance to eliminate poverty, the new mission statement wants it "to be a respected leader and partner in the business of catalyzing knowledge and financial resources in the fight against poverty."

Though Wolfensohn's tenure has been controversial, most people give high marks to the leadership development program he fostered, particularly where he has pointed the way to the institution becoming the knowledge bank as opposed to just the financial institution. And, he has definitely set the tone for the Bank's commitment to be a learning organization.

Five guiding principles were identified by which the Bank would carry out its mission and begin the change process. The Bank would be more responsive to clients, accountable for changing results, efficient and cost-effective, able and willing to work in partnership, and committed to professional and managerial excellence.

In the mid-1990s, to solidify the move toward change, Wolfensohn created a strategic compact between the Bank's management and its board. In this compact, he laid out the change process that the Bank would follow for the next three to five years. He asked that the 180-member board approve this compact and the additional funds he would need to create this change. The compact, which called for a new way of doing business, was unanimously approved. The Bank would focus much more on results, be more responsive and interactive with its clients, and reshape the role played by the board.

The compact also asked for the Bank to focus on increasing its institutional capabilities in three areas: strategic and transparent budget management, flexible and fair human resources policies, and integrated and responsive information systems. The *budget management initiative* began with a forum on strategic priorities and emphasized that all resource allocation decisions would henceforth be made on complete, accurate, and transparent information. The *human resources initiative* committed to employment policies, managerial selection, and professional development procedures that were fair, consistent, and based on skill, innovation, problem-solving, and getting results. The *information system initiative* determined to supply managers with integrated and responsive information for making decisions.

The positive results from Wolfensohn's changes are already evident in the organization. Record performance has been achieved in a number of areas, and feedback from clients has been excellent. Along with the good news, however, challenges do remain. One of the greatest of these is to maintain the high standards and levels of performance.

The Bank continues to focus heavily on building talent within the organization and creating leaders to carry out its mission. Out of this change, it made a large investment in recreating executive education efforts. The result has been the creation of the EDP, which all of the managers in the Bank will attend by the end of the strategic compact. The EDP, which includes five weeks of classroom training and a special project, was created to address the specific needs that leaders would need to make the Bank a relevant world leader.

The Cost

The Bank realized that to foster such a change and to recreate a new language for leaders, the price would be high. The initial investment for creating the program was approximately $20 million. The cost for each manager to attend the EDP is around $22,000, which includes all travel, lodging, and professor fees, for all three modules and the Grass Roots Immersion Program (GRIP). This fee is not charged back to the business groups but is funded centrally through the $12 million Executive Education budget. Usually about 10 percent of the class comes from outside the Bank, and they pay the expenses themselves.

This is a larger budget than any observed among the best-practice partners that participated in the global best-practices study sponsored by APQC and ASTD (1998).[7] Jim Wolfensohn, coming from investment banking, obviously believed in spending big money in order to get a big return. The Bank wanted absolutely the best program imaginable—the costs of which can be difficult to justify at the beginning, but never at the end.

Identifying the Leadership Pool

A formal set of managerial competencies was defined in 1994 with the help of an external consultant. These competencies were fairly generic skills, qualities, and characteristics. However, they were not specific to leaders or to the type of leader that the Bank seeks to create.

Consequently, it began to evaluate its leadership skills. It became evident that the majority of the leaders within the organization had strong technical skills but were too focused on technical excellence. Their managers were lacking other competencies that the Bank outlined as important for the change process—things like people orientation and organizational capability.

Figure 7.1   A New Way of Doing Business

New country compact
–Driven by client needs
–In consultation with partners
–Sets:
  –Results indicators
  –WSB services
  –Country budget

New role for board
–Focuses on broad policy and country strategy
–Reviews results
–Delegates most project approvals

Better results
Assessed by:
  –Client feedback
  –Independent evaluation
  –Board updates

Strong country manager
–Dedicated to client
–Holds budget strings
–Can make decisions
–Accountable for country results

Delivering services through teams
–Contracted by country manager
–From groups with critical mass
–Subject to few but focused checks

To document this situation, Alberto Bazzan, manager of Leadership and Development, interviewed managing directors and vice presidents to determine their criteria for leaders within the Bank. These leaders made it clear that they wanted technically competent, closure-oriented managers who were willing to make tough decisions. This description reflects the old style of leadership—a description that must change as the Bank changes. The Bank needs to lose its "technical arrogance" and shift to a new type of leader, one open to new ideas and willing to develop his or her strategic-leadership, people-management, and client-orientation skills.

The next step in the leadership development journey is to define leadership competencies. EDP graduates often suggest this as a result of attending the program. Such a list of competencies should be generated with input from the managing directors and vice presidents. They should not, however, be used as a narrow rule of thumb but should be included in a list demonstrating the diverse skills necessary for effective leaders across the World Bank Group.

Leadership Pools

Everyone at the manager level and above is eligible for the Bank's EDP. This includes the 6 managing directors, 27 vice presidents, 110 directors, and approximately 250 managers that make up the management ranks of the Bank. In addition, the board of directors consists of 180 representatives from the member countries, and 24 directors are in residence on a full-time basis. All are eligible for the EDP.

The Bank has about 200 quasi-managers who have no one reporting to them. Presently, this group is not eligible for the EDP, but that issue is being reconsidered. In many cases, the quasi-managers are considered to have the highest potential for future leadership positions and, therefore, need the training.

Almost all managers now express interest in attending the EDP as soon as they can be nominated by their managers. Because everyone is expected to go through the EDP, the choice as to who attends is determined more by the makeup of the class than any individual selection criterion.

Lately, when the Bank considers the question of selection, discussion has focused on how managers are chosen. In the past, there had been an "old-boy" system in place for hiring at the Bank, but that has changed dramatically. The Bank is now a competitive place to acquire a position. All manager positions are posted internally and externally, and there is a formal hiring process. This new system works much better, but will need to be honed to ensure that those not hired do not lose face in the process (as most are internal applicants). Only 23 managers did not rise through the Bank system. This makes the EDP process even more important in creating organizational change.

Addressing Diversity Issues

By its nature, the Bank has a diverse work force. Only 40 percent of the management carry U.S. passports. There are more employees from the United States, Great Britain, Italy, and India than any other countries. This is due in large part to the Bank's longstanding history in those countries. Countries such as Germany, Japan, and Russia have less representation, but that is changing, and the Bank continues to diversify its leadership and use cultural differences to its advantage.

The Bank chose an academic-based, executive education program because of the culture within which it works. There are many Ph.D.s within the organization, who required that highly respected professors and universities conduct the programs. Additionally, the academic setting gets managers away from their daily routines and provides the freedom to think, create, and discuss new concepts and ideas.

Organizing to Develop Leadership

The Bank is a "natural gymnasium" for developing leaders. It employs some of the greatest minds in the world, who work independently to structure creative loans that address the needs of impoverished nations.

The Bank wants to give managers a chance to step away from day-to-day operations to discuss the latest leadership ideas and trends. Relying heavily on universities, the Bank staff for the EDP remains small, consisting of just one to two full-time staff members. The manager of this program reports directly to the vice president of human resources development.

The EDP equips executives to meet future leadership challenges head on. In lectures, case discussions, study groups, and team workshops, participants develop and apply new approaches to management. They have opportunities to broaden their perspectives and enhance their managerial and leadership skills.

The first two-week academic module is held at the Harvard Business School, with the second and third modules held at the Lansdowne Conference Center in Virginia, nearer to Bank staff. Between modules, participants return to the workplace to begin applying what they have learned. Upon returning to the program, participants reassess their business strategies and refine their action plans based on their experiences and interactions with participants and faculty. In fact, all participants must immediately apply their learning to a specific issue or challenge for the Bank and its clients. These group projects, presented at the end of the course to Wolfensohn, are a critical link between learning and results.

The EDP curriculum addresses the following topics:

1. Strategy and Competition:
   + Poverty and Environmental Sustainability
   + The Bank in Context
   + Customers and Customer Focus
   + Crafting Strategy in a Competitive Environment
   + The Role of the General Manager
   + Integrative Exercise on Strategy and Competition
2. Strategic Management of Operations and Services:
   + Analysis of Service Delivery Processes
   + Analysis of Resource Allocation Systems

   ♦ Management of Large-Scale Projects
   ♦ Business Process Reengineering
3. Relating Performance Measures and Incentive Systems to
   Strategy:
   ♦ Team Effectiveness
   ♦ Managing Alliances and Partnerships
   ♦ Integrative Exercise on Organizational Effectiveness
     and Design
4. Leadership, Culture, and the Learning Organization:
   ♦ Leadership as a Force for Change
   ♦ Crafting Effective Corporate Culture
   ♦ Managing and Capitalizing on Diversity
   ♦ Behavioral Change versus Structural Change
   ♦ Integrative Exercise on Sustaining Change

Most case studies and lecture materials are based on actual situations of companies and public-sector organizations. They include issues and challenges being confronted by the World Bank Group. In order to broaden participant perspectives, materials highlighting similar situations facing organizations in dissimilar industries are studied as well.

Problems in Knowledge-Based Development

It was originally assumed that an international development institution like the Bank would be in a perfect position to discover the best and worst ways to go about development either regionally or globally. It was further assumed that what the Bank learned could be disseminated to other eager learners. In practice, however, several significant holes appeared in these neat assumptions:

   ♦ The *educational approach* that prefers to think of knowledge being passed from teacher to passive student is inapplicable in the development world. Development assistance must be based on learners taking an active role in what they are learning.

♦ The assumption that *external incentives* move people and nations is not dependable. Conditions of loans might bring about some surface changes, but they are unlikely to change underlying attitudes. Effective development promotes change in underlying institutions.

♦ *Knowledge is fluid.* It is not tangible like money or material aid. It comes in different types, which are perceived and received differently by persons in different knowledge institutions.

♦ *Two very different models* exist for an international, knowledge-based, development institution. A development institution could function as a development church, espousing the one best way, or it could function more as an open-learning institution in which different theories are allowed to publicly contend and collide, and in which experimentation is encouraged to see what is locally most appropriate.

Dependence or Independence?

An old Chinese story says that instead of giving people fish, it is better for them to learn how to fish. This is now an internationally recognized aphorism extolling the virtues of self-reliance and autonomy. Perhaps it is best to first make the point in the modern context of a business enterprise. A company has a specific problem to solve, and it does not have the required knowledge. It could take the initiative and expend the time and resources of people in the company to learn how to solve the problem. But that is a time-consuming process with an uncertain outcome sometime in the future. Perhaps it is best, in view of the time pressures and relatively low costs, to hire outside experts to solve the problem quickly. The next time the problem arises, the same time pressures will lead them to opt for the same quick fix. The company will develop a dependency relation, and the internal capability to learn will not develop.[8]

The same generic dynamics of dependency can develop between bilateral or multilateral development agencies (including the Bank) and developing countries. The dynamics can be even more tempting in this case, as the outside development expertise is offered as a public good at below cost or for free, and the problems of a country's underdevelopment are always immediate and pressing. Development institutions, like consulting companies, are often tempted to appear to have the answers. Funding and management pressures in development agencies push for the quick and easily monitored solution of giving out fish (i.e., giving out the answers to the clients' problems), as opposed to the time-consuming, difficult, and hard-to-monitor process of helping the clients learn how to fish for themselves (i.e., learn to find the answers themselves).

Another version of this approach might be called the "jug-and-mug" style of training. This name comes from the perception of training as pouring knowledge or answers from the big jug into the little mugs—from the large container of the trainers into the small mugs of the trainees. Like an empty stomach that needs to be given fish, there is a target population that needs to have its human resources developed by training programs. Unfortunately, little thought is given by the big jugs to any self-directed initiative on the part of the little mugs. Education is seen essentially as knowledge transfer from those who know to those who do not.

Even when policy-makers do learn and apply important lessons through well-designed, active-learning programs, this might be criticized as a waste of time and money. International experts may think the policy-makers could have quickly learned the same lessons just by reading the experts' studies. Local ownership of policies comes from local discovery and reappropriation of the policies, not from being tutored by the proper experts. "As Paul Samuelson says, the best way to get a student to learn and appropriate a theorem is to provide the result in a half-proven form, so the student will then have to work out the proof by him- or herself."[9]

Changing the Bank's Culture

In providing his analysis of the Bank's program, Ellerman[10] identifies characteristics of the church-like organization and contrasts them to the open learning organization in Table 7.1.

This type of leadership in "learning how to learn" has always been the mission of the Bank. Yet, its management could see its internal culture needed a return to its original fervor for global economic development. Wolfensohn began emphasizing that, in order to restore the Bank as an international leader of economic development, it would have to break the bureaucratic

Table 7.1   Church Model vs. Learning Organizational Model

Theme	Church-like Organization	Open Learning Organization
Educational philosophy	Truths are promulgated to passive recipients. Giving out fish.	Induce active learners to reinvent and reappropriate knowledge. Teaching how to fish.
Motivation for change	External or extrinsic motivation for short-term behavior change (Taylor).	Internal or intrinsic motivation for long-term sustainable change (Deming).
Scope of knowledge	Focuses on general or universal knowledge or best-practice recipes.	Recognizes need to reinvent local adaptations of best practices.
Explicitness of knowledge	Explicit or codified knowledge (tip of the iceberg) is promulgated in vertical or top-down fashion.	Recognizes rest of iceberg is tacit or implicit knowledge to be transferred by horizontal methods.
Knowledge management philosophy	The one best way is presented as official branded knowledge.	Competition of different views in free market of ideas is coupled with experiments seen as best ways to continuously advance knowledge.

Source: David P. Ellerman, "Global Institutions: Transforming International Development Agencies into Learning Organizations." *Academy of Management Executive* 13 (Feb. 1999), pp. 25–35.

gridlock that had evolved within the Bank over the years. To do this, he pointed to the need to improve client relationships, make a quantum leap in bank managers' financial analysis skills, and develop a culture committed anew to performance and results.

Changing the Bank culture was understood as a major undertaking. Executive education was seen as critical because Bank staff, who had participated in executive education programs, felt that high-level educational experience was most important in making a difference in the organization. Of significance also, there was consensus on the importance of giving managers opportunities to interact with diverse groups of peers from outside their normal base of contacts.

In order to keep a consistent corporate focus, the leadership development process is handled at a corporate level. The EDP was created and is funded by the Bank, not charged out to the businesses. This decision was made to ensure that all managers in the Bank would attend the EDP—without concern for individual budgets. Furthermore, most of the Bank staff is located in Washington, D.C., which makes it easier to handle the task at corporate headquarters.

Leaders vs. Managers

The Bank makes a clear distinction between managers and leaders. Managers are seen as the people who implement a process through predetermined procedures and protocols. Leaders are those who move others forward and inspire others to create better results.

To address this distinction, the third module of the EDP is entitled "Leadership, Culture, and the Learning Organization." The concept is still a bit fuzzy to participants, as they question whether their role within the organization is that of a manager or leader. Current practice is much closer to that of managers, and the EDP process aims to define leadership and move the participants toward leadership within the Bank.

Linking EDP to Business Strategy

The EDP is analytical in nature. Managers discuss current thoughts and trends with other managers and professors. They work through case studies and individual projects. The EDP modules were developed independently of the Bank. Nevertheless, it is confident that because the modules were developed by the best schools in the world, the information will be relevant to the Bank.

The Bank takes care to ensure that programs are aligned with one another, especially since they were created at different times and are taught by different faculty members at different universities. A formal review is done to ensure that the programs are integrated with one another.

Achieving Buy-In

The Bank is also careful to balance its desire to have all managers attend the EDP without appearing too forceful in its approach. The Bank has not had to force anyone to attend, perhaps because the creation of the program in conjunction with the top business schools gave it immediate credibility. In addition, by communicating the expectation that all Bank managers attend the program and explaining why it wants managers to attend, the Bank's invitation has been well accepted. The presence of top managers and a few board members at the program conveys the message of commitment. In fact, a few of the resident board members have completed the EDP themselves. The goal is to have all of them attend.

Even though EDP is off to a good start, the Bank continually tries to create the right conditions for participation. Now that many people have gone through the course and the word is out about the quality of the program, a different problem is beginning to occur—everyone wants to attend. Attendance is now considered a perk of the job.

Lastly, the GRIP has been a tremendous program for solidifying manager support of the EDP. In this program, which is the final module of the EDP, managers are sent to a Third World country to gain first-hand experience of living in a poor community. They return so excited about their experience that their excitement rubs off on team members and others within the Bank. From this experience, they are able to share relevant information with those inside the Bank who are working with the country they visited. This provides invaluable insight, and the entire process frequently results in a stronger relationship for the Bank in that country.

Grass Roots Immersion Program (GRIP)

The final module, which has initially been optional, does not take place in a classroom. It is a week-long immersion of the Bank manager in a poor community to provide a firsthand experience of how others are helped by the Bank. The idea is to increase the participant's appreciation for the social richness of the community and to help him or her realize the daily challenges faced by these impoverished individuals. The Bank managers enter these villages as ordinary people, not as technical experts, to get a broad perspective on poverty.

The purpose of the "Poverty Module" is to encourage the application of the analytical and strategic skills (gained during the academic weeks of the program) to the Bank's mission of poverty reduction. The intense classroom sessions provided by the intellectual exposure of the first three modules sharpen awareness of global competition and emphasize the importance of being client-focused. The Poverty Module gets participants closer to the Bank's real "clients," and it forms an appreciation of the challenge of poverty reduction and of the importance of partnership in that venture. Understandably, Wolfensohn is particularly keen about the GRIP component of the EDP.

The GRIP module has three components. First, there is a role-playing simulation, which provides a safe environment in which participants learn more about listening to their Bank "clients." Second is the opportunity to live and learn in a poor community and to experience life from the perspective of the poor villager or slum dweller. And third, some time after returning to their desks, participants review their experience and search to integrate what they have learned into their work. The objective is "to help us reexamine how we work and to explore other methods of achieving our mission of poverty reduction." The exposure is intended "to provoke in us some doubts about the efficacy of our current approaches . . . to produce in us some respect for the capacity and resourcefulness of poor communities."[11]

Much of the discussion during EDP focuses on the huge challenge of poverty reduction. GRIP is dedicated to providing the Bank's managers with a firsthand experience of living in a poor community, whether rural village or urban neighborhood. The week-long immersion is all about participant observation. The EDP participants join in and share the day-to-day activities of their hosts. They are challenged to ask themselves how they can put all their new managerial knowledge to the service of the poor and to the challenge of reducing poverty.

Another objective of the program is to increase the visitor's appreciation for the social richness of these communities, and they enter the villages as regular people, not as technical experts. During the week, they are not expected to develop a project, provide any service to the host community, do any work in their area of specialty, or to solve problems. The aim is to free the managers of their expertise and give them a broader, more comprehensive perspective of poverty itself.

One participant from operations reported that being free of a "Bank agenda"—not having to push any one line or look only at education, transportation, or agriculture—allowed him to "hear" much more than he had in his 20 years of Bank work.

President Wolfensohn places a great deal of emphasis on executive education, and enthusiastically supports GRIP. In his view, this opportunity "to get close to the ultimate beneficiaries of our work and to further appreciate their communities is of vital importance to ensuring the relevance of the Bank's work."

Managing Those Outside the Leadership Pool

For the quasi-managers (project managers who do not supervise people) and those below that level, the Bank has another segment of management training offerings. Over 1,200 staff members have benefited from these offerings during the past ten years. These courses are divided into three modules that address issues such as group dynamics, interpersonal skills, client interaction, systematic problem-solving, project management, and negotiation skills. Beyond this, the Bank looks to create a New Managers Program to bridge the gap between these offerings and the EDP.

Engaging Future Leaders

Every six months an open dialogue is held among the vice presidents and the managing directors. In this meeting, the group engages in a discussion about whether or not the Bank has the right type of leaders. Do we need more leadership? Less leadership? More management? These questions begin a discussion that focuses on the specific needs of the organization. This has worked well, and the intent is to delve further into the organization to include managers and directors in the conversation as well.

In addition to this open dialogue, the Bank has the benefit of all the research and thought generated by the universities that design and develop the EDP programs. The professors continually update their courses and case studies.

Program Content

Although a major component of the program is theoretical, Harvard's inspiration in the creation of the program dictates that frequent case studies facilitate the learning experience. Case studies provide excellent examples from within the same industry, as well as those from industries that the managers might not work with on a regular basis. The professors bring a wealth of knowledge to the program, exposing the students to issues of many different cultures and entities.

In addition to classroom discussions and case studies,

everyone who participates in EDP is given an assignment on a task team. These tasks are based on real issues at the Bank, such as developing incentives for promoting knowledge management. Once the team determines its project, it must find an executive sponsor. The sponsors are vice presidents or other top officers who assist the team in its efforts and in its final presentation to the managing directors. Of the results presented to date, approximately 40 to 50 percent have been acted upon, and the remaining ones have not been used. If budgets are necessary, they are created by the team and funded by the executive education budget.

EDP saves the most powerful experience for last. The GRIP program immersion is an incredible experience. Most of the managers come from relatively affluent backgrounds, and this is their only firsthand experience with poverty.

While there is a mix of classroom discussion, case studies, team projects, and an immersion activity, the Bank feels that the missing piece is in the implementation. Therefore, the Bank is looking for ways to ensure that each participant applies the content at work.

The Bank is also spending about $1 million this year to add the element of coaching to the process. Two hundred and eighty projects will take place, with 15 internal experts and 4 consultants helping these leaders work better in teams. Lastly, the Bank is investing in researching methods or developing leaders into teachers, because these are great ways to use what they have learned.

Learning Technologies

The EDP is a residential program that takes place on the university campus of the school that delivers the module. For a time, the Bank considered having the professors come to Washington, D.C., but participants found that to give the program their full attention, they needed to be away from their offices. Due to this focus, the use of technology has been minimal. A distance-learning infrastructure that the Bank has in place is not employed for the EDP.

The only technology used so far has been chat rooms to facilitate discussion by participants and their project teams during the time between the modules. In the future, the Bank expects to use technology as an enabler for this program. In fact, it is considering the use of technology to create a quarterly learning forum, during which EDP graduates and others will share learnings and applications of their team projects.

The Role of Current Leaders

While Bank leaders are going through the EDP, their role is that of participant. Even a few of the resident directors have gone through the EDP, and the rest are now invited to attend. Senior leaders do become more involved in the EDP while coaching teams on various projects. Leaders at the vice-president level and above are approached by the project teams to be their executive champions or coaches. These leaders are chosen for their organizational knowledge, and they work with the teams as they create solutions and recommendations.

Succession Planning

The Bank has a fairly simple succession-planning process. Every six months, the vice presidents evaluate those reporting to them. This evaluation is an open process and aids promotions and salary increases. At the same time, it creates an accurate picture of the talent within the Bank's organizations.

Currently, the EDP does not play a role in the succession process, except that all of the current leaders are expected to go through it. The strategic compact, however, makes the issue of succession planning very important. The Bank recently created a policy that anyone over age 50, with at least 18 years of experience with the Bank, can retire immediately with a full pension. If everyone eligible decided to retire, the Bank would have to replace half of those people currently occupying the executive ranks.

This is cause for concern, especially since the vice presidents noticed a lack of young talent during their last meeting. The Bank will try a bigger push to seek out such talent, which will mean taking a closer look at those in the quasi-manager level. This group has been ignored for quite some time, even though some of the highest potential candidates probably fall in this area. It will be up to the EDP to develop the skills in these individuals that they will need to perform in new leadership roles.

Impact of the Experience

Reflecting on the program experience as a whole, EDP director Tariq Husain noted, "It has been among the most educational experiences of my work life—the partnership with faculty is seamless and the outcomes are impressive, way beyond expectations. It feels like a family engaged in joint work with common goals. Such a partnership is what we are attempting to accomplish within the Bank."

With regard to the program's impact on participants, Husain went on to say, "The content is relevant, the pedagogy is outstanding, and the impact on participants is magical. We felt this on March 14 when Cohort 1 graduated and Jim Wolfensohn visited. The learning experience produced a change in a dramatic way—it transformed a group into a team."[12]

A program participant echoed Husain's reflections, noting, "The program is about poverty. It is about the clients. What we learned is not about what to say, it is about what to do."[13]

Expanding on that view, another participant summarized the impact of EDP by noting, "For me, the World Bank's EDP was the most outstanding executive education I have received, and even far exceeded my initially high expectations. It is a watershed for the institution, an enormously far-sighted and effective investment in cultural change that will expand our capacity to carry out our vital mission."[14]

The overall impact of the experience and the value of the consortium delivery model was summarized by another participant: "I can already see the group cohesion that is building up among us. Working together for long hours has built a strong feeling of shared goals. We are starting to use the same language; we are, in fact, changing our corporate culture within the group as a result of what we learned. . . . Several elements of the program design contribute particularly to this: coming back together several times, with intervals in between, but not too far apart, is proving to have a great impact; having a wide range of faculty, brought together from the different training institutions gives a richness that would not be available with only one institution."[15]

Wolfensohn also believes the lessons of EDP are taking root: "From the outset, I think everyone agreed that the enhanced education of the Bank Group's staff was fundamental to change the way we do business in today's challenging development environment. What we have witnessed, in less than two years, is a complete overhaul in our approach to seeking and achieving that education; one that is evolving with each intake to meet our institution's needs; and one that has sent a veritable breath of fresh dynamism and enthusiasm throughout the institution. Thanks to the EDP, we are now equipping more and more of our managers with a level of training that will not only improve their client orientation, but will allow them to harness and develop the technical skills of their teams. This, to my mind, is crucial if the Bank is to be the responsive and effective development institution it was created to be. This has been a bold initiative that has paid off, and I know the end results will bring in enormous dividends for the 4.7 billion clients served by our institution."[16]

Measuring Outputs

Since the upper managers of the Bank are all participants in the EDP, they will immediately change the program if they are not happy with it. To ensure that all reaction to the program is captured, the EDP staff collects feedback from all EDP participants.

The EDP aims to make people aware that change is possible and can be managed to introduce humility and to open the mind to asking for help. To ensure that these qualities and other skills learned in the EDP are being applied, a measurement task team within the Bank evaluates participants six to eight months after completion of the EDP. This information, combined with the actual results achieved by the project teams, adds to the participant-reaction data to paint a strong picture of success for the EDP.

In the late-1990s, WESTAT Corporation, a firm that specializes in assessment of education programs, conducted an interim evaluation of the EDP that was based on the experiences of the first two cohorts to participate in the program. WESTAT found that it was very effective overall, and that six to eight months after attending the program, 20 percent to 30 percent of participants were usually changing something. WESTAT's major findings included the following:

♦ *Positive overall assessment.* Most positive results relate to three EDP objectives: willingness to learn, client focus, and the importance of leadership in implementing strategic change and achieving continuous learning.

♦ *Most valuable learnings* included humility and the human side of organizational renewal.

♦ Two positive factors cited as facilitating the transfer of EDP learnings were *simultaneous attendance* by members of the same management team in the same cohort and *networks formed* among EDP alumni across Bank units.

♦ *Focus on results and accountability* was seen as conflicting with partnership concept and with the Bank's new management structure.

♦ There was *concern* that work environment and overall Bank culture would not allow for the application of EDP learnings. Some felt an insufficient number of managers encourage workplace applications. Others expressed skepticism about true cultural change. Some felt participants were not held accountable or rewarded for change.

In addition, the WESTAT group developed a number of recommendations for changes to the program. These include recommendations to

- Restructure the project to focus on real Bank issues
- Modify case mix to increase relevance
- Increase involvement of external participants
- Establish work climate that nurtures application of EDP lessons
- Address gaps in skill and operational application

Tracking Leaders

The Bank maintains a central file of managers who have participated in the EDP and those who still need to attend. This electronic file connected to PeopleSoft, and the information is part of the public record that can be viewed by anyone in the Bank.

In addition to external studies, 360-degree feedback is also used to ensure that learnings are applied back on the job. After a three-year battle to approve the use of 360-degree feedback, this has become an more important tool in crafting the kind of leaders needed at the Bank. With the Bank's inclusive culture, where most meetings are discussions, 360-degree feedback works well to ensure that managers are effectively leading and constantly improving.

Communication

Though there is no internal marketing effort for the EDP, the desire to get into the program is greater than ever. Because of the great expense of the program, it sometimes seems that the popularity of the program is a mixed blessing. However, the quality of the Bank's management is so crucial that the organization remains committed to putting all managers through it. There is a level of accountability on the EDP part of graduates to "get the learnings out." Each participant is expected to communicate his or her learnings and help in the transformation of the organization.

Key Lessons

Successes of the Bank's EDP include:

 ♦ *Making a large investment for change.* The Bank was fortunate to have the ability to make a large investment in the EDP. In the strategic compact, Wolfensohn said that to create real change would take a large investment, and it has. The investment is starting to pay off, and the changes are being felt.

 ♦ *Planning within the organization.* Careful planning pays off as it does for any new venture. Tying the program to the culture of the organization was key for the Bank. It has an inclusive culture, so involving many people from the start and tying the results to career planning was a key to the success of the EDP.

 ♦ *Creating the right attitude toward learning.* The Bank was fortunate to start off with a high concentration of intellectual power. This excitement to learn is a first step to the success of a program like the EDP. Without this willingness from the managers, the EDP would likely fail.

The primary challenge surfaced by the Bank's EDP is:

 ♦ *Moving learning from the individual to the organization.* The intellectual prowess of the leaders has also proven to be a challenge, as the learning has remained on the individual level. The Bank needs to impress upon the leaders the power of shared learning and the need to build organizational capacity.

James Wolfensohn will leave the Bank a very different institution. It will be less bureaucratic. It will have fewer layers of management. It will be more streamlined, more transparent, and more eager to distribute knowledge than to hoard it.

Wolfensohn can take pride in having brought a new mindset to the Bank. In his brief time at the helm, it has become the "Knowledge Bank." His aim is nothing less than what he calls "the end of geography as we at the Bank have known it. 'My goal,' " he told a recent annual meeting, " 'is to make the World

Bank the first port of call when people need knowledge about development.' "[17]

Summary

The World Bank has supported more than 6,000 development projects in 140 countries with $300 billion in financing for 50 years. The challenge is that the old ways are not working anymore.

James Wolfensohn, who joined as president in 1995, set the new learning direction for the Bank. He disbanded the old leadership development program and created the Executive Development Program (EDP). EDP is a program that all managers are scheduled to attend in order to hone and develop their leadership skills, characteristics, and qualities.

The positive results from these changes include record performance in a number of areas and excellent feedback from clients. However, of the many challenges that remain, the greatest is to maintain high standards and levels of performance.

The desire to get into the program is great, but it is expensive, so this popularity is a mixed blessing. However, the quality of the Bank's management is crucial, so the organization remains committed to requiring all managers to go through it.

James Wolfensohn will leave the Bank a very different institution. It will be less bureaucratic. It will have fewer layers of management. It will be more streamlined, more transparent, and more eager to distribute knowledge than to hoard it.

Notes

1. James Smalhout, "High-Wire Act That Changed the Bank," *Euromoney* (Sept. 1999), pp. 178–181.
2. Ibid.
3. David P. Ellerman, "Global Institutions: Tranforming International Development Agencies into Learning Organizations," *Academy of Management Executive* 13 (Feb. 1999), pp. 25–35.

4. David Luff, "On the Ground: In Washington," *Global Finance* (Nov. 1999), p. 6.
5. Ibid.
6. Smalhout, "High-Wire Act That Changed the Bank," p. 178.
7. American Society for Training and Development, "Leadership and Executive Development," Trends, ASTD Benchmarking Forum, April 1998, p. 2.
8. Ellerman, "Global Institutions," p. 25.
9. Ibid., p. 25.
10. Ibid.
11. From the description in an anonymous World Bank document, "Grass Roots Immersion Program," circa 1998.
12. A. A. Vicere, R. M. Fulmer, "Leadership by Design," Harvard Business School Press, Boston, 1998, p. 221.
13. Ibid, p. 222.
14. Ibid.
15. Ibid.
16. Ibid.
17. Smalhout, "High-Wire Act That Changed the Bank."

8

Corporate Universities

A Source of Competitive Advantage— Saturn as Model

The corporate university movement extends far beyond McDonald's "Hamburger University" with which the American public is jokingly familiar. Corporate universities consist of more than renaming and revamping companies' training departments. The corporate university represents business leadership's growing commitment to continuous learning as a source of competitive advantage. (A number of Internet Web sites are available to provide more information about corporate universities. See Appendix B.)

Corporations are realizing that their most important assets are not equipment, technology, or machines, but rather human capital and the know-how that resides in the minds of their employees. Corporate universities are linking employee learning to overall company strategy, and as a result corporate universities are becoming the connective tissue of organizations. At some organizations, corporate-learning programs are even beginning to drive businesses.

For years, wise companies have gladly paid for their employees to attend continuing education classes at nearby colleges and universities. And while that practice continues to have a place in the corporate university movement, it is now even more likely that you will find college-sized, educational organizations existing within corporate domains for the purpose of making the organization into a "learning organization."

As one executive phrased it, "People really are the last true competitive advantage. Everyone knows about fast-to-market, quality, and re-engineering. They no longer provide a competitive advantage, merely entry onto the playing field. Innovation and people are the only edge, and companies that recognize that fact and organize their systems and structures around it will enjoy success—as Saturn has. No one believed world-class, small cars could be built profitably in the U.S.—but Saturn people proved them wrong."[1]

In 1994, Jeanne C. Meister, the publisher of *Corporate University Xchange*, identified 30 companies that share the common goal of seeing "training as a process of life-long learning rather than a place to get trained."[2] Just two years later, she updated the research and found that almost 1,000 firms were involved in the process, and today, she estimates that 1,600 groups call themselves "corporate universities." These firms recognize that prominent players in the twenty-first century will be those who turn a smarter workforce into a dollar-and-cents competitive advantage. They also know that educational investment will not pay back through casual and accidental educational programs at nearby colleges and universities.

In their commitment to smarter workers as a bottom-line advantage to the company, these companies have organized themselves as learning systems. They have integrated aspects of hiring, training, recognition, and advancement into an educational system that is widely publicized and promoted, and in which participation is high. The resulting individual and collective learning have reinforced the original hypothesis and led to even more extensive financial investment and leadership commitment.

Business-leading organizations value their people highly and conceive of corporate education as an investment in human capital that makes their businesses more competitive. In the same way, several of the partners participating in the global best-practices study sponsored by APQC and ASTD (1998)[3] indicated that they actively seek to promote from within, thus capitalizing on the depth of experience that already exists within the organization. For example, at Andersen, the company-wide use of an existing knowledge-management system has impacted the design and delivery of training, because knowledge and expertise are readily available on its Intranet.

A Growing Phenomenon

Although the average operating budgets for corporate universities had grown to $12.4 million by the mid-1990s, 60 percent of the groups reported budgets of $5 million or less. Of course, the budgets of giants like Motorola, GE, and Andersen significantly increased the "average" figure. Perhaps more significantly, organizations with corporate universities reported spending 2.5 percent of their payroll on learning. This figure is almost twice the national average.[4]

When Bob Miles of Emory University[5] analyzed leading corporate universities at Motorola, GE, Andersen, and Apple Computer, he discovered that they shared similar strategic orientations for their corporate universities. Their common focus was on aggressive growth and continuous innovation.

The differences between these trailblazers of industrial-strength, corporate education seemed to be differences of emphasis—some emphasized the career development of their employees, while others emphasized the addressing of key business issues through corporate education. For example, Andersen has a carefully designed career ladder, and specified courses are required at each stage in an employee's career. Its career-tracking system maintains an up-to-date record of the educational progress of each of its employees throughout the world. At the other extreme, GE has organized its famous Crotonville educational facility on the assumption that certain educational "moments of opportunity" carry valuable paybacks for individual leadership and organizational performance.

One writer has ventured a definition of the corporate university as "a function or department that is strategically oriented toward integrating the development of people as individuals with their performance as teams, and ultimately, as an entire organization by linking with suppliers, by conducting wide-ranging research, by facilitating the delivery of content, and by leading the effort to build a superior leadership team."[6]

For our purposes, we will define a corporate university as any entity established by a corporation to deliver a curriculum. That is to say, it provides a series of courses designed to develop a set of skills or competencies in its people—as opposed to stand-alone courses that are unrelated to other offerings. While corporate universities cover everything from statistical techniques, to basic personnel policies, to high-level action learning, we will focus primarily on the use of the corporate university to develop leaders.

Creating Knowledge Capital in the Organization

The corporate university is a powerful tool for the creation and management of knowledge capital within the organization. When asked to indicate the reasons for the creation of the corporate university, 77 percent of the APQC-ASTD screening-survey respondents indicated that either knowledge management or the creation of knowledge was a driver.[7] Business leaders reported that the creation and management of knowledge drove the development of the corporate university, and that their corporate universities are responsible for knowledge management within the organization to a great extent.

No matter how you define "knowledge management," it is clear that the corporate university holds great potential for the creation and effective use of knowledge capital within the organization. Some think of themselves as "learning organizations," constantly increasing and updating knowledge. Others actively use the existing knowledge of internal subject matter experts to design and facilitate courses. The corporate university can also take the pulse of the organization, bringing to the surface employee and business concerns and providing an information feedback-mechanism for the company.

The corporate university is the logical and most effective

tool for grounding new hires in the corporate culture. It is also a natural for the regular reminding and re-energizing needed by other employees. Many of Saturn Motors' salespeople think of their training visits to Spring Hill, Tennessee (Saturn headquarters) as pilgrimages to the "holy land," taken to become more enlightened about the company. Every new Saturn employee begins his or her indoctrination with a full week at "Saturn ground zero" (in Spring Hill) learning skills and company values. The same is true for car builders, retailers, and suppliers. The result is that Saturn's learning organization gets first shot at shaping those who will shape the company.

According to the Meister study, Andersen uses its St. Charles facilities to immerse new consultants in the culture of the firm. Dana University was founded in 1969 to reinforce "the Dana style." Eddie Bauer University teaches its culture in every course it offers to associates in the field. In sum, whether courses are offered at dedicated learning facilities or over the Internet, the corporate university plays a pivotal role in teaching and reinforcing the culture of the company.

Lynn E. Densford has described another vital value of the corporate university.[8] Besides improving business results and spreading the corporate legend, corporate universities help attract and retain top-flight employees. In-house training is one of the biggest carrots in corporate America. *Fortune* magazine's annual listing of the "100 Best Companies to Work for in America" always places a high value on the educational opportunities available through its top companies. According to *Fortune*, "extensive and ongoing training and development" is second only to stock options as a primary means of attracting and keeping talented workers.

"The 100 best are making major investments in employee education at multi-million-dollar facilities and through generous reimbursement programs," *Fortune* states. "On average, the 100 best lavished 43 hours of training on each employee in 1998—almost a full day more than last year. Some companies have begun to advertise these learning labs in their recruitment materials."[9]

Of course, the ability to attract and keep good workers has always been a mark of strength in determining companies' financial standing. Institutional investors naturally gravitate toward companies with stable, skilled workforces.

Several Styles of the Corporate University

As corporate universities have evolved, they have taken a variety of forms. Some are far more "corporate" than they are "university." Others are only warmed-over training departments with college course numbers tacked onto the old courses.

For some companies, the *in-name-only formula* works fine. A training department in sheep's clothing can make everybody feel more up-to-date and innovative, without bringing on the undue disturbance of comfortable corporate traditions. The added attention might even result in some new equipment, improved presentation skills, and more interesting classes. But, unless the studies are generated by and connected to the corporation's goals and objectives, it is unlikely that dramatic contributions to profitability, strategy, innovation, or competitive advantage are going to accrue.

A far more appropriate and excellent model could be called the *"initiative-driven" educational program*. This type of corporate university exists to facilitate the accomplishment of a corporate-wide initiative, business plan, or project. Motorola University successfully drove the quality initiative throughout Motorola. It was even involved in Motorola's strategic planning and entry into various global markets. Emerging functions of corporate universities now include advancements in thinking on globalization, productivity, process improvement, and empowerment.

The *change-management corporate university* concentrates on facilitating major changes and transformations within a company. However, a university with this goal must be prepared to reinvent itself once the change has been accomplished. There will always be new idea worlds to conquer and new changes to be managed, but the change-management university must expect to go through a metamorphosis each time the corporate goals or leaders change. As an example, National Semiconductor University drove a change-leadership program through its company in the mid-1990s and then shifted to a skill-development program.

The *leadership development corporate university* is best exemplified by GE's Management Development Institute at Crotonville, New York (discussed in Chapter 3). This institute, which had historically focused on developing managers and leaders for GE, took on new life when CEO Jack Welch made it his tool for orienting and assimilating new managers. Crotonville has driven programs such as Work-Out and the Change Acceleration Process (CAP) and illustrates the principle that the most successful corporate universities have been those with CEO support and a single, clear focus.

A *business development corporate university* is chartered to help develop opportunities and explore possibilities. If an organization is opening international offices, its corporate university can prepare employees; educate them about the new country; do research, recruiting, and development; and generally support the process. Interestingly, these kinds of activities require quite different skills and capabilities from the normal training department.

The *customer/supplier relationship management corporate university* is similar to the business development approach. It focuses on educating and managing employees, leaders, and suppliers about customer and supplier relationships. This is a practice common among manufacturing companies such as Ford and Motorola.

The *competency-based, career development corporate university* focuses on individual skill development and the process of career development in a company. It may include developing a performance management system or career development activities.

Most corporations require the corporate university to provide evaluative metrics to senior managers or to the board of directors. The metrics required are usually different from those used for the evaluation of other business units. Examples of metrics required include percent of payroll, student days, tuition fees, courses delivered, programs conducted, reduction in turnover for those receiving training, increased productivity (pre- and post-behavior assessment), increased skill in managing savings, instructor payroll cost-savings, increased sales due to train-ing targeted on key selling programs, expectation versus proficiency, expectation versus performance, expectation versus importance, and profits versus performance.

Saturn—A Shiny New Model

Throughout this chapter, frequent references will be made to the exemplary corporate university serving Saturn Motors. Saturn is a wholly-owned subsidiary of General Motors (GM), specializ-ing in small to mid-size vehicles. Seen as an innovator in new car development, pricing, and manufacturing, Saturn is moving from a "first-car" company to a more diversified provider of transportation with the new "L" series mid-size and a sport util-ity vehicles.

Saturn came into existence a decade ago. It was the result of a team of GM people who took as their mission the design and implementation of a plan to build a car company that could produce and sell a compact car to compete with imports. Con-ceived in the early 1980s, Saturn began producing cars at Spring Hill in 1990.

Saturn employs approximately 8,200 people who are orga-nized into three divisions, the largest of which is manufacturing. Many employees came from other GM plants to work at Saturn. Saturn team members had to buy into a unique United Auto Workers (UAW) agreement, in which both management and workers share management responsibility.

As has been well documented over the past ten years, Sa-turn's Spring Hill headquarters has been the subject of numer-ous articles and features, and it receives requests for hundreds of visits each year. Its design, manufacturing, and people processes have won acclaim and awards from all over the world. Saturn's unique training goal, which requires each team member to take 92 hours of training per year, and development of leaders through teamwork and collaboration, made this unique com-pany a force to be reckoned with in the small-car business. Sa-turn credits its success to its people and their strong belief in Saturn's mission, philosophy, and values.

GM, the world's largest company, began a planning process in the early 1980s that led to its first American car nameplate since the 1920s: the Saturn Corporation. It was intended to be experimental and to forge new territory for GM. It was created largely as the outcome of an intense benchmarking effort by "the Original 99"—99 managers and union employees from GM who were brought together as a team to explore the possibility of GM competing in the small-car market.

It was immediately apparent to the Original 99 that this could only happen through a major emphasis on training, really on retraining, that connected with the evolving mission, vision, and strategic goals of the organization. These values are clearly visible at Saturn today. The sense of enthusiasm and excitement at being a part of a new kind of car company is not just a theme of Saturn's advertising. The targeted values can be seen in the organization, from the posters and placards that adorn every wall in the corporate offices, to the smiling faces and hand waves that greet a visitor on a tour of the manufacturing facilities. There is a sense of enthusiasm and excitement at being a part of a new and different kind of car company.

The company's mission is simply stated: Earn the loyalty of Saturn owners and grow our family, by developing and marketing U.S.-manufactured vehicles that are world leaders in quality, cost, and customer enthusiasm, through the integration of people, technology, and business systems.

And They're Doing It!

Skeptics doubted that this new corporation could achieve its goal and manufacture a small car comparable to that of Toyota or Honda. But Saturn quickly began winning awards for quality, customer service, and innovative management practices. In the mid-1990s, the company was ranked first in overall small-car value by *Consumer Reports,* and Saturn overtook Ford's Escort to become the best-selling small car in the United States.

A recent benchmarking study of companies with well-known, and in some cases award-winning "Career Development" programs, revealed that Saturn is at the forefront in terms of the development opportunities and resources available to its people. "Saturn does more training per team member on an annualized basis than any other company around."[10]

Corporate training's traditional role has been a function of the human resource department. The success of corporate universities has demonstrated that the learning experience needs to be kept separate from traditional human resource processes. Many human resource functions operate on credits and annual reviews. In a corporate university, it is important for learning to be the primary focus. The employee should be taking courses to learn and improve his or her job performance, not simply because of a requirement. The relationship with human resources should not override the corporate university's day-to-day operations.

Saturn's corporate training function encompasses four main training areas:

1. Retail training
2. Supplier training
3. "Car Builder" training
4. Saturn Consulting Services

Every new Saturn employee spends a full week in orientation, learning skills and company values, before participating in additional training. Each employee has an Individual Training Plan (ITP) designed to meet that individual's needs for his or her job for the coming year. This ITP may include classes on UAW history, Saturn's culture and values, technical training, team skills, and more.

The training, education, learning, and development of Saturn people has been a cornerstone from its beginning. There never was much selling to do. It is because of Saturn's outstanding attitudes and performance in corporate education that we will refer so often to the company as a positive role model. One manager stated: "Saturn doesn't have a 'university' per se, because training is the blood running through the veins of the corporation. It is so much a part of the fabric of the organization that it cannot be separated out as a free-standing entity."[11]

Most of the learning organizations in the APQC study are

funded by their corporations and operate as cost centers. They usually exist as line items in the corporate budget or are supported through charge-backs to the business units for training services. There are good reasons for either approach. The line-item approach is preferable when business units decide to spend their money on other things. On the other hand, the charge-back system clearly demonstrates that the university's products are considered "worth paying for" by the business units. Because the Saturn Corporation believes so strongly in education as the key to building a happy and proficient workforce, Saturn University maintains its own budget and funds corporate training. There is no system of charge-backs to the business units. For Saturn corporate training, delivery is funded centrally.

Benchmarking the Corporate University

In 1997, APQC developed a consortium benchmarking study to investigate best practices in corporate universities.[12] The purpose of APQC's multiorganization benchmarking study was to identify and examine innovations, best practices, and key trends in the area of corporate learning initiatives and to document the processes involved. The goal was for participants in the study to be able to direct their own training processes more effectively and to identify any performance gaps. Saturn was benchmarked again in 1999 as a leader in developing leaders at all levels.

Twenty-nine businesses participated in the APQC study. They cooperated in the planning, completed surveys, and hosted on-site interviews. Of those 29 organizations, 5 were identified during the consortium as having strong, innovative corporate universities: Andersen, Dana, Digital Equipment, Eddie Bauer, and Saturn.

The APQC project team set its work scope to determine whether the corporate universities were creating value, designing their learning processes, delivering their promised product, and creating organizational structures that would last.

To evaluate the design of each corporate university's learning process, the project team looked for alignment of the curriculum with business needs; application for international audiences; and clear definition of boundaries, degrees, and credits.

Measures of actual delivery of the universities' promised products included whether or not they were using traditional versus nontraditional methods, using technology to reach their audiences, and partnering with their local resource providers.

The APQC project team considered corporate universities to be creating lasting organizational structures if they were systematically developing their university infrastructures and their relationships with their corporations.

The project staff organized its report according to four aspects of the corporate universities' programs: their corporate influence, their structures, their learning processes, and their management of information:

1. *Corporate university's influence on the corporation.* Best-practice corporate learning systems should extend beyond the narrow concept of the corporate university and dovetail smoothly with the mission, values, and culture of the organization. They consciously and constantly involve business units in all aspects of the learning process. A critical component of this involvement must come from above—a strong commitment by senior management to the development and education of the workforce. A core philosophy of learning is a theory of knowledge acquisition that drives course design and delivery, as well as interaction with business units. The core philosophy of learning is usually synonymous with, or closely aligned to, the mission of the corporate university.

2. *Corporate university's structure and organization.* Obviously, the entire corporate structure cannot and does not adjust itself to the ideal scenarios of the corporate university. The university must fit within the corporate chart and still be able to reach its highest potential. The business strategy of the organization not only drives the structure of the leading corporate universities, it is the reason those universities exist. On the other hand, most of the outstanding corporate universities were freed long ago from the restrictive domain of human resources and given the authority, responsibility, and respect to function as separate and productive cost centers.

3. *Corporate university's learning processes.* Outstanding corporate universities follow no universal process map for designing their systems and approaches to their learning interventions. They more often determine their training goals and their related requirements only after identifying and focusing on expected outcomes. In short, they make the teaching technique fit the learning challenge. They rarely make blind rushes toward the latest educational technologies. While they are not uninformed about or opposed to technology, they utilize automated training devices only when these devices uniquely facilitate the training process. Saturn's People Development mission is simply stated: "to provide world-class programs and tools that support development of the skills people need to successfully achieve Saturn's mission and business strategies, and also to support the realization of individual career fulfillment and personal growth."

4. *Corporate university's management of information.* If any truism characterizes the corporate university perfectly, it is "knowledge is power." The corporate university is a powerful tool for the creation and management of knowledge capital within the organization. Benchmarking rises to the top frequently in searches for techniques for managing knowledge and information.

When asked how his organization defines a corporate university, an Andersen representative replied, "We don't." This statement represents the corporate universities' wisdom in ignoring existing corporate university models and creating a one-of-a-kind organization that reflects and reinforces the culture, mission, and values of their companies. Leadership corporate universities define themselves clearly and go as directly to the achievement of their goals as possible.

Support from the Top

One of the most important keys to corporate university success is the strong commitment of senior management. In some of the more successful universities, the education effort has been driven by senior managers who understand the long-term value of shaping an organization by constant communication and education. In others, management has supplied strong support financially. The fact that the financial support has continued even during economic downturns is further proof that these managers recognize that the corporate university is no budget frill.

Saturn corporate university leadership is somewhat at a loss when asked about management level buy-in. They have never been without it. Training, education, learning, and the development of Saturn people were a cornerstone when the company was created. At one point early in Saturn's history, senior management's support of training was put to the test. Word came down from GM that Saturn had to break even by the end of the year "or else." Every person at Saturn was mobilized to find a way to reduce costs and improve the bottom line. Many companies would have cut training until the crunch passed. But Saturn's president declared that Saturn needed people to be in a learning mode more than ever. His expressed philosophy was "the more they know, the quicker the company will become profitable."

What They Teach . . .

The business strategy of the organization almost always determines the structure of that organization's corporate university. The corporation, not the university, establishes organizational hierarchy. This enables the company to perform educational needs analyses and facilitate the implementation of the strategy. The corporate university can then ensure that the workforce has the necessary skills and knowledge to accomplish the identified tasks. It is clear that what drives the continued support of corporate learning is a corporate-culture commitment to the development of people.

The mission of Saturn's People Systems Training and Development (PSTD) is to provide opportunities in partnership with the UAW, for individuals and teams in the Saturn community to learn, grow, and continuously improve. PSTD focuses on devising strategies that support Saturn's corporate values: customer enthusiasm, commitment to excellence, teamwork, trust and respect, and continuous improvement.

At Saturn, when a learning need is identified, a writer is assigned to the team requesting training. The writer then drives the development of that training module and pulls together the necessary resources for a training development team within the business unit that needs the training. The training content is then driven by Subject Matter Experts (SMEs). A task analysis is done, and learning objectives are established. A standard Saturn instructional design includes: developing a delivery strategy, using train-the-trainer competency-based instruction, creating "modularized" training, and creating reference materials.

Saturn's emphasis on the development of its employees is evident everywhere. It is in the corporate training facilities and on the floor of the manufacturing plant. Every Saturn team member has an individual training profile and a personal goal of attending 92 hours of training annually.

To keep track of its employees' training progress, Saturn has a central Education Tracking system (ET), a mainframe computer system offering worldwide access to more than 1,900 users. ET houses all employees' individual training plans and progress toward their annual goals. The system also contains course abstracts, class schedules, and instructor/faculty schedules. The system is accessible to every training-point person on every team throughout Saturn. Even car builders on the plant floor can access the ET system and see the training report of a vice president.

Within Saturn's Manufacturing Business Unit, Work Unit Counselors (WUC) are the first level of leaders. WUCs are elected team leaders of 10 members and are responsible for representing the work unit in the decision-making process. Operations Module Advisors (OMA) represent the first level of partnered leadership (one OMA is union, the other management) and are responsible for a module (10 teams) with a crew of 100 members. OMAs are in charge of the development of self-managed teams and day-to-day production initiatives. Crew Leaders (CL), who are management, and Crew Coordinators (CC), who are union, work side-by-side to run three rotating crews, six days a week, 20 hours each day. CLs are management team members and are responsible for daily production and quality targets. CCs are elected from the union and are held responsible for daily production goals and the fair representation doctrine. Area Module Advisors (AMA) oversee two modules and three crews and are responsible for business-plan achievement, strategic planning, and decision-making processes. Figure 8.1 provides a chart representation of these relationships.

Within the Saturn Learning Organization, three of the main areas have advisory councils that guide curriculum development and course offerings. The only area that does not have an advisory board is Saturn Consulting Services.

How They Develop Their Training

One of the most interesting observations of those who have studied the corporate-university movement is that they must take care not to become too much like regular universities! Unfortunately, some companies are only creating neat logos and sweatshirts for their reengineered training departments and labeling all their training courses as "101s." But the bottom line is that they make no fundamental changes in their approaches to the training and development of their employees.

Anyone who has ever attended a traditional university is aware of the ivory-tower syndrome and the tendency toward territorial protectiveness through entrenched tradition. Colleges have not typically been viewed as the most flexible, progressive, or change-oriented of institutions. This is humorously illustrated by the claim that, in the time of Orville and Wilbur Wright, there were college courses being taught in Aeronautical Engineering, courses that concentrated primarily on explaining why a heavier-than-air machine could never fly. The innovation of flight had to come from two bicycle mechanics who had not taken such courses.

While colleges and universities continue their struggles to break the tradition-kills-innovation reputation, corporate universities know that their activities must continually prove themselves in view of their companies' bottom-line objectives. Any organization's establishment of a corporate university must be

Figure 8.1 Organizational Chart from APQC Site Summary

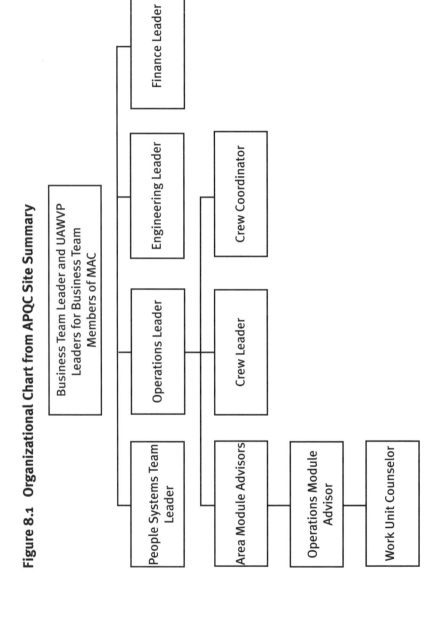

monitored, flexible, and focused on the strategic imperatives of the sponsoring organization. To add real value, a corporate university must become a generator of learning and innovation, but never a stodgy, academic repository of dead information to be parroted by the students.

There appears to be no standard approach or process for designing learning interventions. Corporate universities have to maintain the flexibility to adapt to the changing demands of their business environments. Every university has its own methodology. The design process, whether it be for discrete courses or entire learning programs, is thought of by many as the scientific part of the learning process within the corporate university. From needs analysis, to course design and development, to the eventual delivery, each corporate university remains distinct.

Every year there is heavy competition for top educational designers from recognized universities in the field of instructional design, such as Florida State and Syracuse. Saturn has a distinctively different approach to hiring designers. In addition to the traditionally trained designers, it hires a number of musicians, comedians, and actors as designers to ensure that the learning process is fun and interesting.

Benchmarking is a key driver in the creation and innovation of the corporate university. Benchmarking has become a widely used practice within most corporations, especially in the creation or re-creation of new products or processes. Learning best practices from others has not been lost in the corporate university world either. Following the Motorola credo of "stealing shamelessly," leading corporate universities use benchmarking as an initial step before implementing their own practices. Whether it be for designing courses or the corporate university itself, benchmarking has proved to be a valuable tool for beginning the change process. The corporate learning community even welcomes other corporations to benchmark, realizing the potential to learn from them as well.

How They Teach Their Lessons

Every Saturn team member is required to complete 92 training hours annually. That represents five percent of the average work year. In an average year, Saturn University will deliver training to over 10,000 Saturn team members (both permanent and contract employees), for an average of 112 hours per employee.

To ensure that Saturn employees receive the right training within their 92 hours, Saturn constantly compares the training to five specific values. All training must develop commitment to customer enthusiasm, commitment to excel, trust and respect for each other, teamwork, and continuous improvement.

Each employee has an ITP that ensures that within these values, the right skills are being taught to enable that employee to perform his or her job. In fact, the ITP is developed by looking at an essential list of requirements and factors. Every educational experience must meet federal/state requirements, Saturn requirements, business unit requirements, work unit modules and work unit requirements, job-specific skill requirements, and optional and career growth opportunities. The Saturn ITP may include classes on UAW history, Saturn's culture and values, technical training, team skills, and many other types of learning.

Car-builder training is funded centrally and is not billed back to the manufacturing units. The training takes place at the Northfield Development Center at Spring Hill and at locations within the plant. Central to car-builder training is the ITP process, whereby every Saturn employee plots the course for his or her own training program for the coming year. Each person's plan is stored on a central system, and progress is tracked. The ITP database is available to 1,800 of Saturn's 9,200 local employees, from senior management to each team's training point-person. One manager stated: "The biggest challenge with the ITP is overcoming the ego—getting people to admit they need to improve in some area."

Many operations and functions of the corporate university are informal and are pushed out to the business units—specifically, to the team level in which decisions are made about the individual training each needs for the coming year. Each team has a training point-person.

There is a training profile for most job groups at Saturn. The profile tells which training is needed for which job or functional area. This includes technical, legally required, Saturn-required, and team-required training. When a person changes jobs, his or her training profile is changed as well.

Who Does the Teaching?

Wise universities keep their full-time staffs to a minimum and gain double value by using part-time or short-term teachers from throughout the company. By recruiting from within the organization or using line personnel as SMEs or teachers, they capitalize on unmatched experience that upgrades the educational offerings and build increased commitment to the corporate university itself, as former teachers return to work in all parts of the company.

Training at Saturn is delivered by process owners and SMEs. External vendors are used as well. Internally, there are different deliverers, including facilitators, coaches (OJT), instructors, teachers (human skills courses), and the T3 process.

Saturn's T3 (train-the-trainer) process identifies leaders within the organization who are capable of teaching and trains them to deliver. The T3 process includes attending the course as a student, observing the course with an instructor or guide, reviewing requirements with T3 coach, co-teaching and receiving feedback, and teaching the course and receiving feedback. After this process is complete, the T3 instructor is qualified to deliver the course.

Leaders at Saturn are not just asked to teach; they are required to do so. Teaching, or facilitating training, is counted as training hours for the leaders. Saturn uses this model to capitalize on the knowledge that exists within the company.

Saturn University continues to push many of its operations and functions out into Saturn business units. It is not surprising that Saturn training is spread by those who have been trained.

Emphasis on Leadership Development

As a result of feedback on employee surveys, Saturn has put in place more training on leadership skills. A second survey specifically addressed what people wanted. The leadership courses are directed mostly at the corporate level, but some retailers are taking leadership classes, as well. Saturn does not have any hard measurements of leadership effectiveness; leaders are evaluated based on the effectiveness of their teams.

The Human Resource Management (HRM) function, in coordination with the business teams, decides who should be included in the leadership development process. Each business team has an HRM group that owns the leadership piece. HRM is ultimately responsible for identifying potential candidates for the leadership development process within the teams but does rely on input from the individual business teams to help guide their decisions about who should be included.

The current selection process at Saturn uses a position requirement description (PRD) process. Union and management positions both have PRDs. For management team members, crew leaders, crew coordinators, and area module advisers review resumes and check references to decide who will get interviewed. Union team members who want to become leaders must go through a prescreening process before they are eligible to join the OMA pool. This prescreening process reveals the most qualified team members based on required skills. On the management side, Saturn typically gets ten resumes for three open spots; the union side often has 120 people for each job. An interview process follows the prescreening for both union and management candidates. This process helps build a pool of prequalified team members for selection later on. These team members are responsible for their current jobs but will participate in enhancement training while they are in the pool. Saturn is looking to move toward a more complex, up-front assessment tool that relies more on competencies and input from team members that have experience working with the candidate.

Diversity and Communication among Potential Leaders

One of Saturn's requirements of leaders is that they "appreciate the power of diversity." Saturn looks closely at its pool of leadership candidates to ensure diversity of gender, race, experience and cross-functional representation. Diversity issues are considered to be a part of the selection process for all levels of leadership.

Saturn follows a fairly traditional and informal communication process for high-potential team members. Unlike many organizations, however, it does not give up easily on its lower-performing team members. Instead, it spends quite a bit of time identifying strategies to improve a team member's performance through training, mentoring, and/or coaching.

Likewise, team members in leadership positions, as well as those considered high-potential with great futures, receive significant amounts of training. Saturn does not advertise who the high-potential group is to the rest of the team member population, because it does not want to "de-motivate" others. This knowledge can and does get out, but this has not been a problem, as Saturn team members tend to feel in control of their own destinies with training and job issues.

Methods for Building Leadership Capability

As stated earlier, every team member has an ITP that promotes continuous learning and requires 92 hours of training per team member per year. Saturn offers hundreds of courses and conducts about 1.5 million hours of training per year. A team's compensation is tied to the way each team member pursues his or her ITP. Saturn team members must perform 65 percent of their training hours in classes listed on their ITP, as well as the 92 total hours of training, teaching, or going to school. Team members who fail to meet the 65 percent put others in jeopardy of losing pay. Each team member puts 12 percent of his or her total pay at risk each year, of which 4 percent is for training incentives. If even only one team member does not meet plan, the whole team loses some of that money.

What does that mean for team members in leadership roles? When a team member is selected for the OMA leadership role, he or she sits down with his or her manager to customize and adjust his or her ITP so that training is based on the criteria and profile of the OMA role.

There are many ways available to reach the 92-hour goal. Classroom-based training, facilitator-led courses, on-the-job training, job experience, and video-based courses to mention but a few. Another way Saturn team members can earn training hours is to teach one of the available courses. In fact, Saturn staffs most of its tremendous number of training classes by making all leaders responsible for teaching a certain number of courses per year.

"OMA Boot Camp" is one of the best programs that Saturn offers. It brings together OMAs (new and old, union and management) to use tools such as the Learning Styles Inventory (LSI) and Situational Leadership® to gather feedback and develop critical leadership skills. LSI is a feedback instrument that helps team members see themselves as others see them.

With all of the courses Saturn offers, it has had to develop an education and training team that is responsible for designing the tools and classes that help team members accomplish Saturn's goals and mission. The education and training team (about 35 team members) is comprised of in-house writers, developers, and subject matter experts from all over the company. Outside experts and consultants have been used in the past as well.

Mentoring and Coaching

Saturn encourages informal mentoring to take place throughout the organization. Certain departments and divisions have formal mentoring programs, but Manufacturing Leadership and HRM have identified this as an important area to solidify. HRM looks for team members who have been successful in different aspects of work, such as balancing personal and professional lives, leading teams, and managing conflict; and then point people with those issues or interests in their direction. Additionally, African-American and Hispanic men's and women's groups that have come together informally and naturally for the purpose of mentoring are supported internally.

The unique nature of the OMA role lends itself to natural mentoring and coaching relationships. Typically, a new management OMA will be paired with an experienced union OMA on the job to help ease the transition and foster knowledge sharing. Currently, HRM looks for mentoring fits between the partners by using such tests as the Meyers-Briggs personality inventory and the LSI. This role highlights the importance of the unique relationship between the union and management at Saturn, because one could not accomplish its goals without the other.

Coaching is a requirement of all leaders at Saturn, and it is the biggest aspect of training for leaders. Coaching ties directly to each leader's performance evaluation. In fact, Saturn requires its leaders to take many of the outside courses that Saturn offers, such as those at the Center for Creative Leadership or The Covey Leadership Center, before it will allow that leader's team members to attend them. This helps ensure that coaching takes place and supports the program.

Whom They Teach

Today's more successful corporate universities set up their training programs after they know what needs to be accomplished. Though this seems to be a common-sense approach, it has been woefully absent in the history of corporate training. More common has been the establishment of courses that were destined to stay on the class schedule forever, even after they were no longer needed. Most organizations conduct measurements of students' individual learning and organizational learning. Whether the corporation chooses to focus on individual learning or overall corporate performance, the underlying focus is to use training to improve its particular business situation.

Saturn University is also involved in the education of the company's sales forces. Retail training falls under the areas of wholesale, sales, and service. It focuses on the retailer or franchise operations. Typical of its orientation, Saturn refers to its franchised sales outlets as "retail" or "stores"—not dealerships. Retail training includes sales, repair and parts, and leadership and culture training. All Saturn retail employees come to Spring Hill facility for training. The company believes that having all Saturn employees come there ensures a consistent training experience and fosters the sense of being part of one big family. The company has also found a high correlation between training and good customer satisfaction index (CSI) scores. This correlation has resulted in a high demand for the Saturn orientation course from retailers. This core orientation course includes a ropes course (called Excel); a plant tour; and a "ride-and-drive" experience, during which retailers get to experience the Saturn product firsthand.

Supplier training is the newest part of Saturn's corporate university. The idea for supplier training came from benchmarking with Motorola University. Saturn's supplier training goals are to improve the quality and business performance of suppliers, to share the Saturn culture of team skills and leadership, and to orient suppliers to Saturn (culture, standards, processes, and so on). Supplier training is not mandatory but it is recommended. Some supplier courses are "stock" Saturn courses, such as the Introduction to Saturn Culture and the Excel ropes course, but approximately 90 percent of the courses offered to suppliers are specifically designed for them. Saturn University delivers supplier training courses at or near its locations across the United States and Canada. The training is primarily done by Saturn employees with a background in supplier management.

Requests for manufacturing training at Saturn go through a prioritization process within the Management Leadership Team (MLT), which acts as an advisory board for training development issues. This process is based on business priorities. Units may also purchase training from outside vendors if the training required is not Saturn-specific. Other areas, such as Saturn University supplier training, retail training, and Saturn Consulting Services (SCS) manage prioritization of training requests in a variety of ways.

SCS was set up to answer external questions about the company's training programs and to share information with GM groups. The focus of the consulting group is to foster leadership and team building within Saturn. Consulting is seen as a core value throughout the organization—team members must continually consult with each other to assess performance and improve processes. SCS consults with customers in order to understand them and meet their needs, and it is run as a profit center.

What about Educational Technologies?

Saturn offers 800 courses and delivers over 10,000 classes for a total of over a million training hours a year. It utilizes several training facilities for the delivery of training. The Northfield facility has 16 classrooms, 4 computer labs, 2 computer-ready technical labs, a conference center and theater, a distance-learning facility, a robotics lab, a video editing suite, and a workplace development center. In addition, the manufacturing facility at Spring Hill has 24 classrooms for car-building classes and 180 "team centers" where car-builder teams can meet. Saturn has several other facilities for specific training needs; it also utilizes space at GM and rents space when necessary.

In most corporate universities, the use of technological teaching devices begins only after a close examination of the business process itself. It is rare to see a thoughtless automatic rush to commit training to the latest forms of media. For example, Saturn stores all individual ITPs in a huge database. This database, which was designed by Electronic Data Systems (EDS) and Saturn, keeps track of all 8,200 team members' 92 hours of training. Saturn uses the database to follow how many hours and what kind of training each team member has accomplished toward his or her goal. The database also shows whether it has enough teachers, classroom space, and registration for each class.

One effect of technology has been the rapid pace with which it enables change in business today. The changes affect not only the products or services provided by a corporation, but also the way in which they are organized. As this is seen throughout the corporation, it is mirrored in the infrastructure and delivery of learning within the corporate university.

Much is seen and heard about online registration for courses and the cost savings associated with distance learning.

Most corporate universities realize the need to implement new applications but, to this point, have resisted the urge to simply replicate the current way of doing business and automate it. Instead, leading corporate universities have opted to examine closely the learning process itself and only make use of new technologies when it makes sense. They have discovered that using an Intranet and new software applications will increase the visibility of the offerings of the corporate university, and that distance learning forces the reevaluation of the learning process and can change not only the delivery of the learning intervention, but the design as well.

Using an Intranet for course catalogs and employee registration holds a great deal of interest and value for all corporate universities, especially as virtual offices and telecommuting become more popular. Most have moved to online course catalogs and will be making the shift to allow registration online in the near future. With the implementation of new technology, trailblazing organizations have been able to market their programs better and meet the needs of their employees.

While the movement to implement new technology within corporate university infrastructure has taken off, the implementation on the delivery side has been much slower. The classroom remains the most popular method of delivery.

Most corporate university leaders admit that some form of distance learning will eventually dominate their delivery of learning experiences. However, there remains initial resistance to this new technology. Employees feel more comfortable in a classroom setting. To overcome this resistance and to add more social interaction to distance-learning approaches, some corporate universities are busy improving the interaction of their distance learning offerings. Saturn does not make heavy use of distance and computer-based training (CBT). Distance-learning programs have been offered by various providers, including the University of Tennessee, Columbia State Community College, General Motors Corporation, GMI/EMI, and others. The company is social, and face-to-face learning is the preferred mode.

Measuring Results

Saturn is a values-driven company. Its corporate university is constantly checking its behaviors, techniques, and progress against Saturn's five values: commitment to customer enthusiasm, commitment to excel, trust and respect for the individual, teamwork, and continuous improvement. If the training under scrutiny is not obviously supporting those values, that training is dropped. Training is an example of how Saturn distinguishes itself from GM and the traditional, auto-manufacturing culture. Saturn has designed and created a culture in which training can stay focused on the strategic goals and values of the company. Training is the "currency in the human equation." Every new Saturn employee spends one full week in an orientation process—learning skills and the company's values—prior to participating in additional training. Saturn uses its five values as a constant check—all training is held up against those five values and the question is asked: "Does this training initiative feed these values?" If not, the training is dropped.

Staying in touch with customers is essential to any business. Many corporate universities are able to provide educational activities that help business units understand customers better and bring them innovative and targeted service. The universities involve the company's business units in tailored learning experiences relating to design, delivery, and other critical processes. The benefits of this specially designed training accrue in two directions. The business units discover the answers and new strategies they need, and corporate university staffs become more conversant with the overall business and more meaningfully centered on the customer-first philosophy that needs to be a part of all of their courses.

If a corporate university cannot be justified in terms of the business and cannot forecast an improvement to the bottom line of the business (over status quo), there probably should not be a corporate university.

From the beginning, Saturn Corporation has been able to get its union leadership to work with its management in making business decisions. This has been possible, in part, because of the significant role education has played in developing and spreading the culture and strategy of the organization. The business strategy for the entire organization is to build good cars, focus on the customer, and empower the employee. Saturn's new manufacturing facility in Spring Hill was largely staffed by UAW members who had been laid off by GM and who had elected to relocate to the new Saturn site. Saturn's mission reflected the expectation that both General Motors and the workforce would benefit from the investments.

Saturn does not have hard numbers on the impact of the corporate university on retention. However, it emphasizes the commitment to training and development as a tool in recruiting. In addition, Saturn has found a high correlation between training and good CSI scores. This correlation has resulted in a high demand for the Saturn orientation course from retailers.

Saturn does not view the corporate university as an entity that needs to justify its existence. All of Saturn's educational functions are service organizations that support the corporate values and mission. The former president of Saturn has now become the president of GM University. He has a much harder road to travel there, because learning—while increasingly valued at GM—was not a building block of GM culture.

Of course, the hardest thing to measure is the learning. But it seems evident to Saturn's PSTD that the achievements of the corporation have been supported to a great extent by the environment of learning that exists there. PSTD is making efforts to put measurement systems in place. For example, there is a "touchback" process being piloted in a new course.

Measurement and evaluation of courses at Saturn center on tracking course and class data (quantitative) and gauging the success through surveys and questionnaires. Evaluation criteria are based on four levels:[13] reaction "smile sheets," performance checklists for both pre- and post-tests, post-training survey of transfer of training to job, and return on investment.

At Saturn, evaluation is built into the course design process. An evaluation specialist often serves as a resource to each design team. Saturn is currently looking at ways to follow up, so that training "takes hold" in the business units. Saturn benchmarked Motorola for evaluation methods, which was a catalyst to gain more knowledge and in-house skill about evaluation. The company brought in a measurement specialist to do a study on courses offered. The study looked at both quantitative and qualitative data and supported the continuation of even the most expensive courses. Saturn uses a database to evaluate qualitative feedback from all courses, particularly in the retail and supplier training programs.

To tell the story of its successes, Saturn University now produces a *People Development Annual Report* to congratulate those who have achieved major developmental milestones, such as educational degrees. It also communicates Saturn's development programs to the rest of the organization.

Saturn has set up a radically different approach to training from that of its parent company, GM, which offers little training to line employees as compared to that of management, salaried employees, and executives. At GM, most training is on-the-job. There is almost no training in the auto industry itself or on financial and economic issues. Workers at GM had to demand more training, and it was the first item to be cut during downturns.

One of the most important lessons Saturn's educational leaders have learned is to have a strong answer to the question, "Why do we need a corporate university?" The corporate university must be an integral part in achieving that vision. It is equally vital to understand the culture and to be able to do a gap analysis to identify in which areas training and education are needed.

Saturn has built strategic business plans that are visible and can be pushed out into the organization. Education is a palpable and important part of each of those business plans. It has also been crucial in getting employees involved in shaping the strategy and business plan for the company. The team representatives have input, and that empowers all of the employees.

Saturn is confident that the payoff of its education effort is evident in the skill level and accomplishments of its workforce. Its outstanding software assessment and planning tool (Career Point) is available to most team members and indicates the proficiency of Saturn trainees. Saturn is providing ever-increasing numbers of team members with opportunities for global development and believes that the opportunities for the development, challenge, and continuous improvement of its team members is without peer in U.S. industry today. The Saturn philosophy of People Development continues to be that it must be member-driven and leader-supported.[14]

Summary

Business leadership's commitment to continuous learning as a source of competitive advantage is evidenced in the corporate university. These universities link employee learning to overall company strategy, and as a result corporate universities are becoming the connective tissue of organizations, and their learning programs are even beginning to drive businesses.

Saturn Motors has an exemplary corporate university. Every employee has an Individual Training Plan (ITP) designed to meet that individual's needs for his or her job for the coming year, and each employee is required to take 92 hours of training per year. To keep track of the training progress, Saturn's central Education Tracking system houses all ITPs. The system, which is accessible to every training point-person in Saturn, contains course abstracts, class schedules, and instructor/faculty schedules.

Training is delivered by process owners, internal Subject Matter Experts, and external vendors. Internal training is delivered by facilitators, coaches, instructors, teachers, and Saturn's T3 (train-the-trainer) process.

A values-driven company, Saturn's corporate university is constantly checking its behaviors, techniques, and progress against Saturn's five values. If the training under scrutiny is not obviously supporting those values, it is dropped.

Notes

1. Saturn executive Peggy Berger, as quoted in American Productivity and Quality Center, 1997 *Saturn Site Visit Report*, p. 17.
2. Jeanne C. Meister, *Corporate Quality Universities*, New York: Richard D. Irwin, 1994.
3. American Society for Training and Development, "Leadership and Executive Development," Trends, *ASTD Benchmarking Forum*, April 1998, p. 2.
4. Jeanne C. Meister, "Future Directions of Corporate Universities," *UNICON Conference*, March 17, 1996, pp. 2–5.

5. Robert H. Miles, "Corporate Universities: Some Design Choices and Leading Practices," Emory Business School, Atlanta, 1993.
6. Kevin P. Wheeler, "The Uses and Misuses of the Term "Corporate University," 1999/2000, www.glresources.com/corp_ed/whatcu. htm, Global Learning Resources, Inc., Fremont, CA.
7. Consortium Benchmarking Study, "The Corporate University: Learning Tools for Success," APQC Institute for Education Best Practices, Houston, 1998, p. 67.
8. L.E. Densford, "Front Lines: Corporate Universities Add Value by Helping Recruit, Retain Talent," Corporate University Review, Mar/Apr 1999, from Web site http://www.traininguniversity. com/magazine/mar_apr99/front.html.
9. *Fortune* Jan 10, 2000.
10. Saturn Training's Annual Report, 1997.
11. Anonymous, "The Corporate University: Learning Tools for Success," Consortium Benchmarking Study: Best-in-class Report, American Productivity & Quality Center, Houston, 1998, p. 18.
12. Anonymous, "The Corporate University: Learning Tools for Success," Consortium Benchmarking Study: Best-in-class Report, American Productivity & Quality Center, Houston, 1998.
13. Donald L. Kirkpatrick, *Evaluating Training Programs: The Four Levels* (San Francisco: Berrett-Kohler Publishers, 1994).
14. For more information about Saturn, please see George Hollenback & Wesley Vestal, editors, *Developing Leaders At All Levels* (Houston: American Productivity & Quality Center, 1999).

9

Universities

Learning to Listen

T he interest of colleges and universities in the executive education market is nothing new. *Bricker's International Directory of University-Based Executive Development Programs*[1] lists nearly 500 executive education programs offered by business schools throughout the world. What is new is that some leading universities and other innovative academic institutions are finally leading the way into meaningful service to the business community. Research has indicated that corporate customers have historically characterized business schools as "unwilling to listen" to their potential customers. Now, that tide has apparently turned, and the authors believe that a few leading business education practitioners have gotten the message and are developing gold-plated abilities to hear, to anticipate, and to meet the needs of the corporate community.

The changing business scene has continued to value the extra wisdom that can be gathered through years of formal study but has been unwilling to wait around for the traditional timetables of higher education. Corporations have basically said to their rising leaders, "Be sure you get all the education that's available, but don't take very long doing it." While spending billions for executive education,[2] companies have been channeling only about 25 percent of those billions through university based business schools.[3]

University-based programs were in big trouble. They knew they had valuable knowledge to share but found business unwilling to bow to the idol of academic tradition. In the words of a former business school professor who headed the executive development function at a major corporation, "[university] programs are too long. They're not flexible enough. They're too expensive, and they lack action learning."[4]

Executive education customers were pleading for specific educational help but finding few institutions willing to alter traditional offerings to address their needs. Business wanted:

1. Traditional, general management programs
2. Traditional focused programs
3. Custom programs
4. Organizational problem-solving assistance

Universities were comfortable enough with general management and focused programs, but somewhat out of their element when required to customize and solve problems. Consulting firms, on the other hand, were good at custom programs and problem-solving but lacked the ivy-covered credentials of academia. A major market was waiting for whoever could create the product the market was requesting.

A 1999 survey by *Business Week* indicates that the universities have gotten the message.

The unquenchable thirst for learning means that it's a great time to be in the executive education business. The average company spent about $10 million on internal and external executive development in 1998. Of those responding, 76% said they were sending the same number of execs or more to B-school programs than they did five years ago, while 79% said the same about private companies. Overall, spending on U.S. corporate training and education for managers rose to $16.5 billion, up 17% from last year, according to *Train-*

ing magazine. Moreover, 1998–99 revenues at the 63 providers surveyed by *Business Week* averaged $11.9 million, up 97% from 1994, with 43% of revenues coming from custom programs designed for one or a group of companies.[5]

Five Global Innovators

It is clear that the message has now been received. The changes have been accomplished. The fastest learners among learning institutions are already cashing in on their new and innovative offerings to business. The remaining institutions are scrambling to get in on the lucrative game. Today, over 75 percent of all executive education dollars go to some form of customized program. Most companies plan to focus more on such programs in the future. Executive education of the future will be unacceptable unless it is shorter and more focused. And it must feature action learning projects with measurable results.[6]

Some 78 percent of those responding to the *Business Week* survey said that the quality of executive education had improved from five years ago. The elite business schools, however, no longer have the monopoly they have enjoyed for so long. Asked who is the most effective provider of executive education, "53 percent of those surveyed said that consultants were tops."[7]

Universities now know that their traditional "business model," featuring time on campus in classrooms, is on quicksand. The Internet's "clicks-and-mortar" approach spells change for executive education. "We have been functioning and operating in the ultimate elitist environment for 1,000 years," says Meyer Feldberg, dean of Columbia Business School. "[The Internet] is the instrument for democratizing intellectual capital."[8]

In this chapter, we will look at five of the universities that have gotten the message and successfully responded to the market's call: the Harvard Business School, London Business School, Institute for Management Development, Thunderbird, and the Graziadio School (Pepperdine). There are, of course, others, but these five represent a cross section of today's most exciting and promising approaches to executive education. As other universities and consulting organizations mix, merge, customize, and create new formats, the future of executive education and academia can only get brighter.

Harvard Business School

We will begin with the Harvard Business School, which is almost always referred to as "venerable." This often conveys the idea of stodginess or conservatism, but that has been far from the recent record of executive education at Harvard. Ranked "most highly respected" in *Business Week*'s survey,[9] Harvard continues to be a provider of excellent executive education. Under the leadership of Associate Dean Earl Sasser, who is an authority in the field of service management, the school has gained recognition as the leading purveyor of the "top end" of the executive education market.

Harvard has long been a leader in open-enrollment executive education programs, but it broadened this commitment in 1995 under Dean Kim Clark. He re-appointed Professor Earl Sasser as Associate Dean for Executive Education, hired Bob Fogel as Executive Director of Executive Education, and gave the two of them the charge to "grow Executive Education in the right way."

They wisely began by commissioning McKinsey to conduct a study of the executive education market and then began to study existing Harvard programs. They discovered that there were a number of short, focused programs that were generally offered once a year and were primarily driven by faculty interest. They further learned that the increase in attendance at these programs was not a result of student satisfaction and word-of-mouth recommendation but of aggressive marketing.

The study also revealed that the most significant growth in open-enrollment programs had occurred in the first two programs developed in over 20 years! The new Program for Global Leadership (PGL) and The General Manager Program (TGMP) were extremely well received and were far more popular than the programs that had been on the docket for years. PGL had a true global focus and a split format. It was first offered in Singapore in 1998, where it exceeded its targeted enrollment and was successful beyond all expectations. TGMP had a split format, with two months between its first and second modules. In a Harvard first, distance-learning technology was used to continue the learning between the two modules. The program reached full capacity in only three years.

Today, Harvard's program is riding a five-year growth of 124 percent. Revenues for 1998–1999 were $65 million for the 69 programs offered, one-fourth of them custom programs. It ranked number one in general management instruction and number two in leadership.

Harvard's innovative programs are complicated to operate. Staff scheduling is more difficult. There is also the problem that the new programs sometimes cannibalize some previous curriculum offerings. Even so, Professor Sasser has wisely observed that he preferred that "we do the cannibalizing rather than someone else."

In spite of its successes, Harvard has begun to realize that global executive education is a much tougher and more competitive market than sitting back in ivy-covered halls and waiting for students to come. As one Executive Education administrator observed, "U.S. companies in particular seem less enamored with the Harvard name, and they can't afford to have senior people absent for long periods of time."

Harvard's Custom Programs for a Demanding Market

The World Bank approached Sasser in November 1995 to see if Harvard would customize a program for its leaders. The result was not only a success, it was the beginning of an important new emphasis in customized, global executive education. (This story is developed in greater detail in Chapter 7.) In the next four years, customized programs skyrocketed to approximately 25 percent of Harvard enrollment. It was clear that tailoring learning to students' needs and schedules was the future of executive education.

From that World Bank beginning, Harvard has customized programs for DaimlerChrysler, IBM, Johnson & Johnson, Compaq, Ernest & Young, Bank of Thailand, Novartis, Merck, Unilever, and Bertlesmann. The relationship with Novartis alone resulted in a $2 million gift to the school. The Harvard faculty found new life in its involvement with an additional 1,700 senior executives and managers of organizations that were leading the world in leadership development.

Custom programs are also gold mines of networking. They frequently open up unforeseen opportunities to work with other leading business and professional schools around the world. The World Bank Program involved Harvard with Stanford, INSEAD, and IESE. The Bertlesmann program had the faculties of Harvard and IMD teaching together. Plans developed for the Telefonica custom program to be taught jointly by Harvard and IESE faculties in both Argentina and Spain.

In October 1997, Harvard established the Executive Development Center (EDC) as a nonprofit corporation to handle its mushrooming customized programs with Fogel as its president. William Fulmer was hired as the first full-time employee of EDC—as Senior Fellow and Senior Vice President—to help with assessment and design of customized programs. EDC allowed the school to pay faculty competitive rates more easily. Its intention was to spread the custom teaching opportunities across the Harvard business faculty and to make sure that this new thrust did not become the tail that wagged the venerable old university dog. But corporate demand for the new approach would not be denied. Within a year, some faculty members exceeded the intended EDC cap and became heavily involved in client assessment and course design for corporate clients.

Impact of Custom Programming

From 1994 to 1998, EDC's annual program starts increased from 32 to 78 and enrollment per full-time equivalents (FTE) from 83 in 1994 to 149 in 1997, reflecting in part larger sections. The number of program weeks continued to increase each academic year. Today, there are five times as many off-campus, focused programs as there were in 1996. Custom programs have Harvard personnel off campus for almost 30 weeks of the year, including 10 weeks in Washington, D.C., 3 weeks in Asia, and 3 weeks in Europe.

These changes have resulted in a 40 percent increase in customer-service activities in just two years. The phone calls, faxes, and e-mails continue to increase, as does the number of applications. Executive Education personnel make 250–300 corporate visits a year, many to Europe and the Pacific region. Today, at least two-thirds of participants in comprehensive management programs are from outside the United States. The number of participants from Asia and the Pacific now exceed those from Europe.

The Executive Education staff has increased from about 25 full-time employees to about 70. They work to meet increasing demands for new and custom programs, and new partnerships. Executive Education's financial contribution to the school rose from $14 million in 1996 to $36 million in 1999.

Executive Education also contributes significantly to research and development. EDC funds its own three-person research and development group "to improve the quality of executive programs, by supporting the faculty in research and providing tailored, up-to-date materials for participants." Most of this research has been international, with a strong emphasis on Asian and Latin American businesses. Research and development's field-based cases, library cases, supplements, videos, and customized exercises are already in use in the Executive Education programs.

Harvard's Executive Education even took the lead in conducting a special, four-week Senior Executive Program in South Africa for the future leaders of the region. The 60-person class was composed of government officials, executives of state-owned enterprises, and private-sector executives. According to Sasser, "almost to a person, faculty members have described their experience in the program as one of the most significant things they've done in their career."

Constraints of Custom Programming

Even with its major activities off campus, the school's on-campus activities began to reach capacity in housing, dining space, office space, and classrooms. EDC's on-campus housing utilization (McArthur Hall) remains at approximately 90 percent, and the program's success keeps it in the musical chairs competition for allocation of campus residential space.

Of course, the most serious resource constraint is faculty time. A significant number of faculty members who had been particularly active in building and teaching in executive education programs have recently retired. And there is the serious, unresolved issue of faculty workloads. Although faculty members who teach in custom programs are compensated through EDC, there are limits to what a faculty member is able and wants to do. Sometimes, it is hard to say "no" when colleagues tell you they want you on a blue-ribbon team they are assembling. Sasser and his staff have to balance the need for faculty power with the diminishing returns when faculty members begin to exceed reasonable limits.

As custom programs have grown, the need for flexibility has increased, especially for faculty time spent off shore. Setting up a program off shore involves far more than faculty travel. There must be needs-assessment visits; organization of faculty leaders and teams; program design; and staff support to handle logistics, materials, and supplies several time zones away.

Even conducting domestic programs can be a major challenge. Corporate requirements for multi-million-dollar training programs cannot be rehashes of previous offerings. They require major time commitments to research the client company, its needs, and the right faculty and approaches to meet those needs. The time demand for preparation is often so great that EDC wisely brings in consultants to coordinate the study and assist the faculty leader in designing the program.

A New Harvard Business School Initiative

Dean Sasser and EDC have begun to blaze a trail into a new and uncharted region of program preparation. Previously, most courses were assembled through what one administrative person called "plug-and-play" course design. Beginning with two key subject areas, "leadership" and "leading change," EDC is working to do more than simply plug in courses that already exist. Sasser is working with a core faculty in these fields to develop leading-edge theory and practice to keep Executive Education course material up-to-date and to involve a greater number of faculty members.

In developing an offering on "leadership," Sasser conscripted Professor John Kotter and Dr. Gary Hamel. Kotter and Hamel identified faculty, both at Harvard and at other institutions, and began developing new materials for executive education and for Harvard's MBA Program. They even planned a meeting of the world's leadership thought leaders on the Harvard campus in 2000. Also planned are a three- to four-day open-enrollment program on leadership for 330 people and several CEO forums on leadership in different locations around the world.

Other topic areas being considered for this "start-from-scratch" program development approach include leading change, brand management, disruptive technologies and corporate strategy, and performance in emerging markets.

Harvard Business School Executive Education in the Twenty-First Century

Without doubt, Harvard's "Team EXED" has achieved Dean Clark's mandate. Now, as it enters the twenty-first century, it is clearly at a crossroads. The number of new requests for custom programs continues to increase, and yet, the previous clients do not simply get educated and go away. On the contrary, every success in executive education seems to generate new demands for new work with previous clients. And, as clients become increasingly sophisticated, they demand more customization and more experiential learning, which requires more time-consuming hands-on teaching by the Harvard faculty.

Harvard recognizes a growing necessity to prioritize. It must decide which activities will allow it to have the greatest influence on the practice and theory of management. In the words of Bob Fogel, "Which segment best contributes to the future intellectual capital of the school? Where do we best add value to the institution, and then how do we serve it?" Harvard also realizes that it can only continue as a leader in management education by being a leader in the hottest segment of the market. Hard choices always come with major successes.

London Business School

On the other side of the Atlantic, the London Business School (LBS) is an interesting combination of pragmatism and scholarship. Both LBS and Harvard support a more pragmatic approach to research than many of their colleagues. LBS is especially challenged by the concept of having faculty members who compete in the traditional academic arenas, while maintaining a presence in executive education—a presence that reflects action learning, pragmatism, and the needs of the marketplace.

LBS was founded in 1964. Its first nondegree, executive education programs were introduced two years later. Initially located close to Trafalgar Square on London's Northumberland Avenue, the school soon moved to its present elegant and historic building overlooking Regent's Park. In a short time, it has risen to number 18 in *Business Week*'s survey ranking the best of management education.[10] In 1998–1999, LBS offered 59 programs, 50 of which were custom programs. This produced revenues of $20.3 million, a 122 percent growth in five years. Those surveyed ranked the program number five in global business.

The success of LBS has been a result of pleasing customers and clients. In surveys, former students give the school much higher rankings than other groups surveyed in the overall business community. That means that the school is popular with those who know about it, but not everyone thinks of it when answering a survey—a clear challenge for LBS, as it continues to build its reputation.

Evolution of LBS General Management Programs

The school's first two executive programs were the Senior Executive Program and the Executive Development Program. The Senior Executive Program is for top managers. It concentrates on corporate strategy and is four weeks long. It continues as one of the school's flagship programs. It focuses on transforming futures through growth, innovation, and leadership. It runs twice yearly and is designed for a class of about 50 participants, typically drawn from close to 20 countries.

The Executive Development Program was aimed at middle managers and originally lasted 12 weeks. In 1974, it was shortened to ten weeks and had its name changed to the London Executive Program. In 1989, it was replaced by the four-week Accelerated Development Program, which is aimed at high-potential managers who are ready to move from function assignments into general management. True to its name, the program "accelerates" their transitions by developing and polishing their technical, people, and strategic skills. Highly successful, the Accelerated Development Program now runs four times a year for groups of up to 50 from multiple countries and cultures.

By the end of 2000, LBS plans to extend its portfolio of general management programs to four. The two new programs will be for younger high-potential professionals in their twenties and for seasoned top managers (probably age 40 to 60) who wish to pursue new directions in their careers and lives. This will complete the range of programs for very different stages of the life and career cycle of the participants.

In 1973, LBS launched its first brief course, the International Business Program. This one-week course was for senior executives with international responsibilities. Since then, the LBS has developed a wide range of short courses that are typically aimed at top or high-potential managers and respond to the needs of the current market. These short courses can be grouped in the following key areas: strategy, leadership innovation and change; marketing; finance; sector-specific issues; and e-business challenges.

The programs on industry-specific issues have proved to be an area of high market demand, and LBS continues to systematically add new programs to its industry-specific portfolio. Programs that are already successful include the "Agribusiness Seminar," "Managing Professional Services," and "Managing Innovation in Service Businesses."

A New London Business School Initiative: "Masterclasses"

Over the past few years, LBS has become increasingly aware that managers want to access, as quickly as possible, the knowledge and management tools produced by the school's innovative faculty. Consequently, LBS has developed a series of two-day "masterclasses" that get right to the point of recent, leading-edge research that is both practical and relevant to business people.

The first four masterclasses focus on hot topics about which business leaders need immediate and knowledgeable assistance: corporate culture and its effect on business performance; performance measurement; lower pricing; and strategic innovation. LBS believes that it offers a comparable quality program at a 30 to 40 percent lower price than its major competition.

The London Business School's Custom Programs

In 1975, LBS set up the Centre for Management Development to design and run company-specific programs. Among the earliest programs was a four-week middle-management course for British Petroleum and a three-week senior-management course for Royal Dutch Shell.

The Centre has grown significantly, more than doubling its revenues in its first four years. Its client base has broadened enormously. Relevance is probably the most critical characteristic of a custom program. Companies do not mind paying a premium as long as custom programs meet their key corporate challenges.

The success of the Centre proves the expansive future of short courses that work. It presently tailors programs for international clients like ABN Amro, Alcatel, British Airways, Chase Manhattan, Compaq, Conoco, EDS, Esso/Exxon, Garanti Bank, Glaxo Wellcome, Hong Kong Shanghai Bank, KONE, Lucky Goldstar, Lufthansa, Lloyds/TSB, National Power, Orange, Old Mutual, NatWest, Sonae, Volvo, Whitbread, and WPP Group.

LBS's custom programs are generally designed for senior and high-potential managers. They aim to improve the performance of the individual participants and their organizations. Courses are most frequently in the areas of general management, strategy, leadership, marketing, finance, and e-business.

Key characteristics of the centre's approach are flexibility to client needs, innovative design, and close working relationships with client companies. Even before the program development begins, LBS program customizers look closely at the client's requirements and actually refuse to go forward unless they feel confident that they can meet the client's stated learning goals.

The Centre has also learned to partner with other leading business schools and top training organizations and consultancies to maximize its executive learning products. Some of the entities with which the Centre has already partnered are Duke University, MIL (Sweden), Columbia University, IAE (Argentina), INSEAD, JMW Consulting, the Kellogg School at Northwestern University, Nijenrode (The Netherlands), and the Wissenschaftliche Hochschule für Unternehmensführung (WHU) in Germany.

London Business School's Mission and Key Competencies

The school's stated mission is "transforming futures." Its stated aim is to bring about transformed futures through a focus on six core competencies: scholarship, professionalism, innovation, relevance, internationalism, and transformation.

Scholarship is valued by LBS customers, because it is the surest path to new ideas, new concepts, and innovative management tools. To stay fresh and on the leading edge of knowledge, the school wisely incorporates its faculty's research into its program offerings.

Professionalism and world-class facilities must be supplied as openers in the highly competitive world of executive education. The school has enhanced its London facilities with two world-class lecture theaters and seminar rooms in its main building overlooking Regent's Park, and one wing of the school has been converted into an elegant, self-contained space for company-specific programs. Additional facilities are being developed for use in 2001.

Innovation is at the heart of progress in our digital economy. LBS incorporates innovative learning approaches and world thought leaders in the field of strategic innovation to keep its programs current and relevant.

Relevance is an essential characteristic of any program that stakes its future on its ability to hit the target the client provides. LBS invests the time and study to gain a full understanding of the client company and its culture before beginning to create a program. Relevance is heightened through activities such as one-to-one coaching, masterclasses in special subjects, and occasional periods of quiet reflection.

Internationalism broadens perspectives, expands networks, and helps LBS students prepare for the global business environment. Well over half the school's faculty originates from outside the United Kingdom. Thirty to forty nationalities take part in the school's short courses each year, in one of the world's most vibrant, international cities.

Transformation is the aim in any constantly changing environment. Successful graduates think and act differently from the way they did before they arrived at LBS. Challenging participants to think differently is the recognized core competence of LBS executive education. Says Program Director Liz Mellon, "We need to get rid of our black pin-striped suit mentalities and explore the unknown, the unthinkable."

Scope and Growth of LBS Operations

Executive Education at London Business School now accounts for half the school's program revenues. By the turn of the twentieth century, revenues from Executive Education activities were already over $20,000,000.

The school's faculty of 140 includes 80 full-time faculty and 60 teaching and research fellows, visiting, and emeritus faculty. The Executive Education Department is led by an associate dean (Gay Haskins) and includes a team of 40, who are involved in corporate relations and account management, marketing, client services and business development, and program direction and management.

LBS Innovative Practices

At LBS, some of the most innovative practices include 360-degree feedback, evaluation, creative thinking, computer simulations, action learning, partnerships with other providers, and consortia programs.

The 360-degree feedback method allows an individual to understand how he or she is seen by others at work. About six weeks before a program, LBS sends questionnaires to each participant's supervisors, peers, and subordinates. LBS staffers compile the anonymous data and prepare a report. Unique LBS twists on the 360-degree concept are that the Centre carefully tailors each questionnaire to the particular focus of its program; presents the feedback only in small group settings and only through an organizational behavior tutor; gives individual students, on a confidential basis, an idea of how their feedback compares to the more than 15,000 records in the LBS database; and offers a follow-up survey six months after the program, so that participants can measure their progress.

Creative thinking is fostered at LBS through the inclusion of theater, music, painting, and poetry in program experiences. The Senior Executive Program, for example, uses rehearsal, preparation, interpretation, direction, improvisation, and other basic acting techniques to unlock self-awareness and build group identity.

Computer simulations are particularly useful aids to learning. They can take participants beyond case studies and into the dynamics of the business, enable team learning, and provide a framework that captures the holistic nature of challenges facing business. These simulations give life to strategic issues.

Action learning is used to combine formal training events, on-the-job projects, and informal group reflection. This technique is especially good at developing personal-management skills, since it combines classroom education and problem-solving projects. It also helps to improve organizational performance through participative problem solving. Many of the executive development programs delivered by the Centre for Management Development have action-learning elements.

Partnerships with other providers is a constant aim of LBS, particularly in the design and development of company-specific programs. An example is the LBS Senior Executive Development program developed for Glaxo Wellcome. LBS partnered with Duke University and INSEAD to produce a successful program for the company's top 300 managers. The partnership worked well and enabled Glaxo to draw on leading faculty from each of the three schools.

Consortia programs provide opportunities for groups of companies to learn from each others' experiences. LBS frequently arranges for five or six organizations from different industry sectors to join forces to provide a development program for their managers. Each member company selects four to six managers to take part. Consortia programs provide valuable opportunities for benchmarking and for seeing problems through the eyes of a completely different industry.

LBS has a Global Consortium that brings together senior managers from ABB, BT, LG, Lufthansa, SKF, and Standard Chartered Bank to focus on transnational management. Its European Consortium contains four companies headquartered in Europe: British Airways, Electrolux, Deutsche Telekom, and SmithKline Beecham. It works to develop a business understanding of the issues involved in operating in a European market, by broadening each participants' perspectives on the dilemmas that senior managers face when operating in the multicultural, multinational European market. The LBS UK Consortium consists of five blue-chip British companies: British Airways, BT, Lloyds TSB Group, Marks & Spencer, and Vauxhall Motors. It works to enhance the perspective of participating executives by creating an environment in which they can benchmark with their peers and make cross-organizational comparisons.

Leadership Development in the New Millennium

LBS recognizes the difficulty of staying on top. Gay Haskins, Associate Dean of Executive Education, has warned her colleagues, "We tell top executives to 'be rule breakers, not rule takers.' We tell them not to 'base future strategies on past successes.' We tell them to change. Well, our mission is 'Transforming Futures,' and we have to transform ourselves, as well as transforming others."

To keep from resting in its laurel-covered ivory tower, LBS is committed to staying constantly aware of the marketplace for executive education. They will remain alert to the current growth of business schools in Eastern and Central Europe, Latin America, and Asia. They will work to make their international offerings ever more international. They will remain vigilant to the challenge of being ready to provide development opportunities anywhere on the globe at a moment's notice.

LBS is aware that they, along with other leaders of executive education, face formidable competitors beyond business schools. Consultancies, conference organizers, independent trainers, and the whole realm of distance learning can be very consumer friendly and technologically responsive. For this reason, LBS is constantly exploring ways to facilitate its unique strengths through video conferencing, satellite program delivery, and computer-aided distance learning. A recent alliance with the California-based University Access to facilitate technology-assisted instruction is evidence of this commitment. As one LBS publication describes the situation, "The paperless classroom and the paperless office are no longer just on the horizon. They are very close by."

At the same time, LBS knows that cyberspace is unlikely to replace the personal and adaptable touch of classroom learning. So, while LBS works to always be technologically proficient, it knows where its present great strength lies. Partnerships between business schools and other providers will surely continue. But, corporate leadership will continue to look beyond the corporate walls for the objective, professional, university-based guidance they need. The challenge for LBS, and for all those involved in leadership development, will be to give meaning to the learning they provide.

Institute for Management Development

The Institute for Management Development (IMD) of Lausanne, Switzerland, has been described as a blend between a business school and a consulting firm. It is not a conventional part of an established university, although it does offer a full-time MBA program. IMD also offers open-enrollment executive development programs and conducts business-relevant research. The primary focus of IMD is through what it terms "Partnership Programs." These are customized executive development programs developed in a partnership with 30 to 40 client companies a year.

IMD ranks eleventh in a *Business Week* survey to identify the top twenty management education programs. IMD was ranked third in global studies, fourth in innovation, and fifth in custom programs. Its 1998–1999 revenues were $35.3 million, a 69 percent increase in five years. It offers 74 programs, 57 of which are custom programs. More than 4,000 executives from over 70-plus countries attend IMD programs every year.

IMD was established by industry to serve industry. It is not a traditional business school, but it does offer an intensive, on-campus MBA program. This full-time program is given on campus for 11 months. A general MBA is offered with a truly international flavor, although all instruction is conducted in English. The program is limited to about 80 students by design and represents a small part of IMD's offerings and less than 8 percent of their revenue. Roughly 80 percent of IMD's gross revenue is generated equally by its open-enrollment and partnership programs. IMD tries to maintain a balance between the these programs as both a risk-control measure and an enhanced learning opportunity.

IMD's "Obsession for Relevance"

IMD can be better understood through the formal statement of their values. These are referred to as the "Obsession for Relevance," and their aims are to:

1. Develop strong partnerships with industry
2. Be selective in choice of clients and be customer-driven
3. Maintain and use diversity (countries, industries, functions)
4. Provide general management orientation

This value statement guides all of IMD's activities, and the philosophy of Learning Partnerships with leading companies is both the vision and unifying logic for all of IMD's activities.

IMD has approximately 47 faculty members who represent

over 20 nationalities. These faculty members have traditional academic credentials but are expected to spend considerably more time off the campus of IMD than many of their colleagues would find acceptable. A much larger portion of their time is occupied with dealing with assignments from a variety of global businesses. The typical IMD faculty member has an extensive background in teaching and research, tempered with real-life experience in meeting the educational needs of busy executives. Many faculty also have management experience in the manufacturing and service industries. Professors are paid on merit and are expected to engage in research as part of faculty teams. The goal of IMD research is to keep the faculty up-to-date on real-world management issues, as well as making a contribution to the practice of management. Overall, this approach to faculty selection and practice permits IMD to remain at the forefront of real-world, future-focused business education.

Innovation at IMD

Innovation in program development is an IMD hallmark. One measure of this is that a third of its open-enrollment programs were introduced after June 1995. Another measure of this is programs like Orchestrating Winning Performance. In this program, participants take a role in designing their learning experience from an intensive, six-day offering of recent insights from the entire IMD faculty. These insights are then combined with problem-solving activities. In the future, IDM looks to a greater integration of distance-learning technologies with more traditional face-to-face sessions. Technology will allow extended learning opportunities and information exchange. Face-to-face techniques, though, remain necessary for the rapport and exchange required to learn about behaviors, values, and new perspectives.

IMD's own 1997 study of its faculties' core competencies uncovered the following two core groups: learning process competencies and substance competencies. The learning process competencies were identified as the ability to listen to and understand customer needs; capabilities in fast-tailored executive learning design; orchestration of exceptional collaborative learning processes; effective delivery skills; truly global approach due to no home-country bias; and a general management perspective concerning both strategy and implementation. The substance competencies were identified as the ability to develop distinctive frameworks that provide original insights into business issues and real-world orientation in research.

IMD has built its reputation on top management's increasing commitment to executive development as a company's primary edge in the stiff competition of the era. IMD works as an outside catalyst to facilitate the essential process of ongoing organizational learning. An academic institution like IMD can provide a business with a sense of objectivity, as well as the competencies to help delineate specific learning programs.

Learning Network

The IMD Learning Network is a member organization open to industries worldwide. The Learning Network was established more than 25 years ago and is comprised of some 130 international member companies. Benefits of membership include access to IMD's cutting-edge management research through IMD's 15 annual Discovery Events. Member executives are brought together in a collaborative learning environment. These connections also enhance the relationship between IMD faculty and line executives, which creates opportunities for research projects. Through the Learning Network, IMD is also able to achieve the socially responsible goal of promoting excellence in management development.

IMD believes its learning partnership approach is "perhaps the most promising vehicle available to the CEO who wishes to accelerate a strategic agenda by strengthening creative, opportunity-seeking, business development with an implementation focus throughout the company."[11]

Thunderbird

Thunderbird is the American Graduate School of International Management. Based in Glendale, Arizona, it has a long history of catering to students from a variety of countries around the world and for emphasizing international or global business issues. In the last few years, Thunderbird has risen to prominence in the rankings of executive education because of the unusually dynamic combination of its president and its head of Executive Education. It ranks seventeenth in *Business Week*'s top twenty but earned a number-two spot for its global business program. Thunderbird's revenues in 1998–1999 were $10 million, a 317 percent increase in five years. It offers 122 programs, 78 of which are custom programs.

Starting from Scratch

Drs. Ed Barrett and Roy Herberger came to Thunderbird from Southern Methodist University in 1990. They brought high hopes of building an education business that supported their ambitious goals. At that time, Thunderbird was earning a little more than $600,000 annual revenue, mostly from government-funded, cross-cultural work. Herberger, Thunderbird's new president, asked Barrett to step out of his comfortable position as senior chair holder at SMU and join him at Thunderbird to develop the executive program.

Under Barrett's leadership, the department started open-enrollment programs in global finance, global strategy, global marketing, and those for the oil and gas industry. The department also added the Executive Master of International Management (EMIM) degree program, which is an executive-level version of the accredited Master of International Management (MIM) degree program. It is designed for experienced, mid-career managers, professionals, and individual business owners who wish to complete a master's degree in international management without interrupting their careers. The EMIM program follows the same general curriculum as the MIM program. Course work is required in world business, modern languages, and international studies, but each course has been redesigned to meet the special needs and learning requirements of mid-career professionals.

At the Right Place at the Right Time

In the early to mid-1990s, the economy began forcing the executive education market toward shorter, more focused programs. Companies were searching for the most from their training dollars and "canned," open-enrollment programs lost favor. Custom and consortium programs became more popular, because they allowed the companies more control over program content. In addition, the consortium programs still offered that "cross-fertilization" between participants that was so appealing about open-enrollment programs.

In 1992, Dr. Barrett and Dr. Warren Wilhelm, a former head of management development at Allied Signal, had discussions about how Thunderbird could assist transnational firms to expand business globally. As a result of those discussions, Thunderbird Executive Education formed strategic partnerships with leading firms to meet the needs of their global managers. These alliances are known as the Thunderbird International Consortia (TIC).

TIC programs are two-week, global management overviews offered three times per year. Each member firm agrees to send several of their employees to each program. Because the companies in each consortium are noncompeting, participants engage in rich interaction with colleagues from other industries and cultures. Advisory boards made up of representatives from each member firm meet with Thunderbird often and have significant control of program design.

An Idea Whose Time Had Come

The TIC began Thunderbird's important shift to custom programs for single firms and groups of firms. In 1994, a Global Telecommunications Management Program was added to the Thunderbird lineup. This program provides telecommunication managers with a forum to discuss, analyze, and understand key issues in the rapidly changing global telecommunications environment.

At about this time, North American firms were beginning

significant global expansion, and their learning needs matched Thunderbird's niche, one that had been developing since the school's founding in 1946. Today's Thunderbird campus was originally Thunderbird Field No. 1, an army airfield where U.S., English, and Taiwanese pilots were trained during World War II. Following the war, General Barton Kyle Yount, Commanding General of the U.S. Army Air Training Command, realized that U.S. business was going global and that few Americans were prepared for the challenge this represented. He talked the government into selling him the deactivated base for one dollar and became the founding president of the American Institute for Foreign Trade. In 1968, the school's name was changed to the Thunderbird Graduate School of International Management. After another name change in 1973, the official name became Thunderbird, the American Graduate School of International Management, in 1997.

Thunderbird's High-Flying Mission

Thunderbird's stated mission is to "develop high-potential individuals to serve the advanced management needs of international enterprises." Specific goals of the institution include:

+ To serve international business, government, and non-profit organizations through faculty research and consultation, student internships, and technological facilitation
+ To foster global understanding by seeking a domestically and internationally diverse faculty and student body
+ To maintain close links with leading enterprises so that the curriculum remains responsive to their needs, and the placement process meets student and international enterprise objectives.

Thunderbird—Home of Consistent Diversity

The school's history demonstrates that global business education is a specialty and has been for more than 50 years. Thunderbird's custom programs illustrate its capability to customize educational experiences for many industries, as well as for its global client base. Examples of Thunderbird client and program diversity include:

♦ *A major automotive and aerospace supplier*—a two-week program with instruction in global leadership followed by a project, a field trip, and a report back to the company's management committee with project results

♦ *A worldwide automobile company*—a one-week program focusing on mergers, alliances, and consolidations involving prework, a cross-cultural dinner with Thunderbird graduate students, interactive sessions on campus, and post-program communication

♦ *A major European telecommunications company*—a nine-day workshop in global management for worldwide business unit and area managers to familiarize them with the international telecommunications marketplace

♦ *An international oil company*—a two-week workshop in global management with heavy cooperation between the academic director of the program and an on-site company human resources representative. Considerable tweaking and refining are done during the program to meet the company's internal goals.

♦ *A leading pharmaceutical conglomerate*—an innovative, two-week program for senior company executives designed to enhance marketing skills and global management capabilities. The program is split into two one-week blocks separated by two months. During the first block, participants undertake a complex, pharmaceutical, computer-based simulation. In their teams, they then identify company-specific projects. They return to their jobs, work on the projects, and reconvene two months later. In the second block, participants work on case studies and workshops. The program concludes with project presentations to a member of the company's executive team.

♦ *A large Korean conglomerate*—a three-week, intensive English-language program followed by a nine-week, broad-based, global management program for high-potential managers

♦ *A global tire company*—a three-week program for global

business leaders designed to broaden the mindset of high-level functional leaders and prepare them for global, general management responsibilities. Held close to the company's headquarters, the program concludes with project presentations to the CEO.

Thunderbird's Key Competencies

Thunderbird Executive Education programs (and the school as a whole) share a single, primary competency: global focus. This focus goes far beyond mixing in some global business courses, featuring a few star international professors, or traveling outside the country as part of a seminar. Thunderbird knows that a truly global graduate business school must approach international management education not as a sideline, but as a primary focus.

Thunderbird's philosophy is built on the simple truth that to do business on a global scale, managers and executives need to know not only the intricacies of international business practices, but also understand the customs of other countries and be able to negotiate and communicate with different cultures and peoples. All Thunderbird courses are dedicated to teaching students and executives about the global business environment. Beyond that, all of its executive programs are completely globally focused. The entire faculty of more than 100 members are dedicated to expertise in international management education. They consult with global companies, conduct worldwide research, and develop global business cases. All of this results in a treasury of real-world business tools and practical applications that executives can use on their jobs.

Thunderbird's campus community has a current MIM enrollment of more than 1,500 students. They come from 79 different countries, 50 percent from outside the United States. Students represent Thailand, Russia, China, Kenya, Japan, India, Mexico, South Korea, Germany, Brazil, Indonesia, and Spain. This student diversity brings a wealth of business and cultural experience that enriches the Thunderbird learning community. Alumni of the program work in over 12,000 organizations in more than 135 countries, and this "Thunderbird Network" is the most powerful of its kind in today's global economy.

Every Thunderbird executive education program is specifically designed to prepare managers for the world of international business. Excellence in global focus is the reason *BusinessWeek* ranked Thunderbird's executive education programs "#2 in global business education," ahead of programs like Harvard and LBS.[12]

Under Thunderbird's Broad Wings

The ever-changing and constantly adapted offerings of Thunderbird include the Thunderbird Language and Culture Center, the EMIM program, the Executive Inn (a residence for executive guests and other visitors to the campus), and Thunderbird Executive Education (TEE).

TEE is the largest component. It designs and implements one- and two-week, open-enrollment, custom, and consortium programs. It has grown steadily in revenue since 1989–1990, when revenue was approximately $600,000 and there were 3 employees. Revenue in fiscal year 1999 surpassed 14 million and there were 65 employees. TEE's average annual growth rate was nearly 40 percent from 1990–2000. Custom programs are Thunderbird's largest line of business, followed by consortia programs, open-enrollment programs, the EMIM program, the Executive Inn, and the Language and Culture Center.

Traditionally, Thunderbird has supported management development of first- and second-level management with local or national sponsorship up to the top corporate executive level. Approximately 3,500 professionals attend these programs each year. Programs are held on and off campus. In addition to the main facility in Glendale, Arizona, Thunderbird has two international campuses in Archamps, France, and Tokyo, Japan. Progress is being made toward hosting executive programs at these sites.

The school also runs many on-site programs for organizations that would rather use their own facilities for training. For the past four years, it has given a luncheon lecture series for one of its local clients and simultaneously broadcast the series to other company sites around the country. Another Thunderbird client hosts school faculty members for management and finance programs about 15 times per year at its site in France.

The school's original campus has grown tremendously during the last decade, particularly its executive education facilities. The $6.5 million Executive Inn building was added with 64 hotel rooms, an executive lounge, four large-tiered classrooms, 24 breakout rooms, and a combination office and classroom building. A new dining facility includes three private executive education rooms for guests.

Thunderbird Innovations

Thunderbird's approach has been to provide a select faculty with good teaching skills and expertise in the adult-learner environment. There is also an environment of operational excellence. The tremendous cultural diversity of the campus population is a special strength. Graduate students in executive programs are routinely included in cross-cultural dinners and discussion panels. The majority of these students have business experience in their home countries, and they are glad to share their knowledge with executive participants. Participants and students enjoy these interactions and gain knowledge that cannot be found in books.

Further innovative program components are global projects and action learning. The school's consortium programs are very much alive and well after many years, because clients value the shared educational experiences involving such a wide number of managers at their own levels. Many of the original member firms continue to make the significant commitment to the TIC each year.

Thunderbird has obviously learned the central lesson that, in order for its programs to be successful, it must show its participants how to make sense of their own experiences. It must draw on those experiences and demonstrate to its students how they can turn "what they know" into "what they need to know." Such insights benefit companies and careers. And, as grateful Thunderbird alumni continue to succeed around the world, the school continues to develop an unmatched global network of knowledge, experience, and influence.

Thunderbird expects to continue riding the trend away from open-enrollment programs and toward custom ones. Though the need for executive education is certain to continue growing, there will be less case-based classroom instruction and more "action learning." There will be shorter programs; an increasing use of partnerships and alliances; a reduction in the number of company providers; an expectation of measurable bottom-line impact; a more active role by the client in program design; and profit margins under increasing pressure. Successful executive education providers will use technology well and form partnerships with other educational institutions and providers to best meet clients' needs. Although this is a lot to undertake, Thunderbird was founded on change and therefore looks forward to a changing future.

Pepperdine's Graziadio School

The Graziadio School of Pepperdine University has broken into the top 75 overall business schools rankings in the country only in the past year, under the leadership of Dean Otis Baskin. Yet the school was delighted in November, 1999, to be named in the top 20 Executive MBA Programs. This came as no surprise to Pepperdine or its graduates, for the school has placed major emphasis on this area.

Beyond its geographic advantage of having five campuses in Southern California, Pepperdine has developed a special Presidents and Key Executives (P/KE) program that uniquely appeals to those who hold these positions in corporations. The classes of this program are especially popular because all faculty who teach in the program are present for the first four-day workshop, where they meet the students and explain how their portions of the course will fit into the overall design and curriculum; students work together on integrated projects that will have an actual impact on the operations of their businesses; and, as a final project, each student makes a presentation to share the real difference the program has made to his or her firm. There have been a number of instances in which new businesses were formed as a result of these presentations.

A course adviser, usually a graduate of the program, attends every class for the seven trimesters. This course adviser not only handles much of the administrative details for the faculty member but also serves as an interface between the students and the faculty. Even though Pepperdine now has over 100 classes that have graduated from the P/KE program and 40 from its more traditional MBA executive designs, these student advisers continue to stay in touch with graduates. They can often help with academic or professional problems long after graduation. The Pepperdine business-alumni network is now 24,000 strong, with more than 1,700 business school graduates leading businesses throughout the world as presidents, vice presidents, and CEOs.

Pepperdine is widely known for the fact that the main campus is located in Malibu, and, while this makes it attractive to a certain category of undergraduate students, it has not caused the university to receive a great deal of positive press in terms of business schools. What many people fail to realize is that, over the past 20 years, Pepperdine has established a network of campuses throughout Southern California, campuses that emphasize the education of the mature working professional.

Pepperdine has taken some aggressive and nonconventional approaches to the education of executives, particularly in what has been described as their "boutique programs." These include the MBA for Presidents and Key Executives, more often referred to as P/KE, and the school's Master of Science in Organizational Development (MSOD) has been consistently ranked first or second in the nation in this specialized area. Pepperdine also offers an Executive MBA program in several locations beyond Southern California and a Master of Science in Technology Management in the heart of Silicon Valley.

The Graziadio School of Business and Management focuses on the development of values-centered leaders and managers for a rapidly changing global business environment. It provides seven distinctive master's-level programs and one undergraduate degree-completion program designed for students at all levels of professional development. Students gain the professional and personal skills needed to manage growth and change in their organizations. Students in all programs have the advantage of being taught by a faculty rich in academic and professional experience.

"Behavioral Science Applied to Management Practice"

When the Pepperdine University School of Business and Management was founded in 1969, it offered the only business programs in Southern California designed specifically to meet the education needs of executives. Classes were held on evenings and weekends, so that students could maintain their professional status while earning an MBA or bachelor's degree.

The founding deans and faculty placed an emphasis on knowledge and skills for successfully dealing with individuals and groups, so that all business programs of Pepperdine begin with a communications workshop as part of the course Human Behavior in Organizations. This course provides both theoretical and experiential knowledge of group dynamics, personal leadership style, and teamwork. The Graziadio School is unique in having been built upon principles of behavioral science as applied to management practice.

Courses are taught from a global perspective with an emphasis on managing change, whether personal, organizational, or technological. Teaching methods include case analyses, discussions, simulation exercises, and lectures. Instructional technology is used in ways that enrich the learning experience and develop skills for the workplace. A high degree of student participation is required in all of the school's programs, and most courses include team projects. Success is contingent upon students' competency in developing and demonstrating effective team skills in classroom activities and projects.

Many faculty are qualified both academically and professionally in their field, having enhanced their academic credentials with decision-level responsibility as entrepreneurs, executives, and consultants. Complementing this focus on business practice, class size is limited to 25 students to foster discussion, interaction, and teamwork.

Eight Distinctive Business Degree Programs at Pepperdine

The Graziadio School enrolls more than 2,700 students in eight distinctive business degree programs. The largest program is the Fully-Employed MBA program, which graduates some 600 students per year. Perhaps the school's most widely recognized program is the MSOD program, which focuses on managing change in organizations. For the past two years, this program has been ranked number one in a national survey of managers and organizational development practitioners.

The Graziadio School's P/KE MBA program is still the only MBA program designed exclusively for presidents and key executives. In the P/KE program and the Executive MBA program, students learn to assess vital information, evaluate industry trends, make strategic decisions, and provide visionary leadership. Among the unique features of these programs, students are required to attend a communications workshop at the beginning of the program; develop a major research project focused on a business opportunity; and attend a seminar on ethical dilemmas, issues, and consequences at Nellis Prison in Nevada.

Other programs include the Bachelor of Science in Management (a degree-completion program) and the Master of Science in Technology Management, which is designed to give managers a competitive edge in the global technological environment. Full-time students can choose among an MBA, a Master of International Business, or a Juris Doctor MBA offered in concert with the Pepperdine School of Law. The school has recently introduced a joint Master of Public Policy/MBA degree. The Graziadio School is also developing an increasing number of learning opportunities at partner institutions and corporations around the world. Of the school's nearly 3,000 students, over 60 percent are enrolled in the full-time MBA program.

The Graziadio School offers a noncredit, business preparatory program designed for international students who lack the communication skills or need other preparation for Pepperdine's business degree programs. The school also offers specialized programs in entrepreneurship, process mapping, transit management, management-organization development, managing in the twenty-first century, and call center management. Annual study-abroad programs were introduced in 1998 in Oxford, England, and Antwerp, Belgium, for fully-employed MBA students, alumni, and others in the business community.

A significant acknowledgment of the business school's success came in 1996 with a $15 million endowment by successful businessman George L. Graziadio, chairman and founder of Imperial Bancorp. The school was renamed the George L. Graziadio School of Business and Management in his honor. Graziadio also worked with Dean Baskin to create a Board of Visitors, comprised of some 100 leaders from business and public life, who have significantly supported and directed the Graziadio School during the self-evaluation process.

In less than three decades, the Graziadio School has become one of the ten largest professional business schools in the nation and is the leading provider of MBA talent on the West Coast. Currently, the school has an alumni network of more than 23,000 worldwide, including 1,000 who currently lead organizations as vice presidents, presidents, and CEOs.

Summary

Universities and other innovative academic institutions are leading the way into meaningful service to the business community. Today, over 75 percent of all executive education dollars go to some form of customized program.

In this chapter, we looked at five universities that represent a cross section of today's most exciting and promising approaches to executive education: Harvard Business School, the London Business School, the Institute for Management Development, The American Graduate School of International Management (better known as Thunderbird), and the Graziadio School of Pepperdine University.

Harvard Business School has broadened its commitment to open-enrollment executive education programs since 1995 when Dean Kim Clark re-appointed Professor Earl Sasser as Associate Dean for Executive Education and hired Bob Fogel as Executive

Director of Executive Education. In 1997, Harvard Business School established the Executive Development Center as a non-profit corporation to handle its customized programs. Today there are five times as many off-campus, focused programs as there were in 1996.

The London Business School (LBS) is an interesting combination of pragmatism and scholarship. The school's programs include the Senior Executive Program, the Executive Development Program, the International Business Program, and a series of two-day master classes. The Centre for Management Development designs and runs company-specific programs. The Centre has grown significantly, and its success proves the expansive future of short courses that work.

Described as a blend between a business school and a consulting firm, the Institute for Management Development (IMD) is not a conventional part of an established university. Established by industry to serve industry, IMD is known for innovation in program development. IMD works as an outside catalyst to facilitate ongoing organizational learning, and to provide a sense of objectivity, as well as the competencies to help delineate specific learning programs.

The American Graduate School of International Management, better known as Thunderbird, caters to students from countries around the world, and emphasizes international business issues. During the last few years, Thunderbird has risen to prominence in the rankings of executive education. The school's 50-year history demonstrates that global business education is a specialty, and its programs illustrate its capability to customize educational experiences for many industries, as well as its global client base.

The Graziadio School of Pepperdine University focuses on the development of values-centered leaders and managers for a rapidly changing, global business environment. It provides seven distinctive masters-level programs, and one undergraduate degree-completion program. Courses are taught from a global perspective with an emphasis on managing change, whether personal, organizational, or technological. In less than three decades, The Graziadio School has become one of the ten largest professional business schools in the nation and is the leading provider of MBA talent on the West Coast.

Notes

1. *Bricker's International Directory 2000: University-Based Executive Development Programs, Peterson's Guides* (Lawrenceville, N.J., Nov. 1999).
2. Lori Bongiorno, "Corporate America's New Lesson Plan," *Business Week* (Oct. 25, 1993), R4. See also Jennifer Reingold, "Learning to Lead," *Business Week* (October 18, 1999) pp. 76–80.
3. Albert A. Vicere and Robert M. Fulmer, *Crafting Competitiveness* (Oxford: Capstone Publishing, 1996), p. 272.
4. Quoted in Bongiorno, "Corporate America's New Lesson Plan," p. R4.
5. Jennifer Reingold, with Mica Schneider in New York and Kerry Capell in London, "Learning to Lead," *Business Week* (Oct. 18, 1999), p. 77.
6. Vicere and Fulmer, *Crafting Competitiveness*, pp. 294–301.
7. Reingold et al., "Learning to Lead, p. 77.
8. Ibid., p. 78.
9. Reingold et al., "Learning to Lead," p. 76.
10. Reingold et al., "Learning to Lead," p. 80.
11. P. Lorange, "Creating a Learning Partnership: A Key to Competitive Advantage," IMD: Perspectives for Managers, Nov. 1995.
12. Reingold, et al., "Learning to Lead," p. 80.

10

Leadership Development Firms

New Faces of Competition

T he increased demand for leadership development has been coupled with the increased demand for online delivery of demonstrable results. This combination has brought a new breed of leadership development firms to the forefront of the business education field. These firms are not a new phenomenon, but they are uniquely constituted and prepared for the opportunities of a clientele that cannot and will not wait. Everyone from the general public to business leadership has become so accustomed to immediate responses and instantaneous results that the upstart leadership development "speedboats" are running circles around the traditional "ocean liners."

Multiple external consulting firms have come roaring into the spotlight and made solid names for themselves in the field of strategic leadership development. This chapter takes a closer look at the work for six such firms: the Society for Organizational Learning, the Center for Creative Leadership, the Center for Executive Development, Linkage, PROVANT, and Keilty, Goldsmith & Company.

Society for Organizational Learning

It is appropriate to lead off with the Society for Organizational Learning (SoL), because it is not a university or a consulting firm in the traditional sense. SoL and others like it are hybrids of a university and a consulting firm. This phenomenon is a natural result of the opportunities in the field, the growth of the market, and pressures from businesses.

Such hybrids are not truly business schools, but they do have some of the strengths and some of the resources of business schools. For example, Cam Danielson is president of Kelley Executive Partners, which is an executive education arm of the Indiana University Business School. It was spun off as a separate organization in January 1999. This is not unlike the way that Harvard set up this quasi-independent firm to run executive education. As this kind of evolution continues, we come to something like SoL, which began as a part of MIT, but for various reasons was spun off.

How SoL Began

The Center for Organizational Learning was founded in 1991 at MIT in Cambridge, Massachusetts. Its twofold mission was to facilitate collaboration among corporations committed to fundamental organizational change and to advance the state-of-the-art building of learning organizations. The Center's initial focus was on developing new learning capabilities in the areas of systems thinking, collaborative inquiry into tacit mental models, and nurturing personal and shared vision.

The consortium grew rapidly, and by 1995 it included 19 corporate partners: Amoco, AT&T, Chrysler, EDS, Federal Express, Ford Motor Company, Harley Davidson, Hewlett-Packard, IBM, Intel Corporation, Lucent Technologies, Merck & Company, National Semi-Conductor, Pacific Bell, Philips, the Quality Management Network (a consortium of healthcare organizations), Shell Oil Company, Texas Instruments, and US West.

Working in partnership with researchers at MIT, some of these companies engaged in a variety of significant organizational experiments. Through these experiments, the consortium explored the possibility of building learning capabilities in intact teams, developing new organizational learning infrastructures, transforming the assumptions and practices of executive leadership, and developing internal learning communities. Over time, companies have involved thousands of people in these experiments.

The group gradually came to understand that the goals and activities of such a diverse learning community did not fit into any existing organization. It became clear that there was no established theory and few models for organizing for learning, which could complement the theories and methods for developing new learning capabilities.

This led a group from MIT, the consortium companies, and affiliated consultants to embark on an extended process of reflection and inquiry into the Center's underlying purpose, organizational concepts, and structure in June 1995. This process was guided by Dee Hock, founder and former CEO of Visa International. The result was the creation of SoL, a nonprofit member-governed organization, that was designed to maximize the potential for self-organizing and continuous evolution.

What Is SoL's Purpose?

It was pretty clear to informed observers that MIT was uncomfortable with the pragmatic, consulting-based operation of the group that Peter Senge founded. The group was therefore spun off and is now functioning as an independent membership organization, but one that still attempts to bring together university-based researchers and consultants to accomplish some of its objectives.

SoL is a global learning community dedicated to building knowledge about fundamental institutional change through integrating research (disciplined pursuit of discovery and understanding); capacity building (developing new individual and collective capabilities); and practice (the application of concepts and tools in pursuit of specific ends).

Its purpose is to discover, integrate, and implement theories and practices for the interdependent development of people and their institutions.

SoL—A Mutual Benefit Society

SoL members are linked together as a network of colleagues. The intent is to bring them together in an effort to invigorate and integrate the knowledge-creating process in the area of fundamental institutional change. It is self-governed by a council elected by the members and composed equitably of the three membership groups.

SoL takes in funds through membership fees, meetings, educational offerings, services, products, and research contributions, as well as allocating funds to innovative research ideas in line with the overall research agenda. The intent is to link the researcher, practitioner, and consultant communities to realize their full potential and develop funding support as new ideas mature.

The members of SoL pool their efforts to participate in and contribute to a mutual learning community. This community effort functions under SoL's purpose and guiding principles. Becoming a member of SoL starts with commitment to its purpose and principles.

SoL has corporate, research, and consultant members. A fourth membership category, member-at-large, has been added to recognize individuals who, over time, have made or currently are making a significant contribution to the SoL community and do not fit into the other categories. This membership is by invitation. Working together, these various members contribute to SoL's in-depth projects that advance knowledge about fundamental institutional change. Such knowledge includes improved theory and method, enhanced capabilities, and enhanced practical results. Conceiving, undertaking, and sharing results from such projects is a core activity within the SoL community.

Members of SoL participate in a variety of community-building activities, including the Annual Members' Meeting, the Practitioners' Conference, and peer-learning processes designed by the members to enhance the continual learning. Members also participate in a self-governing community guided by the

SoL constitution. The constitution is SoL's legal foundation, and the processes laid out in the constitution govern SoL's operation. The society functions effectively only if SoL's members understand and are committed to their application, as well as to their continual testing and improvement.

SoL corporate members can derive the following benefits:

• Participate in a dynamic consortium of world-class companies collaboratively creating best practices in the area of organizational learning for sustained competitive advantage

• Develop internal capacity in the form of individuals and groups with competence in basic learning disciplines, including systems thinking, working with mental models, dialogue, personal mastery, and others being developed by SoL's members (corporate membership includes approximately $40,000 worth of slots in organizational-learning-related educational programs)

• Undertake significant organizational initiatives, both for the purpose of improving organizational learning capabilities and to contribute to general knowledge

• Gain access to outstanding capacity-building help and research support from SoL's consulting and research members

• Gain access to leading tools and methodologies under development within the SoL community

• Gain access to peer relationships with other like-minded practitioners striving for similar changes, from whom they can learn and gain support

SoL research members can derive the following benefits:

• Contribute to the continuing advance of theory, method, and empirical foundations relevant to SoL's purpose

• Have the opportunity to contribute to and study significant learning and change processes in member corporations

• Gain partnerships with other researchers, consultants, and practitioners to explore collaboratively critical "research domains" identified in SoL's integrated research agenda (such research domains include organization-wide transformation, assessing impacts of significant learning initiatives, and the role of leadership in transcending the barriers to such change)

 ♦ Access to organizational-learning-related courses and conferences

SoL consultant members can derive the following benefits:

 ♦ Contribute to the application of theories and methods, to their continuing development, and to building the capacity of member organizations to do likewise

 ♦ Collaborate with researchers and corporate members in long-term significant projects in member corporations (although membership is not a requirement for and does not in any way assure paid work in such projects)

 ♦ Become part of SoL's continuing capacity-building processes, with access to SoL's organizational-learning-related courses and conferences, in order to advance their professional skills and to develop the capabilities of others

SoL's Current Work

Members of SoL have the opportunity to participate in community-building activities, capacity-building activities, governance activities, and research initiatives.

Community Building Activities

 ♦ Annual SoL Members' Meeting—Provides the forum for members of the SoL community to come together to elect its governing council, set direction for the membership as a whole, and develop SoL's capacity for self-governance.

 ♦ The Annual Systems Thinker Conference is aimed at enabling cross-organizational learning and sharing the work and activities of members of the SoL community. It enables members to stay informed of the learning occurring within the practitioner community as well as the community as a whole.

Capacity building activities

◆ Five-day programs, four times a year, intended to provide an experiential exposure to organizational learning, concepts, methods, and tools, and to begin building capacity to support ongoing work. Corporate members are entitled to ten tuition-free slots per company.

◆ Executive Champions' Workshop—A small (fewer than 20 participants), three-day course, held twice a year (in the United States and in Europe), designed for executives (top one to three levels of their organization) who are in a position to champion organizational learning work in their organization. This course is intended to establish a network of senior executives able to support one another, as well as accelerate the spread of learning capabilities throughout large organizations.

◆ Foundations for Leadership—This workshop places a strong emphasis on the core-learning competency of creative orientation and the discipline of personal mastery. Participants spend significant time developing their personal and organizational vision. The special contribution of this leadership course comes as people discover the deep connections between personal mastery and systems thinking.

Governance Activities

◆ Elected representatives from corporate, consultant, and research communities meet approximately four times a year to deliberate key strategic issues for the entire community, establish an integrated research agenda and other over-arching goals, admit new members, and reflect on current governing processes.

◆ Quarterly meetings are held with two to three designees from each corporate member to insure alignment of the companies and the overall direction of the SoL community. They also provide infrastructure and processes for the community and capacity-building work of SoL.

SoL research initiatives fall into three major areas: large system change, leadership, and organizational learning assessment. For example, an initiative at Shell Oil involves senior executives, consultants, and researchers focused on understanding the transformation process required to produce a company-wide learning environment that enables outstanding business results. One component of the Shell project focuses on the profound shifts in the work of top management in a learning culture.

Ford, Harley Davidson, and Lucent have been working collaboratively for over two years with MIT's System Dynamics Group, with financial support from the National Science Foundation (NSF), to understand better the factors that determine success or failure in process improvement initiatives. This project is now entering a second phase to test whether new learning tools and methods can lead to more systemic approaches to process improvement.

In the area of leadership, an initiative is under way that includes a number of SoL corporate members focused on researching the forces that interact and the leadership roles required to initiate and sustain fundamental institutional change.

The Shell Foundation has allocated funds to support research in the area of "assessment," improving methods for understanding the personal, cultural, and economic impact of organizational learning efforts. A number of SoL member companies are participating in this research. This project builds on and extends the "learning history" research started at MIT.

Another initiative, "Creating Sustainable Learning Organizations," focuses on how present industrial organizations can meet their economic and social needs without compromising the ability of future generations to meet their own needs. The initiative derives its inspiration in part from a collaborative environmental movement started in Sweden, called "The Natural Step," which links business, scientists, government, and consumers. Several SoL companies have begun to work together to develop the conceptual framework and practical tools that would enable applying organizational learning principles to build healthy organizations for the long term.

Each of these initiatives includes a research component aimed at gaining generalizable new insights; a capacity-building component in which there are focused efforts aimed at developing new individual and collective learning capabilities; and a practical application component intended to produce significant business results.

Center for Creative Leadership[1]

When companies were asked to rank the providers of business education, instead of doing what they had traditionally done—talking about business schools—they ranked the Center for Creative Leadership (CCL) number seven overall and first in leadership. This nonprofit group has $56 million in revenue and has long been known for its strength in sharpening leadership skills. CCL does a great deal of research but also has profitable training programs with locations in Greensboro, North Carolina; San Diego; Colorado Springs; and Brussels.

CCL is a nonprofit educational institution whose mission is to advance the understanding, practice, and development of leadership for the benefit of society worldwide. The Center was founded in 1970 in Greensboro, North Carolina, through support from the Smith Richardson Foundation. H. Smith Richardson was a North Carolina native who ran the international Vick Chemical Company, producer of Vick's VapoRub. He was a visionary who believed that the success of an organization depended upon the ability of management to respond to change. Today, the Center is a leader in executive and management education.

In the 1970s, CCL began experimenting with feedback-intensive leadership development programs—programs that provide participants with a heavy dose of feedback in a supportive environment. Over the years, CCL has refined these programs and added new components to them, developed more sophisticated feedback tools and methods, and studied the impact of programs on participants. CCL has tried to understand how managers learn, grow, and change throughout their careers—not just from formal programs, but from the challenges in their working and non-working lives, the relationships they cultivate, and the hardships they encounter.

CCL provides a broad range of programs, including leadership course offerings, management publications, assessment tools, and organizational research. The program offerings address the needs of profit-making and nonprofit corporations, as well as government, military, and educational organizations. More than 21,000 executives and managers participated in CCL's programs in 1999.

The Center offers open-enrollment and customized programs drawing from 150 modules it has developed, which can be tailored to meet an organization's objectives. Courses are available for all levels of management and are delivered to small groups at one of CCL's offices or on site.

Courses include the following:

◆ *Leadership at the Peak*—an open-enrollment program for top managers, designed to help them analyze their leadership abilities and opportunities as they assume top management roles. Self-assessment tools are used to assist the executives in establishing developmental goals. This course uses multimedia simulation, one-on-one consultations with staff, and mock television interviews. *The Wall Street Journal* rates this course highest in the leadership development category for public-enrollment executive education.

◆ *Leadership and High-Performance Teams*—focuses on upper-middle to upper-level team leaders to build and lead successful teams and to create an environment and strategies that will foster team development

◆ *Looking Glass Experience*—helps experienced managers gain personal insight into strategic thinking, change management, teamwork, and interpersonal skills.

CCL is a leader in the development of assessment tools. It pioneered the use of 360-degree assessment and feedback in leadership and development programs. The center's Benchmarks tool uses staff, peer, and manager feedback to evaluate leadership skills.

The Campbell Development Surveys™ are standardized assessment instruments that assess leadership, team leader profile, team leader development, and organizational climate. The value of these tools is that they provide an objective evaluation of an individual's or organization's strengths and weaknesses. The results of the assessment evaluation are used to define development goals. These tools allow the individual to identify factors that potentially could derail an individual's career and assists them in creating a plan to strengthen weaknesses.

These assessment tools are incorporated into many of the center's classes. They are also available for an organization's internal use if administered by a certified testing professional.

CCL's Purpose

CCL defines *leadership development* as the expansion of a person's capacity to be effective in leadership roles and processes. *Leadership roles* and *processes* are those that enable groups of people to work together productively and in meaningful ways.

Three things are particularly notable about this definition of leadership development. First, CCL tends to see leadership development as the development of capacities within the individual. Most of CCL's research and educational programs are directed toward the individual. Even when CCL's interventions are directed at teams or at organizations, the primary goal is enhancing individual capacities.

Second, CCL tries to look at what makes a person effective in a variety of leadership roles and processes (rather than what makes him or her "a leader"). The assumption here is that in the course of their lives, most managers must take on leadership roles and participate in leadership processes, in order to carry out their commitments to larger social entities: the organizations they work in, the social or volunteer groups they are part of, the neighborhoods they live in, and the professional groups they identify with.

These leadership roles may be formal positions infused with authority to take action and make decisions (for example, a manager, an elected official, or a group's representative at a meeting), or they may be informal roles with little formal authority (the team member who helps the group develop a better sense of its capabilities, the person who organizes the neighborhood to fight rezoning efforts, the whistle-blower who reveals things that have gone wrong). Leaders may actively participate in recognized processes for creating change (such as serving on task forces or project teams, identifying and focusing attention on problems or issues, getting resources to implement changes) or in more subtle processes for shaping culture (telling stories that define organizational values, celebrating accomplishments). Rather than classifying people as "leaders" or "nonleaders" and trying to develop individuals into leaders, the center has assumed that everyone can learn and grow in ways that make them more effective in the various leadership roles and processes they take on. This process of personal development that improves leadership effectiveness is what the center understands leadership development to be about.

Third, CCL believes that individuals can expand their leadership capacities. The key underlying assumption in all of their work is that people can learn, grow, and change. CCL does not debate the extent to which effective leaders are born or developed. No doubt, leadership capacity has its roots partly in genetics, partly in early childhood development, and partly in adult experience. The focus is on how adults can develop the important capacities that facilitate their leadership effectiveness.

CCL—Scope and Scale

CCL's *Publications Guide* offers for sale more than 80 CCL books and reports on leadership, executive and management development, creativity, and human resource topics.

There is ongoing research by CCL's staff to identify new management issues and to develop tools and instruments to assess and evaluate issues. Recent research topics include global leadership, high-performing teams and emerging leaders.

In addition to its corporate headquarters in Greensboro, CCL has program offices in Brussels, Belgium; San Diego, California; and Colorado Springs, Colorado. There also are 20 affiliate groups around the world.

Center for Executive Development

The Center for Executive Development (CED), not to be confused with Harvard's Executive Development Center, described in Chapter 9, was established in 1987 by four former Harvard Business School professors. They had a simple question: Would it be possible to use the teaching skills and knowledge of strategy, leadership, and change to facilitate the learning they had gained over the years to facilitate the learning and growth of corporate clients in a unique way?

They were pretty sure that the answer was going to be yes. After all, for roughly ten years, each of them had been teaching for various corporate universities and other nonacademic executive education programs, in addition to teaching in the MBA and executive programs at Harvard. Furthermore, they were good at it. Their skills were widely sought—both in Europe and in North America.

But the question was not simply, could they make a living? Rather, they wanted to know whether they could make a unique and valuable contribution by forming a corporation and devoting their entire energies and focus to the learning and change needs of leaders in large organizations. There were some important parameters that conditioned this question. They assumed that the world probably did not need another strategy consulting business. What would be CED's competitive edge? They concluded that it had to have something to do with teaching excellence. The business schools were not producing thousands of worldclass case method instructors each year. Could CED use education as a tool to accelerate the strategic change companies so desperately needed?

As the founders of CED developed its business plan, they also saw little advantage in its simply being a speakers' bureau and hiring out themselves and others like them to teach a day here and a day there in corporate programs. Talented professors at leading business schools would continue to do that, as the founders had done during their decade on the Harvard faculty. CED's founders saw few barriers to entry in this niche. They concluded that the day-here, day-there business created no lasting relationships and provided limited impact. They chose to call this the "events" business and decided CED did not want to be in it.

Finally, they wanted to distinguish themselves from the business schools. They had no aspirations to credential their clients, nor did they wish to recreate the rigid, functionally driven focus of teaching and research in universities. Historically, universities have had mixed motives in dealing with corporations as their clientele. They like the extra revenue that their executive education offerings bring in. But they are not quite comfortable adopting a purely commercial mindset. No one ever got tenure at a top-ten school by being the world's best teacher of executives. The research interests of a small group of colleagues are much more powerful determinants of faculty efforts than the learning needs of corporations. Moreover, the academy has a cultural bias against serving corporations. At the university, the focus is on training individuals for positions of leadership in society. CED wanted to make companies, not individuals, its clients. CED's success would be judged by the contribution to the bottom line, by its ability to help client organizations create and sustain competitive advantage.

Their timing was fortunate. The intense competitive pressures of the last decade brought about by globalization and technological change caused every aspect of management, including executive education and training, to be scrutinized. The creation of CED coincided with a demand that corporate learning investments be tied to business need and corporate renewal. Many companies have shifted their training objectives away from building executives' individual skills and toward developing an aligned organization—one in which each member of the management team is energized by a deep understanding of the corporate ambition and a recognition of his or her own leadership role in advancing its common agenda. CED's most demanding clients recognize that the task of executive development is nothing short of changing the corporate mindset and behavior, and no renewal effort can succeed unless that task can be carried out. Consequently, they tie leadership development closely to corporate strategy and aim it directly at achieving specific results.

Education for Change

Doug Anderson, one of the founders and managing partner of CED, believes that the shift from individually based to organizationally focused executive education is fundamental, profound, and long-lasting. It is fundamental in that it causes corporations to rethink all of their training investments and their relationships with universities and consultants. It is profound in that it calls for new content and new learning models. CED predicts that it will be long-lasting in that it will continue to prove more successful in delivering results.

While there is and will continue to be a large demand for individually focused training, CED believes that the integration of strategy and leadership development represents the most exciting and rewarding niche of the executive development market. It has come to call this niche "education for change" and has adopted as its mission to become the world's premier provider. It has found that its content knowledge of strategy, leadership and change, together with its process skills in facilitating strategic dialogues, gives it a competitive advantage over either traditional training firms or strategy consultants. Its clients have come to value its ability to create "learning environments," wherein clients can work together to discover answers to their most important business challenges and opportunities, rather than having answers supplied by some consultant or taught out of a textbook.

Each assignment CED has undertaken is a customized offering and may include developing proprietary, in-house case studies of important strategic challenges. Typically, companies ask CED to develop an integrated set of offerings that may range from facilitating strategic off-sites for the top leadership team to rollouts of three-day seminars for their top 2,000 employees. These interventions are tied tightly to the corporation's most important change agenda. The theme for these programs can be any issue, but the 10 most common tend to be:

- Building strategic advantage
- Aligning and engaging the workforce
- Integrating the organization
- Articulating and enhancing shared values
- Increasing speed to market
- Achieving strategic cost leadership
- Innovating products and services

♦ Developing customer relationships
♦ Creating shareholder value
♦ Forging a competitive mindset

As is clear from this list, the offerings involve a mix of "hard" and "soft" issues. Building new skills can be a part of the development effort, but it is increasingly a smaller, rather than a larger part of the effort. More important are the development of a common mindset and a set of behaviors necessary to execute a new strategy. This is particularly important for companies in need of strategic transformation (as are many of the clients). These are companies that may once have been dominant in their markets but now, because of changed competitive conditions, find they must adapt or die.

Traditionally, consultants have responded to this transformation need in one of two ways, reflecting their professional bias as either content or process experts. Not surprisingly, a strategy consultant begins with a market study to force the client to face external reality. The consultant then outlines a set of strategic options and makes a compelling case for action. If the client buys into the recommendation, the consultant may be asked to recommend organizational changes. Typically, it is assumed that once the client gets the strategy and structure right, the needed behavioral changes will follow.

Process consultants take a different tack. They stress the importance of starting with behavior. If the corporation can commit to new ways of relating, then the clogged arteries of communication will be opened up, and employees and executives will find new energy and commitment to the enterprise. In this model, once the new behavioral paradigms are built, it is assumed that strategy and structure will follow.

CED finds it useful to combine approaches. Both the "strategy-structure" and "behavioral" schools have strengths, but each by itself has weaknesses as well. For example, the assumption that the "right" behavior necessarily follows the "right" strategy and structure is flawed. Getting the strategy "right" is rarely more than 50 percent of the job. Most executives will agree that a first-class job of execution is more important than a first-class strategy. Equally, the notion that a corporation will necessarily come up with brilliant new insights once its executives learn how to "relate" better would be dismissed by most clients as too "touchy-feely." CED believes it is vital to the credibility of the executive development effort to focus learning on the corporation's most important marketplace realities, and on leadership behaviors. CED has helped pioneer new learning methods that integrate both process and content interventions. Two such approaches are commonly referred to as "learn-use-teach" and "action learning."

Learn-Use-Teach

"Learn-use-teach" starts with the presumption that to change the mind of the corporation, the first step is to "get real." Executives must, in Jack Welch's phrase, "see the world as it is, not as they would like it to be." This often requires an exposure to leading-edge strategy concepts to help client organizations reframe their picture of current reality and fashion an action agenda for change. CED has found that strategic alignment is built most successfully when top management teams engage in a rigorous process of strategy development together, model the necessary behavioral changes in executing the new strategy, and then act as instructors in sharing their learning with the rest of the corporation. The final step is critical. By becoming "teachers," corporate executives deepen and extend their own learning. Rather than spinning in place, the "learn-use-teach" cycle, like the wheels on an automobile, becomes a form of locomotion that can take the corporation on a journey of discovery and development.

This approach has been used extensively, perhaps nowhere more successfully than with the Chrysler Corporation. By early 1988, executives at America's third largest auto maker had to face an uncomfortable reality: It was taking twice as long and costing twice as much to produce a new model car at Chrysler as it was at Honda. Moreover, the cars that were in the pipeline were tired extensions of the "K" car platform that would give the company no distinction in the market place. And even at that, Chrysler was not the low-cost producer.

Several CED partners were then asked by Tony St. John, the

corporate vice president of human resources, to develop a five-day program aimed at the top 500 managers of the corporation to help Chrysler get focused on its competitive realities. In developing the program, delivered at the American Club in Kohler, Wisconsin, CED worked closely with the corporation's senior officers, including Lee Iacocca, Jerry Greenwald, Bob Lutz, Ben Bidwell, and (later) Bob Eaton. CED developed separate proprietary in-house case studies on the Chrysler's position in the global auto industry, its product development process, its joint venture with Mitsubishi (called Diamond Star), its supplier relations, and its dealer and distribution network.

The program had a dynamic effect on "unfreezing" the corporation from old assumptions and forcing it to contend with the core realities in the marketplace. After the first session, it became known as "truth week," and there was a general demand that all of the officers of the corporation go through it as well as the senior managers. A separate session was scheduled for the 36 officers of the corporation, the first time they had all been together for a strategy meeting in Iacocca's tenure as chairman. As one wag put it, "the only time Iacocca had had us all together before was at the annual Christmas party."

The officer program was structured more as a strategy off site than as an executive development session. Nevertheless, both sessions were designed as "learning environments," with pre-reading assignments, concept development and breakout sessions, and action planning. Both strategic issues and leadership behaviors were confronted. The consultants' role was to keep the dialogue flowing in a constructive and open way, and to challenge the group when it failed to confront issues as directly or honestly as possible. The interaction with Chairman Iacocca in the final session proved to be especially important. A number of sacred corporate cows were led to the altar of reality and slaughtered, reframing the sense of what was possible for many officers who had previously expressed skepticism, and even cynicism, about the likely outcome of the off site. Even Iacocca sensed the behavioral challenge in adopting the new corporate mindset. Immediately following the officer session in Boca Raton, Florida, he convened a meeting of the top 600 managers at corporate headquarters. After calling on a number of officers to share their learnings from the off site, he added his own perspective on what it was going to take to bring about the strategic changes facing the corporation. In a dramatic conclusion, he declared, with little irony, "Let me put it in my own words: Intimidation is out, and participation is in—and I mean it!"

No five-day dip in the learning pool alone can bring about the kind of change that was to characterize Chrysler during the course of the next five years. But the executive development programs that were to follow and extend deep into the corporation were important catalysts for change. As the top officers began modeling the change, a new sense of excitement and energy flowed into the corporation. Leaders then cascaded their own individual learning as instructors in sessions for middle management, conscious of the power of the "learn-use-teach" model. As top management redirected its efforts and resources, a new structure, the platform team, became key to the effort to shrink the product development cycle. Senior executives who could not adapt their behavior to the new requirements of the platform team were invited to leave the corporation. The success of the concept was proved with the new Viper. The learning gained from Viper was used and extended in the LH program, and then the new truck, and then the redo of the Jeep. By the end of 1996, Chrysler had been selected as the "best managed company in the country" by *Forbes* magazine.

Action Learning

Chrysler's success with "learn-use-teach" could also be an illustration of "action learning." It is a term that is finding increasing use in the executive development marketplace. It is a way of marrying individual executive development with the need to solve a problem for the company. Here is how it works in its broadest application: The company identifies a problem that affects the whole organization, senior management selects a number of executives who form a problem-solving team, the team gets the training and the tools needed to assess the problem as well as the needed time, and it then reports back to senior management with a proposed solution.

In CED's experience, action learning done well can be one of the most powerful approaches to executive education. But it takes a bigger commitment and more resources than most companies are willing to offer, so it often fails.

One place where it did not fail was Citibank, which has employed one of the best approaches to action learning that CED has seen. Citibank called its action-learning program "Team Challenge." The program went into action only after John Reed, the chairman and CEO, and a five-member executive committee agreed on an issue that required action and a senior executive was selected to sponsor the project and report back on action taken. CED partners worked with then-CFO Victor Menezes, on team challenges involving such issues as reorganizing the corporate office, creating a global brand, and defining quality in a financial services environment as a reflection of Citibank's unique culture.

CED consultants involved in preparing for the Team Challenge reviewed reams of company data to determine what had been done before regarding the issue. Five or ten important documents were selected for inclusion in a briefing book designed to give the teams a fast start. The first parts of the book presented a clear definition of the problem and then a list of project deliverables—what the teams could realistically be expected to accomplish. A select group of people in the company who had the best understanding of the problem were also interviewed. The transcripts of those interviews went into the briefing book, and a list of additional interviews the teams wanted to carry out was also provided. A schedule of benchmarking visits was arranged, and three to five companies known to deal effectively with the issue were contacted to arrange appointments for the teams. All of this was done before the teams were convened for their first learning session.

Citibank assigned two groups to each project in order to get a diversity of views and to generate some healthy competition. By the time the teams—each typically eight to ten people—were selected, a 30-day schedule was designed of interviews to conduct and data to collect. The team members were pulled off their regular jobs for the 30 days and given carte blanche to go wherever they needed to in the bank to get their job done. They were in no way limited by the schedule suggested for them, but they first received four days of training to help them meld as a team and understand the issue in context.

As they proceeded with their work, they had two interim reviews with the sponsor and then a final presentation to Reed and whoever else Reed felt was directly affected. Throughout the process CED served as coaches to the teams and facilitators of the interim and final presentations. This form of action learning creates a powerful executive development experience and often results in breakthrough ideas. This is only possible because Citibank has committed many corporate resources into getting its Team Challenges right. What many companies fail to do is:

- Define the problem clearly
- Achieve an understanding of what the deliverables may be
- Scope out the issue in advance
- Give the participants enough time off from their regular jobs to solve the problem
- Make the lines of accountability clear, so the participants know they are reporting to top management
- Commit to take action and follow up to assure change happens

Give people a large and complex issue to solve without the preparation or time to do it, and they will throw up their hands in frustration. Give them the coaching, resources, and time necessary to reflect on their insights, and the problem-solving experience creates not only breakthrough solutions, but new wisdom for the corporation.

Organization-focused strategic leadership development is still in its infancy. One of the lessons CED has learned in their work with corporations is that knowledge alone is not enough. Companies facing new competitive threats and opportunities typically confront the need for deep change. Changing the mind of a corporation requires the development of new strategic understanding and new ways of working together. Insight must move to action. More than "getting real," clients must "get moving." CED managing partner Doug Anderson is fond of quoting the U.S. Army doctrine that "a lesson is not learned until a behavior is changed."

CED has pioneered many of the developments in the education for change market. Their partners have played leading roles in some of the most visible and highly successful corporate learning and transformation efforts of the last decade, including those of General Electric, Johnson & Johnson, Merrill Lynch, the Shell Learning Center, British Petroleum, Lucent Technologies, EDS, Progressive Insurance, Cigna, Novartis, GTE, PricewaterhouseCoopers, United Technologies, Florida Power and Light, and, of course, Chrysler and Citibank.

Linkage, Inc.

Founded in 1988, Linkage, Inc., is a leading global provider of educational programs, training and educational resources, consulting services, and research in the areas of corporate leadership, human resource development, organizational development, and training. Led by Phil Harkins and based in Lexington, Massachusetts, Linkage has grown rapidly in recent years, simultaneously expanding its size, reach, and international presence. Revenues have increased from $4.1 million in 1994 to $30 million in 1999. Linkage has delivered corporate education programs to more than 10,000 individuals, including employees of 80 of the Fortune 100 companies in 1999 alone.

Its comprehensive leadership solutions feature public conferences, workshops, and institutes, including the Global Institute for Leadership Development (GILD). The success of these programs is built in large part on the expertise of Linkage's leadership consultants and their extensive contacts with external thought leaders and management experts.

The Linkage-Bennis Research Study

In 1998, Warren Bennis, now a Linkage board member for more than a decade, conducted a research study with Linkage on the current state of leadership development. The findings of this study became the cornerstone behind Linkage's current practices in leadership education.

Together they found that:

♦ Nearly all respondents recognize the need to create internal bench strength, yet less than 44 percent have a formal process for identifying or developing high-potential employees.

♦ Companies that do identify and develop high-potential employees use structured leadership development systems.

♦ The programs that make a difference include one or more of the following three critical components: formal training, 360-degree feedback, and, most importantly, exposure to senior executives, including via mentoring programs.

The features with highest impact found by the Linkage-Bennis study are incorporated into Linkage's consulting projects, as well as into its workshops, institutes, and customized training programs.

Table 10.1   Highest Impact Features of Leadership Development Programs of Eight Major Manufacturing and Pharmaceutical firms

(in order of impact)
1. Action Learning
2. Cross Functional Rotations
3. 360-degree Feedback
4. Exposure to Senior Executives
5. External Coaching
6. Global Rotations
7. Exposure to Strategic Agenda
8. Formal Mentoring
9. Informal Mentoring
10. Internal Case Studies
11. Executive MBA
12. Accelerated Promotion
13. Conferences

Source: Giber, David; Carter, Louis; Goldsmith, Marshall; Foreword by Warren Bennis, *Linkage, Inc.'s Best Practices in Leadership Development Handbook* (Jossey-Bass/Linkage Press: 2000).

Connecting Best Practices with an Integrated Approach

In order to connect best practices in leadership training and education with the strategy and objectives of the client organization, Linkage provides customized and fully integrated consulting services for leadership development. This approach uses over a decade of best-practice research performed by Linkage.

This approach is known as the Integrated Leadership Development System. The eight-phase approach provides flexibility to allow an organization to choose how far and to what extent it would like to take the implementation.

Phase 1: Identify Need

The first phase is usually a diagnostic step in which the business reasons for creating a leadership system are identified. Critical to this stage is creating consensus and a sense of urgency regarding the need for leadership development. A future vision that is supported by management is key. Most of Linkage's leadership systems use an established model as a focal point for this phase. The best of these models capture the imagination and aspirations of the organization and its leaders. Some of the steps involved in this phase include:

- Conducting leadership diagnostics
- Obtaining input from key stakeholders by interview or focus groups
- Processing results and forming recommendations
- Holding an "implications session" with key stakeholders

Such steps were crucial to Linkage's work at American Home Products and Sallie Mae, in which the committed involvement by senior management teams has proved critical to the development systems' success.

Phase 2: Blueprint

Work at this stage includes creating a blueprint that defines the current state, the desired future state, and the action steps needed to close the gap between the two states. This is the map that helps guide consultants, instructors, and key stakeholders in executing the leadership development system. Some of the key components of this stage include:

+ Conducting a blueprinting session with key stakeholders
+ Identifying critical features of the leadership program or system
+ Building/modifying the existing leadership model

Linkage's work with such organizations as Kraft Foods and Brigham and Women's Hospital demonstrate how this blueprinting process can transform an organization's leadership focus and drive its agenda for change.[2]

Phase 3: Define Best Practices

In this phase, the current best practices in the client's area of interest or identified need (such as succession planning, coaching and mentoring, or diversity). Resources used for this phase include:

+ Research studies
+ Linkage publications
+ Industry surveys and assessments (conferences)
+ Leading consultants and educators
+ Assessment instruments

Phase 4: 360-Degree Assessment and Development Planning

Assessment is also a commonly shared element of all Linkage programs. Clearly, our industries have taken to heart the idea that leaders need to know themselves "from the inside out."[3] Assessments are delivered to both individuals and to teams. The assessment results are used to form development and action plans to drive change in businesses and leaders.

A multilevel battery of assessment instruments are used for this stage, including:

- Leadership Assessment Instrument (LAI)
- Complete Consultant
- Accelerated Competency System (ACS)
- Leadership Output Evaluation
- Personality Profiling Tools
- One-on-One Coaching and Development Planning around Assessment Results

Assessment results, particularly from multi-rater and personality profiling processes, can provoke resistance. Therefore, Linkage emphasizes the importance of individual coaching and feedback sessions to discuss assessment results.

Phase 5: Customized Leadership Program/Competency-Based Learning Experiences

This phase includes the use of existing or custom programs based on a client's identified leadership competencies and/or business issues. At this point Linkage creates a number of program offerings, including:

- Multi-day customized leadership program
- Modularized competency-based training
- Specific job-assignments/rotations
- Self study/online (resource guide)

These customized systems can vary immensely in scale, scope, and scheme depending on individual client needs. Companies like Northrop Grumman and Roche Bioscience have used such programs and focused skill-building courses based on their assessment results and individual development plans.

Phase 6—Action-Learning Teams

One of the most popular key features with highest impact of leadership development programs, alongside assessment and coaching, is action learning. Linkage provides opportunities to practice action learning by using leadership teams to address previously defined business issues. At American Home Products, for example, cross-functional teams work on genuine business issues facing the organization and conclude their projects by presenting recommendations and solutions to the Management Development Steering Committee.

Phase 7—On-the-Job Support and Development

Linkage's benchmark leadership development programs reach beyond the classroom and provide on-the-job reinforcement and support. Work in this phase defines the follow-up support that determines whether the learnings of the program will generalize and transfer to the job. The following tasks are accomplished in this phase:

- Coaches are identified and given focused development
- Mentoring relationships are established
- Coaching processes and systems are implemented

Linkage coaches work closely with leaders and their managers. At Ameritech, W. R. Grace, Scudder Kemper Investments, for example, coaching has played an integral part in leadership development, particularly in ensuring that assessment and classroom learning continue long after a program ends.

Phase 8—Ongoing Evaluation / Measuring the Impact

Evaluation is the capstone—the point at which the organization can gain insights into how to revise and strengthen a program, eliminate barriers to its reinforcement and use in the field, and connect the intervention back to the original goals to measure its success. Linkage provides several levels of evaluation of the leadership development system:

- Customer and employee satisfaction
- Financial measures
- Resolution of business issues
- Training evaluations

Value-Added Leadership Education Offerings

Linkage also provides a full scope of value-added leadership education offerings. These include conferences, public workshops, and satellite programs. The following represent some of the most successful offerings:

♦ *Global Institute for Leadership Development (GILD)*: Co-chaired by Warren Bennis and Phil Harkins, GILD provides high-level programs and services targeted at the long-term leadership development within the world's foremost organizations. One of GILD's programs is the Emerging Leader Program (ELP), which is an accelerated leadership development process.

♦ *The Executive Leadership Development Program*: This program, Linkage's core leadership workshop, is an experiential, interactive session that provides proven models, tools, and processes to help participants become more effective leaders. It is designed to provide an intensive three-day session that helps leaders to continuously improve skills, increase knowledge, and develop their leadership competencies.

♦ *The Leadership Development Conference (LDC):* Held annually in the United States, Canada, and Europe, LDC brings together human resource executives, corporate leaders, line executives, and practitioners who recognize the bottom-line value of developing their organization's existing and future leaders and who are aggressively working to build effective leadership development processes. The conference provides attendees with access to proven tools and techniques, as well as revolutionary approaches to developing leaders and leadership effectiveness.

♦ *Leadership Assessment Instrument (LAI)*: Developed by Linkage in partnership with Warren Bennis, the LAI measures the critical capabilities required for high-performance leadership across all industries and functions. The LAI is available as both a self-managed assessment and a 360-degree assessment.

♦ *Complete Consultant:* Based on the practical experiences of top consultants and research undertaken by Linkage, the Complete Consultant is an assessment instrument that helps human resource and organizational development professionals clarify their consulting roles and target their development efforts.

♦ *Action Research*: Linkage's Research Group provides benchmarking and best-practice research to help guide decision-making on key leadership and organizational development issues, bringing the industries' key leaders and best practitioners to work directly with the client.

♦ *Best-Practice Handbooks*: Linkage Press publishes best-practice handbooks that detail what the world's leading practitioners are doing by way of leadership development, organization development, and human resources development. These handbooks have received critical acclaim by leading experts, senior executives, and thought leaders around the world for being highly informative and clearly written. They include all of the tools, instruments, models, forms, and benchmarking information necessary to successfully implement a best-practice leadership development initiative.

How Linkage Sees the Future of Leadership Development

As organizations become more complex and dynamic, so do their leadership development programs. Globalization, productivity declines, competitive pressures, and customer demands are paving the way for more integrated leadership programs and for correspondingly larger development budgets. Linkage believes that this trend will continue for a minimum of five years. Although the leadership development industry is far from recession-proof, fundamental demographic dictates should counterbalance sudden corporate budget restrictions. The pool of 30- to 45-year-olds will continue to shrink through the year 2015, and corporations that refuse to invest in leadership development will soon find they have no leaders at all.

As for the programs and systems themselves, Linkage sees an increasing move toward higher technology. The attraction of distance and self-managed learning is already intensifying, thanks to the advances in computer technology and the Internet. Linkage has found, though, that high-tech approaches to leadership "soft skills" rarely succeed unless paired with in-person training in the classroom or on the job. Assessment and evaluation, however, are a natural fit for technological approaches, and studies by Linkage, *Training* magazine, and others find that a majority of best-practice organizations do use their Intranet and information technology systems to obtain 360-degree developmental feedback for their leaders. As organizations become more global and electronic communication more ubiquitous, leaders are growing increasingly impatient with papers and forms and increasingly eager to receive feedback and developmental support that are comprehensive, immediate, and readily exploited on a global scale.

Recognizing that every organization's leadership needs are distinctive and discrete, Linkage refuses to provide its clients with inappropriate generic offerings. From world-class institutes to custom-built systems, Linkage's tailored, full-service solutions provide the flexibility and consultative expertise that deepen the specific skills, perspectives, and competencies each organization should expect of its current and emerging leaders. By combining action learning, 360-degree feedback, and clear links to senior-level strategy and commitment, Linkage has committed to building teams of leaders who can understand their customers' demands today and drive strategy and action to anticipate their demands tomorrow.

PROVANT

PROVANT, based in Boston, was established in 1998 with nine operating companies and revenues of approximately $90 million. The initial idea was to bring together a critical mass of training and development content and technology, enabling companies to draw the attention of three stakeholders: Wall Street, large companies who were current or future customers, and future acquisition targets.

PROVANT's sales and growth record have been phenomenal. In one year they became the biggest player in the training and development industry. In 1999, their revenue was $250M and growing.

PROVANT's focus is on "people and performance" issues,

and it was the first "roll-up" in this highly fragmented industry. Several of the operating companies have supporting leadership development consulting and training products and services. These include offerings from J. Howard that specialize in diversity and "inclusive workforces," Educational Discovery's "emotional literacy" and financial products (The Accounting Game), Novations' Four Stages Career Stages framework, MOHR's supervisory training products in the retail industry, and AMI's supervisory and management products.

Recently, the Results-Based Leadership Company was formed as a PROVANT start-up that focuses exclusively on leadership and executive development issues.

Key Competencies

PROVANT's key value proposition is service to their customers. They make it easy for their clients to source a variety of content options through one provider (training, consulting, and the like). They also make it easy for their clients through the technology options provided to them (Internet, CD, classroom, etc.)

PROVANT's program offerings cover the spectrum of "people and performance" issues. They provide strategy and organization design consulting, career management, interviewing and selection, leadership development, sales, competency development, Web-based technology services, project management, public speaking and communication skills, diversity, and culture and change management.

PROVANT clusters its offerings into three categories:

1. *Content providers*—Career management, leadership, diversity, culture, change management, project management, etc.

2. *Industry-focused providers*—Telecommunications, manufacturing, retail, etc.

3. *Technology providers*—Web-enablers, CD-ROM applications, online learning, etc.

Most other efforts, notably Achieve Global and Franklin-Covey, have attempted to integrate operating companies into one "face to the customer." PROVANT does not believe so far that this approach has worked. Entrepreneurs have not integrated with one another easily, and brand image has been lost. Therefore, PROVANT is not attempting to go this route. PROVANT desires to facilitate synergy (versus integration) through sharing technology, sharing of distribution channels, and creating new products and services through collaborative partnerships and through customer referrals.

Investment in a Leadership Start-Up Firm

Jack Zenger, president of PROVANT, and Norm Smallwood, a co-founder of Novations, wrote a book—*Results-Based Leadership*—with Dave Ulrich (professor at the University of Michigan) that was published in May 1999 by Harvard Business School Press. Rather than acquiring a leadership company, PROVANT invested in the creation of a start-up: The Results-Based Leadership Company (founded on the principles described in the book).

Their work creates a leadership-alignment system that increases leadership brand for a company. Accomplishing this involves:

1. Identifying and evaluating current business results and leadership development practices
2. Senior executives establishing clear metrics that link to desired results in four balanced result areas: customer, investor, employee, and organization
3. Aligning leaders at every level by having them prepare an integrated performance and development plan that links to these metrics and identifies critical attributes (competencies) that must be developed to achieve them
4. Ensuring that enabling support processes such as human resources, finance, and information technology facilitate desired results
5. Holding all leaders accountable for results by rigorously monitoring and tracking results

Insights on Helping Executives Change

Like many of the profiled firms, PROVANT has developed a few insights on helping executives change. They are:

1. Importance of having a context for leadership development. It is not about individuals developing more and more competencies, but it is about developing specific competencies related to the delivery of desired results.

2. Importance of action-learning approaches versus traditional classroom training. The best learning occurs when there is a real need and an intent for organizational improvement. Work-Out™ type approaches are real and therefore better than bringing in a parade of consultants and professors.

3. When possible, making the learning real-time and online. Just-in-time approaches to skill building are already possible. AMI has developed a series of CD-ROM products that allow a leader to review the how-tos of difficult situations such as hiring, firing, and interviews.

PROVANT is excited about the concept of integrating attribute development (competencies) with business results—and in the process improving the leadership brand of a company. Recent research (Stern Stewart and others) on intangible factors in determining a price/earnings multiple shows that between 15 and 45 percent of the multiple hinges on leadership factors. The Results-Based Leadership Company of PROVANT will be the leader in moving leadership development from an individual competency-building approach to an organization system that builds leadership brand and improves the value of a stock. PROVANT aims to help shift the leadership agenda in this way over the next decade.

Keilty, Goldsmith & Company

Keilty, Goldsmith & Company (KGC), based in San Diego, is often recognized as a "world leader" in the field of specially designed leadership development, coaching, team-building, and multirater leadership feedback. They are one of the few firms in the field with extensive experience in working with top executives. Since 1981, their clients have included many of the world's leading corporations, and they have been asked to work directly with over 50 CEOs and top management teams. They have also completed major volunteer assignments for national and international human service organizations. A recent publication (by Penn State University), *The State of the Practice: Executive Education and Leadership Development*, listed KGC as one of the seven key nonuniversity providers of customized executive and leadership development in the United States.

Leadership feedback and development processes that KGC has helped to develop or implement have impacted over one million people in over 70 different organizations around the world. The firm is one of few currently performing extensive "before-and-after" studies on leadership behavior (described below in more detail). KGC's clients have included many of the world's leading corporations, such as American Express, Andersen Consulting, AT&T, BellSouth, Chase Bank, Dow Chemical, Enron, GE Capital, Goldman Sachs, Johnson & Johnson, KPMG, McKinsey, Motorola, Pitney Bowes, Pfizer, SmithKline Beecham, Southern Company, Sun Microsystems, UBS, Warner-Lambert, and Weyerhaeuser.

KGC's Structure

KGC is structured in a uniquely "virtual" way. Although led by co-founder Marshall Goldsmith (coauthor of this book) out of San Diego, the approximately 60 KGC consultants live around the country and the world. They each work on projects from "virtual offices" located at or near their homes. This allows KGC to keep overhead costs low—and keep more consultants located closer to the clients.

KGC can "grow" or "shrink" based on client needs. Aside from the core staff, an additional network of experts can be brought on board to serve clients better. For this reason, Goldsmith and KGC maintain excellent relationships with other service providers in the field. In a recent example, KGC secured a government contract for executive development and succession planning. Because succession planning specifically is not KGC's "bread-and-butter," a highly-renowned succession planning expert (and his staff) were added to the KGC team temporarily to serve this client. Larger-scale consulting firms would not have this same luxury of putting together an "all-star" team—they would be limited to their staff on hand. KGC therefore finds this unique "virtual firm" solution to be a superior model.

KGC consultants each run a "business within a business," and each of them is compensated based on their contributions to KGC projects (they do not draw salaries). Most of them also run their own consulting operations both independently of and/or joined with KGC. Consultants can therefore be working on either KGC-sponsored or independent projects. This structure allows KGC to maximize the "intrapreneurial" feel of the firm.

Two standard KGC processes are the Leader of the Future process, used for developing leadership competencies and multisource feedback systems; and the Executive Coaching process, one year of guaranteed coaching for executives and high-potentials (used most often after the Leader of the Future Process).

Approach—The Leader of the Future Process

KGC's Leader of the Future process is designed to help make an organization's vision, values, and change strategy "come to life" in leadership behavior. The way in which the process is implemented varies from organization to organization, but the philosophy is similar. Senior management describes the values of their organization and their vision for the future. The Leader of the Future process helps translate this vision for change into demonstrated attitudes and behaviors.

Individual leaders get confidential feedback on how they are perceived in terms of demonstrating desired behaviors on the job. The corporation gets summary feedback on how the entire leadership team is perceived. The individual and the corporation receive affirmation in perceived areas of strength and develop action plans for change in perceived areas for improvement. The individual and the organization's leaders then follow up with co-workers to ensure the successful implementation of their action plans.

The Leader of the Future process provides a system that helps organizations and their leaders develop in a manner that supports the organizational change strategy. This process has been used in over 70 organizations, and custom-designed Leadership Inventories have impacted over a million people. The process generally includes the following steps:

1. Meet with representatives of the organization to understand the vision, values, broad organizational goals, and change strategy.

2. Work with the organization to develop a profile of the Leader of the Future. This profile is typically composed of two parts. The first part centers on values or principles that are held dear to the company and involve issues such as integrity, quality, and respect for people. (Johnson & Johnson calls these the "Credo Values." American Express identifies them as their "Blue Box Values.") The second part identifies a set of core competencies and leadership behaviors crucial to future success. These might include such issues as communication across organizational boundaries and dealing with individual behavior that undermines teamwork.

3. Help the organization design a Leadership Inventory to reinforce the desired characteristics of the Leader of the Future. This profile aligns organizational goals and change strategy to individual performance expectations of leaders responsible for implementing change in the organization.

4. Design a leadership training process that is consistent with the organization's needs. (The length of leadership workshops varies with corporate needs and resources—from several hours to three days.) The goal is to provide maximum behavioral change with minimal time spent in training.

5. Distribute Leadership Inventories to program participants before the program is conducted.

6. Prepare a confidential, individual feedback report for each participant and a summary of all reports for the team or the organization.

7. Conduct a leadership workshop in which participants learn how they can better help their organization achieve its strategic change objectives, learn how to implement the process, receive confidential one-on-one feedback on their perceived effectiveness, and develop action plans in identified areas for improvement.

8. Follow up with the corporation and team on the summary feedback and on participants' suggestions for the corporation.

9. Follow up with participants (on a regular basis) to help ensure that the individual action plans they developed (in the program) are being implemented. A customized minisurvey process can be used to measure the effectiveness in the areas selected by the individual.

10. Conduct a follow-up feedback process (in approximately one year) so those participants can measure perceived behavioral change. This process has been shown to produce significant measurable positive changes in leadership effectiveness. In a study CED conducted, 89 percent of leaders following this process were seen as more effective. In contrast, over half of those leaders who did not follow this process were seen as unchanged or less effective.

The Leader of the Future process, while quite specialized, can be used effectively with other standard executive education experiences. Johnson & Johnson, KPMG, and Warner Lambert, for example, use the process in conjunction with action-learning exercises in their leadership development programs.

The Executive Coaching Process

Executive coaching has become a major component of KGC's business. In the past several years, executive coaching contracts have made up over 50 percent of KGC revenues. Coaching is not just for the "troubled" executive anymore. Entire senior management teams and "high-potentials" are also receiving coaching attention.

Clients prefer KGC's "money-back guarantee" approach to

coaching. Clients do not pay for a year, and they do not pay unless their executives improve. Finally, improvement is determined by those working with/for the executive, not the executive alone. (This process is further described in the article "Coaching for Behavioral Change" in the fall 1996 edition of *Leader to Leader*.)

In implementing the Executive Coaching Process, KGC:

1. Meets with representatives of the organization to understand the history behind the request for coaching

2. Meets with the person to be coached and the person's manager to help ensure their commitment to the process and that the proper "chemistry" exists between the person to be coached and the person who will be the coach

3. Develops a Leadership Inventory (or use an existing inventory) that is designed to meet the organization's and individual's unique needs

4. Interviews key stakeholders who may interface with the person being coached (as is suggested by the organization). These interviews are designed to both gather information and to help the key stakeholders help the person being coached.

5. Provides 360-degree feedback to the person being coached (using the Leadership Inventory)

6. Helps the person and his/her manager identify key areas for improvement

7. Provides coaching in identified areas for improvement and change strategies

8. Helps the person develop an action plan and follow-up strategy

9. Conducts mini-surveys and 360-degree follow-up surveys to help document improvement and identify remaining areas of concern

10. Provides ongoing coaching

11. Has ongoing dialogue with the person's manager (if desired)

12. Conducts a second 360-degree Leadership Inventory survey (with key stakeholders) in 12 months

13. Works with the person to develop a plan for ongoing continuous improvement

14. Meets with the person and the person's manager to assess the success of the project and reinforce improvement

The Impact of Follow-Up on Leadership Effectiveness

One unique aspect of KGC's work is that they implement ongoing follow-up to ensure that development is a process of continuous improvement, not a "program-of-the-month" or one-time event. Follow-up systems are a critical part of both the Leader of the Future and the Executive Coaching processes.

The graphs below represent composite follow-up data of executive groups from five major companies. At each organization, executives received multisource feedback, selected areas for development, created action plans, and strongly encouraged to respond and follow-up with their respondents regularly.

Approximately three to six months after their original feedback session, the executives participated in a follow-up "minisurvey" (see Figure 10.1 sample). Mini-surveys are short, tailored multisource assessments aimed at measuring change in leadership effectiveness over time. Each mini-survey contains questions relating to the executive's change in overall leadership effectiveness, follow-up behavior, and several specific self-selected items relating to his or her own personal areas of development.

The key item on the survey was, "Do you feel this person has become more/less effective as a leader in the past six months?" Respondents rated the executives on a "-3" (less effective) to a "+3" (more effective) scale.

The results are quite impressive. Overall, 42 percent of the executives improved at a combined "+2" and "+3" level. An impressive 76 percent improved at a "+1," "+2," or "+3" level. Only 4 percent got worse.

However, a striking difference appears when the results are separated between those who followed up with others and those who did not. (Respondents were asked to indicate if the executive had followed up with them or not about what he or she learned from their leadership feedback.)

Figure 10.1   Sample Focus 360-Degree Mini-Survey Questionnaire

Manager: Demonstration Manager

Answer each question below:

1. My relationship to this manager is: (check one)

    _____ Direct Report   _____ Peer

2. In the past six months, this manager followed-up with me on what he/she learned from the Leadership Effectiveness Inventory feedback: (check one)   _____ Yes _____ No

3. Do you feel this person has become more/less effective as a leader in the past six months? (circle one)

    −3 −2 −1 0 1 2 3

    less   more

    effective   effective

Please rate the extent to which this manager has increased/decreased effectiveness on the following areas of development in the past six months (Circle one response for each item.)

Individual Items

1. Genuinely listens to others   −3 −2 −1 0 1 2 3

2. Avoids destructive comments about other people or groups

    −3 −2 −1 0 1 2 3

Additional Comments:

What has this manager done in the past few months that you have found to be particularly effective?

What can he/she do to become more effective as a manager in the areas of development not above?

Forty-nine percent of leaders who followed up improved at a "+2" and "+3" level, compared to 35 percent of leaders who did not. Eighty-four percent of leaders who followed up improved at a "+1," "+2," and "+3" level, versus 66 percent of those who did not follow up.

Clearly, following up with others is key to changing people's perceptions of leadership effectiveness. KGC has also previously demonstrated that the amount of follow-up is correlated

Figure 10.2   Change in Overall Leadership Effectiveness

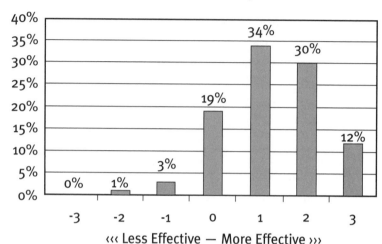

‹‹‹ Less Effective — More Effective ›››

**Figure 10.3   Change in Overall Leadership Effectiveness
Executive Followed Up with Others**

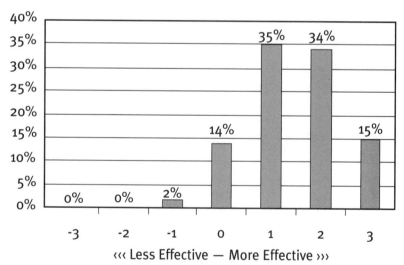

‹‹‹ Less Effective — More Effective ›››

Figure 10.4 Change in Overall Leadership Effectiveness Executive Did Not Follow Up with Others

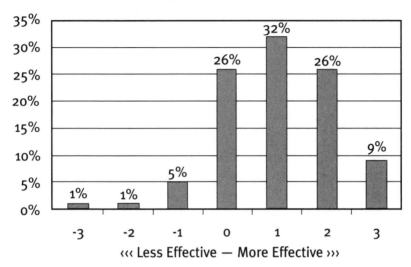

positively with change in leadership effectiveness. Due to these findings, all of KGC's work includes follow-up processes with each program they create.

Six Keys for World-Class Executive Education

Despite the relatively brief history of the move from individual to organization-focused executive development, these pioneering firms offer great insight on what constitutes best practice. The CED says it most effectively with their six pointers for programs that get results:

1. *Distinguish between executive education and other training.* Executive programs typically aim at the top 2 percent of a company's employees. These people have mastered basic management skills, they usually have MBAs or equivalent training, and now they are facing the challenge of providing effective leadership to the company. Their development programs will look

much different from a course in, say, "finance for the nonfinancial manager." As corporations engage in *education for change*—changing the corporate mindset and behavior—programs do not look at all like traditional training sessions.

2. *Recognize that the process and the content are equally important.* Companies can no longer afford executive education as entertainment or simply as a "recognition" event. It is about change, and the process matters. But content also matters. Change will not last outside the corporate university unless it can be translated into action on the job.

3. *Focus programs on creating a shared view of the company's problems and opportunities.* What better opportunity can there be to confront your company's internal and external issues than when you have assembled the company's key managers in a learning environment?

4. *Give top managers a role as teachers.* The best executive education programs are organized around the company's most critical issues. It may be that senior management has not yet formulated an action plan to deal with those issues and is expecting one to evolve out of the program, or it may be that management has a strategy to present during the program. Either way, the direct involvement of the top people is essential. Besides, the presenters frequently learn more than the participants. Often corporate leaders go away from the experience with renewed energy that infuses the entire organization.

5. *Require participants to make tangible on-the-job commitments.* The measure of an executive development program is much greater than those end-of-the-course evaluations trainers like to give out. A series of engaging speakers will evoke high scores, even if no company issues are ever addressed and no change happens. The real impact of the program lies in the participants' commitments to take concrete action back on the job and the mechanisms that are put in place to follow up on those commitments.

6. *Reinforce the lessons of the program in the company's day-to-day operations.* If the choice is between an excellent program with weak on-the-job reinforcement and an average program whose

lessons are nurtured within the company, take the latter. With all the attention that was paid to General Electric's Work-Out™ program, one factor that is often missed is the extent to which the company lives the open and boundary-free values that the program fosters. The program would have led only to cynicism if the company were not ready to adopt those values.

Notes

1. Information about CCL gathered from: Kristine Mayer Brands, "The Center for Creative Leadership," *Strategic Finance*, 5 (Nov. 1997), p. 72; anonymous, "The Search Process," *Journal of Business Strategy*, 5 (Sept./Oct. 1997), p. 4; David W. Bracken, review of "The Center for Creative Leadership Handbook of Leadership Development," *Personnel Psychology*, 52 (Summer 1999), pp. 476–79.
2. Phil Harkins, *Powerful Conversations: How High-Impact Leaders Communicate*, McGraw-Hill, New York, 1999.
3. Kevin Cashman, *Leadership from the Inside Out* (Provo, Utah: Executive Excellence Publishing, 1998).

11

The Strategic Challenge

lthough the organizations profiled in this book have taken different paths to excellence in leadership development, there are principles that account for their success. Saturn may spend less per person on the developmental activities they provide to develop leaders at all levels than the World Bank, but both emphasize the importance of leadership for their future success. The Center for Creative Leadership does not offer degrees but shares a commitment to executive development with the Harvard Business School and other academic institutions we have discussed. They share a focused concern for pragmatic research with a new breed of business schools and hybrid organizations like CCL and the Society of Organizational Learning (SoL). As we have previously stated, each of the groups discussed takes great care to ensure that its leadership development process fits the strategic initiatives and specific culture in which it operates. This chapter focuses on the strategic role of leadership development and how enlightened CEOs use a five-stage model to leverage their efforts to bring about cultural change or to launch new initiatives.

Perhaps the most significant finding of our research and the key focus of this book is that "leadership development is closely tied to and used to support the business strategy of the organization." Each of the best-practice partners profiled in Chapters 2–8 demonstrated the importance of this tie. Support from a CEO is not based on some esthetic appreciation and respect for education or learning. It is based, rather, on a firm conviction that leadership development programs are the powerful levers that will bring about change and strategic alignment. They are an investment, on which the return will be great.

Increasingly, the leadership development process is seen as a source of competitive advantage. During his two decades at the helm of General Electric (GE), Jack Welch used Crotonville as a "staging ground for corporate revolutions." Tremendous growth, shrinking employment worldwide, and significant delayering of the organization have caused an enormous cultural shift within GE. With fewer layers of management, individuals receive fewer vertical promotions. More and more people find themselves responsible for persuading those over whom they have no formal authority. Leadership skills become essential. This had to be reflected in the design and delivery of GE's program offerings. Courses at Crotonville focus on the company's major themes such as globalization and key initiatives such as Work-Out™, the Change Acceleration Program (CAP), and Six Sigma. At the annual Boca meeting, the top 500 operating managers worldwide help set GE's major themes and initiatives for the year. At the end of the year, all corporate functions including Corporate Leadership Development are measured on their ability to support the current initiatives.

Ralph Larsen, chairman and CEO at Johnson & Johnson (J&J), champions the Executive Conference program. While using decentralized decision-making to develop the details of a conference theme, Larsen exercises his leadership by articulating concerns and themes he feels the entire corporation needs to address. Larsen believes that a shortage of leaders is potentially the greatest obstacle to the growth objectives of the firm. He and other senior executives see leadership development as one vehicle to give top leaders from J&J's businesses a new view of their enterprises and of each other. The organization's first formal corporate development programs, Executive Conference I ("Setting the Competitive Standard") and II ("Creating Our Future") focused on developing leadership and new thinking patterns. J&J believes it is critical that any discussion of education and development start with the business objectives of the company.

Larsen has focused on three basic objectives: top-line growth, enhanced competitiveness, and organizational excellence.

At Arthur Andersen, the mission of the Partner Development Program (PDP) is "to help partners worldwide acquire and build the knowledge, skills, and behaviors required to be valued and trusted business advisers in an ever-changing marketplace." To meet the needs of a business that continues to diversify and globalize, the PDP must link closely to Arthur Andersen's business strategy to stay in sync with current objectives.

As Lew Platt saw Hewlett-Packard (HP) moving from its traditional emphasis on measurement devices to a new world of computers and related products, he recognized a need to rethink the way in which the company did business and to reassess the interpretation of The HP Way to maintain its growth and competitiveness. New CEO Carly Fiorina is both a result of this shift in thinking and the cause of continued evolution. As HP's organization becomes more global, its need grows for its leaders to reflect HP's global customer base more closely. Since the generation of leaders who built HP is now retiring, a new cadre of leaders has to be prepared. The Business Leadership Development group created an Accelerated Management Development program to address issues of diversity, the changing mission statement, and how executive education helps create solutions that are in the best interests of the decentralized organization.

Cor Herkstroter, the (now retired) chairman of the Royal Dutch Shell/Shell International (Shell), asked his top 50 or 60 leaders to address the question of how to improve financial performance. It became clear that cost pressures around the world were creating a strain. The leaders initiated a restructuring at the central offices and undertook a service-company review. This review showed that the matrix governance structure needed to be minimized and shifted from a function-and-region (geography) focus to a line-of-business focus.

The Shell Committee of Managing Directors (CMD) decided that a new leadership development process could be a catalyst for organizational change. The Leadership and Performance (LEAP) program was created to be a major enabler of this transformation. Creating leaders at all levels throughout the organization, teaching the hard and "harder" skills (traditionally known as the "soft" skills), and doing it quickly and on a large scale would enable Shell to define a new way of doing business.

As the World Bank (the Bank) celebrated its 50th anniversary, a concern surfaced about the need to change the group's mission. When James Wolfensohn joined the Bank as president, he evolved the mission statement to reflect not only the importance of knowledge and financial resources, but also to address the ultimate goal of world poverty reduction. To carry out this mission and begin the change process within the Bank, the organization articulated its five guiding goals, to be:

1. More responsive to clients
2. Accountable for changing results
3. Efficient and cost-effective
4. Able and willing to work in partnership
5. Committed to professional and managerial excellence

To address the principle of commitment to professional and managerial excellence, the Bank made a major investment in re-creating executive education efforts. The result was the creation of the Executive Development Program (EDP), which all managers of the bank now attend. The program is a unique partnership with the Harvard Business School, the Kennedy School of Government, Stanford University, INSEAD, and IESE.[1]

Making Leadership Development Strategic

The pronouncement of a strategic vision is not enough to bring about change or to tie leadership development to the goals of a CEO. Our data suggest that a five-step process is necessary to make the change a reality. Those five steps are described in the following pages. Table 11.1 summarizes examples of corporate leadership programs that address each of these steps.

Awareness

Creating a process to build leadership skills, abilities, and techniques has pushed best-practice organizations to look inter-

Table 11.1 Strategic Leadership Development

Awareness	Anticipation	Action	Alignment	Assessment
Arthur Andersen: Data Driven (feedback and survey)	**Shell:** Scenario Development	**General Electric:** Work-Out™, Change Acceleration Process	**Johnson & Johnson:** 360-degree Feedback Ties to "Standards of Leadership" and Succession Plans	**Arthur Andersen:** The Search for Quantifiable Measures
Shell: Committee of Managing Directors & Global Research Consortium	**Johnson & Johnson:** Creating Our Future	**Johnson & Johnson:** Action Learning at Exec and Mid Management	**General Electric:** Session C & Corporate Property	**Shell:** The Challenge of 25:1 Returns
	Hewlett-Packard: Preparing a New Generation of Leaders		**Hewlett-Packard:** Strategic Needs for Diversity & New Leadership Models	**World Bank:** Inside and Outside Evaluation

nally and externally for approaches that work. Each of the best-practice leadership development activities demonstrates extensive awareness of external challenges, emerging business strategies, developmental needs within the organization, and other leading organizations methods of meeting the challenges of current and emerging leaders.

The first step in designing leadership development is soliciting direct input from internal customers. Best-practice organizations also study external organizations and opinion leaders when defining their leadership competencies.

Arthur Andersen uses both internal and external data to determine the learning and development needs of its partners. Internal data is sought from client-satisfaction surveys, employee-satisfaction surveys, Arthur Andersen service-category strategies, and upward feedback.

To ensure that Shell's LEAP process does not simply react to the immediate needs of the business, the team has an ongoing conversation with the CMD about corporate transformation. To comprehend business unit needs fully, LEAP staff meets with business executives to understand their needs and explain the program offerings that may fit those needs. LEAP staff and the business executive negotiate a contract for the program; create budgets for the team project; and set time expectations, goals, and outcomes for the process

To gather external perspectives, Shell is a member of the Global Research Consortium. This group gives its members the opportunity to hear and discuss the latest knowledge about leadership and learning. Shell also works with many consultants and professors to stay abreast of the latest in leadership research.

Anticipation

The best leadership development programs emphasize the future rather than the past or present. Future-oriented focus groups, decentralized strategic planning, scenario analysis, and the Delphi method are used as anticipatory learning tools by the masters of developing leaders.

Gary Hamel recommends decentralized planning because "revolutions seldom start with the monarchy."[2] The Merlin

Process is an example of an approach that is participative and future-centered.[3] It requires that managers place themselves at a time in the future and describe what the organization would look like if the approach were totally successful. In contrast to more conventional strategic planning that is top-down, the Merlin Process can be used throughout the organization to create a decentralized strategic plan.

Scenario analysis helps teams of individuals recognize potential external events in advance of their occurrence and plan in advance how they might best adapt to them. The Delphi Method is helpful in forecasting future events. It eliminates committee activity and replaces it with a carefully designed program of sequential individual interrogations interspersed with information and feedback on results from earlier stages in the program. The technique can also be used to assess consensus on "discontinuities" to be pursued.

Planners at Shell contributed early on in the learning movement by developing scenario planning, which is thinking through multiple strategic alternatives—not just one alternative—for the future. These strategic alternatives are assembled from a wide range of role players and a breadth of data and information, to form alternative stories about the future of a company.

J&J's second Executive Conference, "Creating Our Future," looked at where J&J should be in a decade. Groups of J&J executives from around the world worked together for a week with outside consultants to create a future to which they could commit. Participants were expected to challenge conventional wisdom about the evolution of their industry and to focus on action their own organizations might take to create this future. An extended scenario, "J&J 2000," projected a future with multiple trends and discontinuities. Participants assessed the probability and impact of 14 potential developments via a modified Delphi Method. An integrative exercise, the Merlin Exercise, tied the various aspects of the program together by asking participants to apply course concepts to create a future vision of the firm. The program concluded with presentations of this "desired future" to the CEO or vice chairman.

Action

Action, not knowledge, is the goal of best-practice leadership development processes. Best-practice leadership development groups are "bringing the real world into the classroom." Business challenges are complicated and call for innovative, creative solutions. Disseminating the knowledge and building skills can help build a strong foundation, but leadership development is increasingly being used to equip participants with the skills, qualities, tools, and the opportunity to apply knowledge to important, challenging, real-world business issues.

The direction GE takes as a company is influenced by the recommendations of senior-level course participants in its leadership development core curriculum. As a result, participants are highly motivated when a project is a recommendation from the BMC or EDC. Recommendations made by the teams are often implemented and have led to such important changes as the corporate-wide adoption of the Six Sigma initiative.

The goal of another program at GE, Work-Out™, is to overcome resistance to change and persistent habits that are hard to modify. A cross-section of employees meet, typically for two to three days, without their group manager. They review management processes and practices honestly and openly. At the end of each Work-Out™ session, their manager returns to hear the findings and recommendations. The manager either accepts or rejects the ideas on the spot or appoints a team to report back with more data by a given date.

CAP is a systematic attempt to create professional change agents, rather than just managers, by disseminating GE's accumulated knowledge about how to initiate, accelerate, and secure change. If CAP is successful, says Welch, "people who are comfortable as coaches and facilitators will be the norm at GE. And the other people won't get promoted.[4]

At J&J, the purpose of Executive Conference III is to emphasize the Standards of Leadership Model and to tie the standards to specific business issues through action learning. Senior executives in the various businesses sponsor each session of the Executive Conference. Whenever they have a business issue to address, Corporate Education and Development sets up the Executive Conference effort.

Although the principal J&J session is five days, pre-work and follow-up extend the experience. Before the core session, the operating companies discuss the business topic that is the focus of the session. The senior executives who choose the matter for discussion are asked to pick a topic that "can cause significant or transformational impact on the organization." Past program topics have focused on issues such as top-line growth, product-development cycles, new market entries, and developing leaders.

Once a topic is defined, the J&J executive sponsor chooses 50 to 130 program participants. Participants are asked to do additional preparation, such as data gathering and interviewing. After the program, participants are brought back for one day to report on implementation results. Typically, the process takes six to nine months. While the Executive Conference approach includes work teams from the business area with the problem being addressed, action-learning efforts at the middle-management level bring high-potential individuals from throughout the firm to address a critical issue. In a sense, Executive Conference issues aim more at organizational development while middle-management programs are more focused on individual development.

Alignment

As part of the alignment between leadership development and other corporate systems, best-practice organizations demand a tie between their educational efforts and their formal succession processes. Some best-practice partners have leadership development and succession planning reporting to the same executive. Others have a less formal relationship. But all the organizations examined made it clear that a link is present.

In J&J, all development functions use 360-degree evaluations as a part of their leadership development process. In some cases, they are open in admitting that feedback and impressions are used for assessment, although the results are not typically fed directly into the succession-planning process.

While the data were not conclusive, there is a strong indication that the best firms are beginning to formalize this linkage and bring assessment, development, feedback, coaching, and succession planning into one aligned, integrated system. In this new model, leadership development becomes an important part of maintaining a steady flow of information throughout the organization to ensure that top talent is tracked and continues to grow.

GE ties its leadership development process directly to succession planning and is open in making that distinction. As part of GE's human resources planning process, all employees are rated in a nine-block system as part of the annual "Session C" review program. The review includes discussion about performance and adherence to GE values and is later interpreted by someone at a higher management level to ensure fairness and accuracy.

GE believes that "corporate owns the top 500 people in the company and just rents them out to the businesses." To encourage the sharing of business talent, GE includes a negative variable in its performance appraisals for managers who hold back talent. Outstanding business performance and leadership development go hand in hand.

HP provides many opportunities for emerging leaders to develop and grow. As suggested previously, Lew Platt was concerned about the large number of probable retirements among senior executives during the next decade and the need for more diversity in the top management ranks. Leadership Development and Review is not mandated, but it is becoming an institutionalized process across HP. It works by providing a tool to the businesses and by allowing the business to manage the process. The leadership development process links well by providing stretch assignments for the best people and making accelerated-development programs available for individual contributors and first-level managers.

Assessment

Best-practice organizations always assess the impact of their leadership development process. While the range of assessment efforts varied from a strong emphasis on quantification at Arthur Andersen to a more laid-back sense that "we know when our programs are delivering value" at GE, all of the best-practice organizations concern themselves with the perceived value of their efforts.

Shell reports that members of the LEAP staff do not feel their program is adding value unless projects worked on by LEAP teams generate revenues at least 25 times the project costs. During the initial contracting process, a member of the LEAP staff and the leader within the business determine desired project outcomes. As a part of this discussion, the business leader expresses his or her objectives for sending the candidate to the program, and in many cases, those stated objectives define the program and the problem the team or candidate will address.

J&J does follow-up research to determine if subordinates and peers see significant improvement in key performance areas after an Executive Conference. Of all best-practice organizations, Arthur Andersen probably has the most dedicated assessment efforts. Andersen finds that graduates of its PDP return higher levels of client satisfaction and higher per-hour-supervised net fees than partners who have not attended the program.

Since the upper managers of the Bank are all participants in the EDP, they have the opportunity to make suggestions that are likely to result in immediate change. To ensure that all reaction to the program is captured, the EDP staff collects feedback from all participants in the program. An external firm is employed to conduct an interim evaluation of the EDP based on the experiences of the first two cohorts to participate in it.

The old adage "You get what you pay for" seems to apply to the leadership development processes. Each best-practice partner sees value in investing in the future leaders of its organization. Costs are considered in the process, but the larger focus is on the value that the program can provide. When asked to rank the importance of criteria in selecting outside partners or vendors, "fees" were among the least important factors.

In 1997, Arthur Andersen invested $307 million in education, approximately 6 percent of total revenue. Andersen believes that to deliver a best-practice program, focus must be on value rather than on cost. If course offerings achieve their objective (for example, to improve business results), support is likely to be maintained.

The development budget for the Bank's EDP is approximately $20 million dollars. Participant cost is $22,000, which includes all travel, lodging, and business school fees for all three modules and the Grass Roots Immersion Program (GRIP). This cost is not charged back to the business groups but funded centrally through the $12 million Executive Education budget.

The New World—Relevant and Real

The "reality" of business is being redefined. Issues such as globalization, deregulation, and rapid technological change are forcing companies to reevaluate the way they operate. Paradigms that have worked for years are no longer effective, and developing strategic leaders is becoming a critical source of sustainable competitive advantage. Based on observations of best-practice firms known for their excellence in leadership development, this chapter has outlined five steps for making leadership development strategic.

To make leadership development strategic, best-practice firms have instituted development programs that:

♦ Build *awareness* of external challenges, emerging strategies, organizational needs, and what leading firms do to meet these needs

♦ Employ *anticipatory* learning tools to recognize potential external events, envision their future, and focus on actions their organization can take to create its own future

♦ Tie leadership development programs to solving important, challenging business issues

♦ *Align* leadership development with performance assessment, feedback, coaching, and succession planning

♦ *Assess* impact of the leadership development process on individual behavioral changes and organizational success

Gaining and sustaining competitive advantage is increasingly focused on leadership development as an action-oriented, ongoing learning process closely linked to the strategic needs of the organization. In this book, we have explored how some of the world's best corporations have invested to secure the future's only source of sustainable competitive advantage: leadership. These pages are rich with the distilled experience of some of the world's best practitioners of leadership development. Read, reflect, adapt, and use the portions that are applicable to your situation. Above all, keep listening and learning.

Notes

1. See A. A. Vicere and R. M. Fulmer, *Leadership by Design* (Boston: Harvard Business School Press, 1998), pp. 218–223.
2. Gary Hamel, "Strategy as Revolution," *Harvard Business Review* (July–Aug. 1996), pp. 69–82.
3. Robert M. Fulmer and Solange Perret, "The Merlin Exercise: Future by Forecast or Future by Invention?" *Journal of Management Development*, 12, No. 6 (1993), pp. 44–52.
4. Noel Tichy and Stratford Sherman, *Control Your Destiny or Someone Else Will* (New York: Currency Doubleday, 1993), p. 209.

Appendix A: Benchmarking— The Systematic Transfer of Best Practices

The past decade has seen wrenching reorganization and change for many organizations. As firms have looked for ways to survive and remain profitable, a simple but powerful change strategy called *benchmarking* has evolved. Modeled on the human learning process, benchmarking can be described as the process by which organizations learn. A good working definition is the process of identifying, learning, and adapting outstanding practices and processes from any organization, anywhere in the world, to help an organization improve its performance. The underlying rationale for the benchmarking process is that learning from the examples of best-practice cases is the most effective means of understanding the principles and specifics of effective practices.

The most important aspects of benchmarking are twofold:

1. Benchmarking is not a fixed technique imposed by "experts," but rather a process driven by participants trying to change their organizations.

2. Benchmarking does not use prescribed solutions to a problem but is a process through which participants learn about successful practices in other organizations and then draw on

those cases to develop solutions that are most suitable for their own organizations.

Benchmarking is not copying, networking, or passively reading abstracts, articles, or books. It is action learning, as demonstrated in the description of the consortium methodology. Benchmarking is not simply a comparison of numbers or performance statistics. Numbers are helpful for identifying gaps in performance, but true process-benchmarking identifies the "hows" and "whys" of performance gaps and helps organizations learn and understand how to perform at higher levels. For the ASTD-APQC study, the process contained two phases.

Phase I: Selecting Best-Practice Partner Organizations

A list of best-practice candidate organizations was developed through primary and secondary research conducted by APQC and ASTD. Suggestions were compiled from this research, as well as from periodicals and industry journals and knowledge from sponsors. A qualitative screening survey was developed, and more than 50 potential best-practice organizations were contacted. Results from the telephone interviews were compiled. Ten finalists were selected and presented to the consortium for consideration as best-practice partners. Based on the initial data and other information collected by the study team, sponsors selected six best-practice organizations. Each of these organizations accepted the invitation to join the study as potential best-practice partners.

Phase II: Learning from the Best

The sponsor group and the study team developed a detailed questionnaire and a site-visit discussion guide for use as the Phase II data collection tools. Of the six best-practice partners, all hosted an on-site interview. During these site visits, key personnel were asked questions from the site-visit discussion guide. Five best-practice organizations and 19 sponsoring organizations completed the detailed questionnaire. Excerpts from the site-visit summaries are also included throughout this book.

Table A-1   The Benchmarking Process

	Approach	*Purpose*	*Deliverable/Outcome*
Phase I	◆ Conduct primary and secondary research ◆ Administer screening survey	◆ To identify best-practice partner *candidates* ◆ To screen partner *candidates*	◆ List of partner *candidates* ◆ Identification of best-practice *partners* ◆ Screening report
Phase II	◆ Conduct site visits ◆ Administer detailed questionnaire	◆ To extract innovative practices and applicable quantitative data	◆ Site visit summaries ◆ Final report

Appendix B: Web Sites about Corporate Universities

A number of Internet Web sites are available to provide information about corporate universities. They include:

1. Corporate University Collaborative: www.traininguniversity.com
2. American Assembly of Collegiate Schools of Business: www.AACSB.edu
3. On-Site Plus: www.onsiteplus.com
4. WooHoo, Inc.: www.woohoou.com
5. Executive Knowledge Works: www.ekw-hrd.com
6. The Corporate University: www.corporate-u.com
7. Corporate University Xchange: www.corpu.com

About the Authors

Robert M. Fulmer

Currently the W. Brooks George Professor of Management at the College of William and Mary and Distinguished Visiting Professor at the Graziadio School of Business and Management of Pepperdine University, Robert M. Fulmer was a visiting scholar at the Center for Organizational Learning at MIT and taught Organization and Management at Columbia University's Business School. For six years, Fulmer was director of Executive Education at Emory University, where he headed the Executive MBA program as well as public and customized programs for general and functional managers. Dr. Fulmer received his first endowed chair at Trinity University and has served as director of Corporate Management Development for Allied Signal, Inc., with worldwide responsibility for management development ranging from first-line supervision to senior executives. He has also served as president of two management consulting firms specializing in human resource issues.

Dr. Fulmer is the author of four editions of *The New Management, Crafting Competitiveness, Executive Development and Organizational Learning for Global Business,* and *Leadership by Design.* He has served on the editorial board of seven journals and is the author of five other business books and over 120 published articles.

His M.B.A. is from the University of Florida and his Ph.D. from UCLA. His research and writing has focused on future challenges of management, implementation of strategy, and leadership development as a lever for change efforts. He has designed and delivered leadership development initiatives in twenty-three countries and on six continents. Dr. Fulmer has served on the Board of Directors for the Columbia University Center for Research in Human Resource Management, on the National Human Resource Advisory Board of the American Red Cross, and is a Fellow of the Academy of Management. He was founding chairperson of the Executive Education Exchange, president of the Board of Editors for Executive Development, An International Journal, and a past president of the Southern Management Association. He currently serves on the International Research Advisory Committee of the Strategos Institute and is a senior fellow and special adviser to the president of the EastWest Institute. He served as subject matter expert (SME) and adviser for the 1998 and 1999 global benchmarking study of leadership development conducted in collaboration with the American Productivity and Quality Center and the American Society for Training and Development.

Marshall Goldsmith

Marshall Goldsmith is the co-founder of Keilty, Goldsmith & Company (KGC). A recent study by Penn State University listed KGC as one of seven key providers of customized leadership development in the United States. He is also Executive Director of the Financial Times Knowledge-Leadership Dialogue, a process that connects thought leaders with present and future executives from around the world. He is widely recognized as a foremost authority in helping leaders achieve positive, measurable change in behavior: for themselves, their people, and their teams. In 2000, *Forbes* listed Marshall Goldsmith as one of five top executive coaches and *Human Resources Magazine* ranked him as one of the world's leading HR consultants. He has been ranked in *The Wall Street Journal* as one of the world's "Top 10" consultants in executive development.

Dr. Goldsmith is the major developer of the Leader of the Future Process, a process that helps leaders develop in a manner that is consistent with their organization's vision and values. He is one of the few consultants in the world who has been asked to work with over 50 CEOs. His clients include major corporations in a wide variety of industries.

Aside from his corporate work, Dr. Goldsmith has completed substantial volunteer projects for organizations such as the Urban League, the Institute for East West Studies, and the International, Canadian, and American Red Cross (where he was a "National Volunteer of the Year").

Dr. Goldsmith is a member of the Board of the Peter Drucker Foundation and a frequent contributor to the Drucker Foundation journal, "Leader to Leader." He co-edited (with Frances Hesselbein and Dick Beckhard) three books, *The Leader of the Future* (a *Business Week* "Top 15" Best-Seller), *The Organization of the Future,* and *The Community of the Future.* He also co-edited the recently published books *Leading Beyond the Walls* and *Learning Journeys.*

Marshall Goldsmith holds a Ph.D. from UCLA's Graduate School of Management. He is on the faculty of Dartmouth's Executive Education program.

Index